Lockdown Li

A collection of original writing generated by the Rector, members and friends of St Faith's Havant and St Nicholas Langstone during the 2020 Corona Virus Pandemic

To Sreena
with much love and with
thanks for all your support!

Tom Kennar

Published by:
Rev'd Canon Tom Kennar, The Rectory, Havant, PO9 2RP, UK.
www.tomkennar.com

Dedicated to those members and friends of St Faith's & St Nicholas, Langstone who have gone on to glory during 2020:

Douglas Bean
Roger Bryant
Wyn Clinnick
Maureen McAndrew
Ian Normand
Sam Roonan
Daphne Rowden
Janet Schofield
Audrey Whitcombe
Derek Wilkes
and Steve Woods.

and to all those friends, neighbours and members of St Faith's whose generosity and good humour has kept us going.

Contents

Introduction

In mid-March of 2020, it was abundantly clear that our world was about to change. News of the COVID-19 (or 'Corona') virus was rife, and it was apparent that much of what we took for granted was about to be altered irrevocably. A whole season of concerts and social gatherings was about to be culled, in favour of the essential maintenance of 'social distance'. Services were about to be led entirely online, via the strange and unfamiliar worlds of Facebook and Zoom.

As the Rector of this parish, I was especially concerned about how to keep in touch with our parish members and friends. No longer would we be able to swap stories and jokes over Coffee Morning cakes. The annual strawberry tea, and the after-church banter, was all in abeyance. There was a distinct danger that especially those most frail or vulnerable parishioners could find themselves locked away in their homes, with no connection to the church at all (especially if they were not already well-schooled in the use of the internet).

In response to these concerns, the "Corona Chronicle" was born. Initially based on the regular weekly parish news-letter, it very soon grew into a substantial opportunity for parishioners to share their stories with each other, or to express their creativity, whether through the written word or other media. It also offered an opportunity for me and other church leaders to offer thoughtful reflections on both the time of the year, and the implications of the pandemic for this community.

The 'Chronicle' has been produced almost every week of the pandemic (with just a gap for a hospital visit by yours truly). It was sent out electronically to around 200 local people, and paper copies were delivered, by volunteers' hands, to another 70 or so. Many of these were then passed from neighbour to neighbour, all around the parish and beyond, touching the lives of churchgoers and non-church-goers alike. As the weeks rolled by, more and more people felt led to contribute articles, stories, biographies, jokes and puzzles. It was almost like sitting in a paper-version of the famous St Faith's Variety Show!

The volume is a selection of some the original outpourings of those first months of the Pandemic of 20/21 – up to December 2020, including the homilies and sermons preached by me and other clergy-team members at the same time. We have included here only original writings, and not the writings of others which were sent-in for amusement or inspiration, having been culled from the internet or other sources. To keep this volume manageable, we have also excluded eulogies (with the exception of one funeral address, which, being that of a priest, was more theological than personal). We've also excluded articles about other charities, photographic memories, promotions for upcoming events (or celebratory photos after such events) appeals for funding (and updates on the same), letters to the Editor, PCC business summaries, 'who's who' articles, reports from mission partners, prayers, Graham Kidd's weekly column about anthems and organ music, and (of course) service sheets! Sadly, art-works by parishioners have also been excluded, primarily to keep printing costs to a reasonable level (production of artwork being expensive).

The entire archive of 2020's outpourings may be perused at any time via the archive copies of the Chronicle which will be kept in the Parish Archives. Should you wish to access any of the articles in this book, together with their illustrations, a complete archive of all we have achieved together is available at www.stfaith.com/566-2/ - faithfully maintained by our 'webmaster', Colin Carter.

Our sincere hope is that this volume will tell something of the story of the Pandemic, at least from the perspective of the parish church. The Pandemic brought many fears and troubles, but also much creativity. It is dedicated to the tens of thousands of people (we may never know the full number) who lost their lives during the pandemic, and especially, of course to those residents and friends of the parish who passed on to glory during those days.

Funds raised from sale of this book will be used to continue the parish's ministry of maintaining and improving its community buildings, for the benefit of every parish resident (and many from beyond our borders). Our prayer is that once we are able to be together in person again, we may generate the same kind of care, compassion and concern for one another that the Corona Chronicle sought to keep alive, during the darkest days of 2020.

Canon Tom Kennar
Rector of St Faith's Havant with St Nicholas' Langstone
February 2021

Pithy Thoughts

A selection of 'Thoughts for the week' – in chronological order, reflecting on events through the passing the year

The Church Un-resting
by Tom Kennar - 29 March 2020

Being apart from the world is nothing new for the church. Within our many traditions are the ideas of 'Sabbath rest', 'hermitage', 'monastery and convent'. Taking time to separate ourselves from the busy, busy world is something that the great spiritual writers have encouraged us constantly to do.

Anyone who has ever chosen such isolation knows there are immense opportunities available to the church and its people. When we cease the endless round of daily life, and take time to just 'be', there's every opportunity for the still, small voice of God to break through. Jesus himself practiced self-isolation, not least for his 40 days and nights in the wilderness.

It's not easy for us to make the shift. And when the isolation is forced upon us (as in the current crisis), our first instinct may be to resist. Our days feel strange, because they lack the familiar patterns. We resist being told how to live our lives. For a while we try to carry on doing things in much the same way as we always have. But as the days roll by, a quiet acceptance begins to emerge, and new possibilities for the life of faith open up.

Perhaps we begin to see that God calls his church to continue offering worship, but in different and endlessly creative ways. No doubt many of you will have seen the attempts that I (and many of my priestly colleagues) are making to bring the act of worship directly into homes, from our homes. Last Thursday's live-streamed worship from my living room (see the picture) has so far been viewed one thousand, seven hundred times!

But worship doesn't just mean taking part in the Mass, or the Holy Communion (as important as that is). We worship God individually too, perhaps by focusing on a single flower in our window, or a beautiful landscape from a book on our shelves. We also give God his worth (the meaning of 'worship') by expressing God's love to our neighbours, our families and our friends, through keeping up contact, and loving one another, even though we are physically apart.

The church building is closed. But the church itself is open...to all God is saying to us through these days.

Deprivations

by Tom Kennar – 5 April 2020

There are many things to regret about the present lock-down of our shops, churches and homes. For those of us with grandchildren, the inability to give them a cuddle is achingly hard! (We've been keeping up with Lucas by video message - but it's just not the same as being in the same room with him. I'm almost missing having him climb onto my chest to stick plastic toys up my nose!)

For those, like me, who value the traditions of the church's year, the deprivation of such traditions is especially hard. For example, I'm going to miss our annual Maundy Thursday service, where I have the opportunity to wash some parishioners' feet as a sign of my role as servant to the parish. (Mind you, my aching back is not going to miss doing it!). I'm also really sad that our plans for a dramatic reading of the Palm Sunday readings will have to wait for another year. And I'm going to be sad that we can't march from church to church with our fellow Christians on Good Friday. Nor will the Light of Christ be brought into the church - as a sign of the resurrection on Easter morning.

Another deprivation for me will be the annual 'Blessing of the Boats' which was scheduled for Easter Sunday afternoon, down at Langstone. That's been a highlight of my calendar most years since I've been your Rector. I simply love the way the whole Langstone community gathers together on the foreshore, to pray for safety for all at sea in the coming season, and to lustily sing (in various simultaneous keys!) the mariners' hymn: Eternal Father, strong to save. I get to bless each boat belonging to the Langstone Cutters. And in recent years, clubs from other parts of the harbour have joined us too for a blessing. It's always a lovely time! Thankfully, we've all agreed that as soon as the 'lockdown' is lifted, we'll arrange another date to do the blessing...so that's a little light at the end of the Corona tunnel!

Perhaps all this deprivation will do us good. There's definitely a feeling of Lent having been super-charged this year! Perhaps we take all these annual traditions just a little bit too much for granted – and the fact that we've deprived of them, this year, might make us all the more joyful about embracing them in the future?

Loving our neighbours

by Tom Kennar – 22 April 2020

Our Pallant Centre Manager, Will Coulston, lives with his wife Trudie in a small cul-de-sac of houses. Like many such communities, people come and go from their homes with a nod of recognition, or the occasional cheery wave on the way to work. But, in normal times, real connections between neighbours are rare.

At the beginning of the Lockdown, the residents of Will and Trudie's community decided to form a 'WhatsApp Group'. (WhatsApp is a messaging programme, which enables groups of people to easily keep in touch). Through this new connection, the community learned that its youngest member, a little girl, was about to celebrate her birthday - but she could no longer have a party with her friends because of the Lockdown. So, all the residents of the cul-de-sac agreed to open their front doors at the same time, on the little girl's birthday, and to sing 'happy birthday' to her. I'm betting that she will remember that moment for the rest of her life, whereas many birthday parties in future years will fade into dim memory.

I heard of another community, this week, in which a couple of houses were owned by members of the same church. They decided to tell their neighbours that on Sunday mornings, at a certain time, they were planning to stand at their doors to pray the Lord's Prayer, out-loud. To their surprise, everyone, from every house decided to join them. I understand that this has now become a 'lockdown tradition' for the whole community.

This challenging and perplexing time is providing all sorts of opportunities for a renewed sense of community to rise up. Neighbours are caring for neighbours, looking out for the elderly or sick. Carers, medical staff, shop workers, bus & taxi drivers, council workers, emergency service staff (and many more unsung heroes) are going more than the extra mile to keep our society functioning and whole. Sacrifices of time, money and even health are being made every day.

All of these wonderful stories remind me of that line from the Lord's Prayer: 'thy Kingdom come, thy will be done in earth as it is in heaven'. Perhaps the deep desire behind that prayer is finally gaining traction in our lives, community and country?

Thy Kingdom Come - in lockdown

by Tom Kennar – 21 May 2020

To be completely honest with you, dear friends, I'm not usually a huge fan of national initiatives by our mother church, the 'Church of England'. My reticence springs partially from a no doubt over-sensitive fear that the Church might be subject to hijack by either marketing gurus, or by particular sections of our broad range of theologies and practices. I'm also cautious of 'top-down' initiatives, in any organisation whose roots are essentially local (or in our case, parochial).

'Thy Kingdom Come' is just one such initiative, which arrived on clergy desks around five years ago, via an encouraging letter from the Archbishops of Canterbury and York. At the time, I was just settling into life in a new parish, recovering from the extra efforts of Lent and Easter, and while gearing up our commitments to our Mission Development Plan. I confess that I was not overly enthusiastic about a new initiative being foisted upon me between Ascension and Pentecost! So not much was said, by me, at the time or since.

Nevertheless, 'Thy Kingdom Come' has been persistently marketed, by the national church, as an extra opportunity for us all to pray diligently that our neighbours, families and friends may come to know the love of Christ. A worthy aim, no doubt, except that (as I remind the powers-that-be from time to time) this is precisely one of the things for which we already pray on a daily basis – especially in the words of the Lord's Prayer (some of which have been taken as a title for this initiative).

But pray we must - and so, in obedience to the leading of our Archbishops, I warmly invite you to join me, over the coming week, in continuing to pray for God's Kingdom of Love to be ever more firmly established in our lives, in our community, and in our world. You may like to pray the rest of the Lord's Prayer at the same time! Amen!

The relentless self-publicist!
by Tom Kennar – 28 May 2020

In the week when I have announced the publication of my book of talks, stories and journals, I've been reflecting on the place of the 'ego'. It is hard, indeed, to accomplish anything like the publication of a book, or to put on a concert of one's music, without ego having at least a significant role to play.

The word 'ego' is often used negatively (as in the insults 'egotistic' or 'ego-centric'). But of course, we all have an ego…it is a neutral term. Properly balanced, our ego is our sense of ourselves, our identity, our gifts. There is many a light which has been 'hid under the bushel basket' out of an under-developed sense of ego. On the other hand, an over-inflated, or inaccurate, sense of ego can lead to people accepting or seeking positions to which they are wholly unsuited.

During this week between Ascension and Pentecost, we are each asked by church's choice of readings to reflect on the way that Jesus sent his disciples, turning them into 'apostles' (those who are sent). I preached on this theme on Sunday. My invitation, this week, is for you to take a moment to think and pray about what that 'sending' means for you. How can you move from being a 'disciple' (a student of the Master) to being an 'apostle' (one who is sent out by the King)?

Having an accurate sense, through your own ego, of your gifts and talents will be crucial to that question. What gifts has God built into you, over the years that he's been working with you? What talents do you have which God could use in the ongoing work of building his Kingdom?

One of the lovely spin-offs of this lockdown has been the discovery of many creative talents among our congregation - from musicians like Kate and Jude via Facebook, a talent for poetry and writing like Margaret, Clive and both Bills, Chris and Peter in recent weeks. Don't be shy! And don't hide your light under the bushel basket. False, or misplaced modesty has stymied many a move of God's Holy Spirit - when his people have failed to grasp that their personal gifts are just what God is seeking to use!

What's in a name

by Tom Kennar – 4 June 2020

Not so many years ago, black men who worked on the railways of America were universally named 'George' – by a custom and practice which has thankfully ceased. Any black, male, employee of the Railway could be addressed as 'George', without any effort on the part of the passenger to find out the man's real name. The terrible death of George Floyd has therefore had a particular resonance for the Black community in the USA.

We had similar apparently innocuous practices in the UK too. I shudder to remember when the only black people in my home village were routinely referred to either as 'the Sambos' or 'the WOGS' (which I understand originally stood for 'Wealthy Oriental Gentlemen', but which quickly became an insulting catch-all term for everyone who didn't have a white face). The even-more insulting 'N-word' was also heard regularly when I was young.

The use of such terms and names was markedly different from the way we addressed people of our own ethnic group (when we didn't know one another's actual names). 'Sir' was the most frequently used epithet for a man whose name one didn't know. 'Madam' – or 'Miss' for a younger woman – usually sufficed. My paternal grandmother routinely used the Devonian term 'my handsome' when addressing any of us grandchildren and our friends (especially when she couldn't immediately call our names to her mind).

The Bible teaches us that our names are important, though. God's name was considered to be SO holy that it should never be said out loud, and rigorous cleansing rituals were undertaken by scribes before even writing God's name. Even today, we rarely say the word 'Yahweh' (an anglicised rendering of God's actual name).

Our names speak of our identity. Sometimes they are given to us by our families in the hope that we might embody some characteristic of a famous earlier-holder of the name. Or sometimes our families hoped that our lives would be characterised by 'Grace', 'Patience', 'Mercy' or some other similar quality of God. In my own case, humour played its part. My Dad is Harry. I am Tom. And my brother is Richard – though we are completely forbidden to ever call him 'Dick'! The most important thing for us all to remember is that God knows us each, intimately. He counts the hairs on our head – and he knows us all by name. Our heavenly father calls us by our name. We are his. And he is ours. And that's all of us. Whatever colour, race or creed.

Virtual or Real?

by Bishop John Hind – 12 June 2020

During the present lockdown we have been unable to meet our friends and family and many of us have been discovering new and imaginative ways of keeping close. The one thing that lasts for ever is love. This is the ultimate reality and we should thank God for the resources of modern technology that have enabled us to express our love, albeit at a distance. At the same time, we know that "virtual" is not the same as physical contact. We long to be able to be together again. There is something of a paradox here. We know that love, the nature of God himself, transcends all the limitations of time and space and does not need physical expression. And yet in this life physical, personal, face to face contact is a necessary part of showing our love for each other. The present gradual lifting of some of the lockdown restrictions means that we are now beginning to be able to rejoice not only in the love we know we have for each other but also "by baby steps" to express it by occasional and "socially distanced" meeting.

I think this tells us something important about our life as Christians, members of the Body of Christ. One of the wonderful things about our faith is its very physical, human and earthly quality. We know that God is greater than anything he has created; we know that in his love all the limitations of our earthly existence (including sin and death) are overcome. And yet while we live this present life we need physical, practical expressions of his presence with us. This is why however wonderful our ability to worship "virtually" – whether by our online pilgrimage or the regular streamed services from St Faith's – we long for something more. Just as we yearn to hug our friends again, we also need to receive Christ's body and blood sacramentally as well as "virtually" or "spiritually".

For the meantime, let us do the best we can, confident that our love for each other and God's love for us do not depend on physical contact. But let us also remember that we are not bodiless angels, but flesh and blood human beings. Our human desire to be able to meet again echoes our spiritual desire to enjoy the fullness of our sacramental life just as soon as we can.

Are we there yet?

by Tom Kennar – 18 June 2020

Anyone who has ever been on a long journey with a child will know that question! Clare and I once took our then teenage daughter on a 'road trip' up the West Coast of the USA. We were drinking in the vast landscapes as we drove along, but then we turned around to discover that Emily was sitting in the back seat, with a blanket over her head, watching a movie on her laptop! "I'm so fed up of looking at mountains and forests!" she said. "Aren't we there yet?"

For some of us, no doubt, Lockdown is eliciting a similar response. As another Corona Chronicle hits your inbox (or letterbox) I wonder whether you too are heaving a sigh. "Another week of articles from the church!" We hope you're not too bored of it yet...and I thank you all for your many and varied contributions, and encouraging messages over the last few weeks. (I'm thinking about bringing together the best of the Chronicle's articles into a memento edition which we might sell for the Big Build Campaign. Do you think that's a good idea?)

For those who are wondering about when the church might be at least partially open, I can tell you that we have an eye on the weekend of the 5th of July – but that's only IF the recent re-opening of non-essential shops doesn't cause a spike in infection rates. Our church building is closed out of love for our community. We don't want to be the cause of any harm to anyone. Unlike shops, who need customers to survive, the church's work continues largely unabated, via Livestreaming, Zooming, phone calls, socially distanced meetings, and the prayers of our members. It's a different way of being the church – but it's still very much the church, building or not.

Of course we all miss the choir, and the bells, and coffee mornings and concerts and the sheer joy of gathering together in one place to worship the God we all love. But, even if we can't see the end of the tunnel of lockdown, we do at least trust that the end is coming.

So hold fast, stay strong, keep on praying for the world, our Town and for one another. God is at work among us. I see his activity every day, in the love that is shared, the generosity that is experienced, and the friendships that are deepening despite the current circumstances.

God bless you all.

Boris does it again!

by Tom Kennar – 25 June 2020

Bless him. I have every sympathy for any prime minister who has to cope with a crisis such as the one through which we are currently living. I would not be in his shoes for all the chocolate in a Thornton's shop. Nevertheless, allowing for the stress of his position, he does have a frustrating habit of announcing major changes to the COVID-status of churches (and other places of worship) without, apparently, having consulted with any of the members of the Places of Worship Reference Group (Bishops and other senior leaders). It seems they therefore lack the opportunity to prepare the guidance they will need to send out to all local church leaders at the time of the announcement. The result is that after one of our esteemed leader's utterances, a mad scramble takes place in Diocesan offices up and down the land, and new guidance is hurriedly drawn up to be dispatched to anxious clergy and PCCs. Such guidance is inevitably lacking in some respects, so a subsequent cascade of amendments arrives over the coming days.

This is all by way of saying (in answer to inevitable questions from anxious parishioners) that at the time of writing, it is very difficult to say with any certainty whether or not St Faith's will open for public worship on July 5th. We still have much to consider, despite the Government's permission to open. Such considerations include how to limit the number of attendees (should we really turn people away at the door? A booking system perhaps?). Do we really want to meet without singing (or is it better to continue with live-streamed services which can include hymns)? In view of the advice of many scientists, including the retired Chief Scientific Officer to the Government, Sir David King, is it just too soon in the pandemic to consider opening the church? Would we be putting our mainly elderly congregation at risk? And then there's all the practical questions about PPE (should the minister wear a face-mask? What about attendees?).

In short, I am personally erring on the side of extreme caution, and I am grateful to our Standing Committee who share my view. I will, however, update you all on our thinking next week. In the meantime, please be assured of my continuing prayers for all the members and friends of St Faith's.

The moment we've been waiting for…?

by Tom Kennar – 2 July 2020

In this week's Chronicle will be found a statement from the PCC (Parochial Church Council) about our tentative steps towards re-opening first St Faith's, and then other church buildings. As you will know (if you read my outpourings from time to time) we are taking these steps carefully, and gradually. But we are also taking them with great hope in our hearts.

For those who use the church building on a regular basis, for worship, social activities, music and the like, the loss of our beautiful 'gathering place' has been distressing. My experience, however, has been that in almost equal measure, many have found the pause from our normal routines to be quite refreshing. Parishioners have told me, for example, that online worship has helped them to get back into the very act of worship (having perhaps been absent from church for a while). Others have said that they find it rather easier to focus on the sermon when sat in a comfortable chair, without the inevitable distractions of a public place (even the happy noises of my grandson!). Still others have unleashed their creativity, not least in the pages of this Chronicle!

Live-streamed worship has also enabled us to welcome some quite long distance new virtual members. I think the furthest may be Cyprus...but correct me, if I'm wrong. What is certainly true is that our Sunday morning congregation has grown to a steady 100 people (we get around 75 steady internet viewers, many of whom are couples). Sunday evenings regularly attract 20 or more (up from the normal 6 to 8!). Thursday services regularly have more than double the old average attendance in church (currently running at around 37– 40). All these facts mean that once we do eventually return to some form of worship in church, live-streaming will remain a part of our offering both to this community, and others further afield.

Other obvious benefits of this time of pause have been a large increase in the volume of communications I receive from parishioners with perhaps more time to think, ponder and ask questions. This has been a joy – and I've truly appreciated the chance to talk about issues of faith with a very wide number of folks. Long may that continue!

We are not yet at the end of 'the pause'. But, as the end hoves into dim view, I hope we'll hold on to what has been life-giving and worthwhile about these months.

Carefully, gradually, coming together…

by Tom Kennar – 9 July 2020

As we announced last week, it is our intention to open the church for two sessions of private prayer, with effect from next Tuesday (14th). This is part of our very gradual, and careful reopening of the building to our parishioners, always with long-term health and wellbeing in mind. (See the poster on page 1.)

Within a few weeks (exact date to be announced) we hope to open for some limited, socially-distanced public worship (which will also be live-streamed on Facebook, as now). Again, this is being done carefully and gradually, with our eyes very much on the local infection rates. (We are mindful too of the example, only this week, of a local pub which opened for the weekend, and then had to close again immediately because of a COVID infection.)

The Greek word for a gathering of Christians is 'Ekklesia' (from which we get our churchy word 'ecclesiastical'). Originally, it simply meant 'a gathering of people' (for example a gathering of politicians) but it has come to mean the gathering of the people of God. We have been 'virtually' gathering via the internet for much of the past four months – which has been both a blessing and a challenge. A blessing, because it has opened up our worship to many people, near and far, who would not otherwise be able to join with us. A challenge, because some of our core congregation do not have internet connections (and don't want one!) – which means that they have suffered from being 'disconnected' from the 'ecclesia'. It is for such people, especially, that we want to re-commence public worship just as soon as we judge the balance of risk to be in favour of doing so.

We are conscious, however, that attending public worship will be a highly risky activity for some folks – especially those in high-risk groups. We will therefore need to live with some creative tension between those who can, and those who cannot attend. This will be uncomfortable, for many. But perhaps it may serve to remind us that there are many circumstances, around the world, where some of the 'ecclesia' do not dare to gather with their brothers and sisters...especially in those parts of the world where to be a Christian is to invite violence and persecution.

Getting ready to open the church…

by Sandra Haggan – 9 July 2020

On Wednesday Tony, Maddie and myself arrived at Church to begin the cleaning in preparation for when we open for private prayer. It felt rather strange coming into the church, although I have been in a couple of times. On one occasion a few weeks ago when we had a couple of those pesky unwelcome visitors – squirrels!

I stood there and felt as though I was stuck in a moment of time, as in church we were still in Lent with the altar frontal and so on all in purple. The memorial book remained opened on the 24th of March and I felt really sad for all those people who were unable to come in and see their loved ones' names in the book and to light a candle for them. The world had moved on but inside the church we were still in Lent.

Of course with the church having been locked for 100 days there wasn't really any mess as such but a lot of dust and cobwebs, and those little bits of plaster that come down all the time. The cleaning took us much longer than usual and required two visits. We didn't even have a doughnut!

When I went into the porch there was a card under the door, someone had tried to deliver a parcel and we were clearly out! It was left across the road in the charity shop. It did make me smile when I saw the card.

We are nearly ready to receive those who would like to come in to have a chance to reflect, to say a prayer and/ or to light a candle.
It will be good to see you all again.

I despair…

by Tom Kennar – 16 July 2020

I despair. I despair of the politics of separatism which are driving so many nations to the far-right, and people into the arms of hate-mongers.

I despair of any political briefings (from any party) which are short on fact and long on spin.

I despair of prime ministers who respond to respectful policy challenges from other parties with bluster, spin and underwear jokes.

I despair of any nation whose primary economic activity is the service sector (pubs, restaurants, frivolous shopping and entertainment) rather than agriculture, manufacturing, education and science.

I despair of any country which can house all its homeless people when the rest of the population needs protecting from a virus, but which beforehand claimed that housing the homeless was impossible.

I despair of any country which gives its carers a jolly good clap, instead of paying them a real living wage.

I despair of any country whose wealthiest citizens can avoid paying any tax, but who cheerfully drive on roads bought by the taxes of the poor.

But, I don't despair completely. I also rejoice.

I rejoice that people of faith are continuing to pray, and to press for meaningful change, truth and social justice.

I rejoice that people of faith are donating all they can afford (and even what they sometimes can't afford) for the work of the Kingdom, and the relief of the poverty of their neighbours.

I rejoice that people of faith are spending their time caring for their neighbours, telephoning the lonely, reaching out to one another.

I rejoice in the gift of social media which, properly used, enables the housebound and lonely to engage with worship and community life.

I rejoice that in any country which believes that black lives matter and which celebrates gender diversity.

I rejoice that many people realise that real wealth is what you have left when someone takes all your money away.

The Kingdom of God is a real and living thing. It stands in direct opposition to so much that we accept, uncritically, as 'normal' life. Jesus told us that 'the Kingdom is among you' – that it is already a present reality, which exists in direct opposition to the normal life of most nations. Amen?

And…we're back!

by Tom Kennar – 23 July 2020

Well, that was exciting! I've just returned from our first Mass in St Faith's Church since the 19th of March! I have to say that despite the fact that I've now been livestreaming services for four months, I was surprisingly nervous about this occasion. Would I remember to cleanse my hands in the right place? Would my more particular parishioners be concerned at some of the liturgical shortcuts I make (to reduce time overall)? Would people at home be able to hear me? Was I speaking clearly enough, and 'annunciating all my words' clearly, as my old drama teachers taught me?

All in all, it went pretty well. There were a couple of technical hitches (not least with the flickering picture). And it proved remarkably difficult to produce sound which doesn't echo too badly off the stone walls of the building. But I'm reasonably happy that we are ready to fling wide the doors on Sunday to anyone brave enough to join us for a COVID-safe, live-streamed worshipping experience.

Doing anything for the first time in public can be a nerve-wracking thing. Just ask anyone who has read a lesson in church, or led the prayers for the first time! But when it's all over, there's joy – at completing something with only a small number of (largely un-noticed) errors. I can't help but wonder how the Apostles felt, the first time they felt called to stand up in front of a crowd, or in front of the Temple Court, and tell the good news of Jesus. I bet their palms were just as sweaty as the rest of us in similar situations.

But thanks be to God that he promises to walk with us through all the trials of life. The Lord is indeed our Shepherd. His rod and staff do indeed comfort us. And he leads us beside still waters...even when we're terrified out of our minds!

Loving Jesus Christ

by Bishop John Hind – 7 August 2020

During "lockdown" many people have learned how to make an act of "spiritual communion" while unable to receive Christ sacramentally. In live-streamed eucharists from St Faith's and many other parishes, this has been accompanied by a prayer by St Alphonsus Liguori, a great eighteenth century moral theologian and teacher of prayer. This month's reflection came from one of his writings, The Practice of the Love of Jesus Christ.

All the holiness and perfection of a soul consists in loving Jesus Christ, our highest good and our Saviour. Anyone who loves me, said Jesus, will be loved by my eternal Father: "The Father himself loves you, because you have loved me." (John 16.27) "Some, says St. Francis de Sales, consider perfection to lie in austerity of life, others in prayer, others in frequenting the sacraments, others in almsgiving; but they deceive themselves: perfection lies in loving God wholeheartedly." St Paul wrote, "Above all, put on love, which binds everything together in perfect harmony." (Colossians 3.14) Love is what unites and preserves every virtue that makes a person perfect. Therefore, St Augustine used to say, "Love God, and do what you will." This is because by loving God we learn never to do anything that displeases him and to do everything that delights him.

Doesn't God in fact deserve all our love? He has loved us from eternity: "I have loved you with an everlasting love." (Jeremiah 31.3). "Remember, O man, says the Lord, that I was the first to love you. You were not yet in the world, the world was not there, and I already loved you. Since I am God, I love you; because I have loved myself, I have also loved you." It is only right, then, for us to give him all our affections, and to love none other but him.

Seeing that people are drawn by acts of kindness, God determined to win their hearts by means of his gifts. So, "For this reason he said, I shall draw them with the cords of Adam, with the bands of love" (Hosea 11.4). I want to draw people to love me by what usually ensnares them, that is, the bands of love. And all God's gifts to humankind are just like this. He gave us a soul, made in his likeness, and endowed us with memory, intellect and will; he gave us a body equipped with the senses; it was for us that he created heaven and earth and everything else. He made all these things out of love for humankind, so that all creation might serve us, and we in turn might love God out of gratitude for so many gifts.

But God was not content to give us all these beautiful creatures. To win our love for himself, he went so far as to give us the fullness of himself. The eternal Father went so far as to give us his only Son. Seeing that we were all dead through sin and deprived of his grace, what did he do? Out of his immense and overflowing love he sent his beloved Son to pay our debt and to return to us the life which sin had taken away.

By giving us his Son, whom he did not spare precisely so that he might spare us, he bestowed on us at once every good: his grace, his love and heaven; for all these gifts, good as they are, are less than his Son. "He who did not spare his own Son, but gave him up for all of us, will he not also give us all good things with him?" (Romans 8.32)

The Littleness of Mary

A reflection by Bishop John Hind on 10 September 2020

He hath exalted the humble and meek (from the Magnificat BCP cf Lk. 1.52)

The Magnificat, said or sung daily at Evening Prayer, could be described as "the Gospel according to Mary"; it reminds us above all of God's goodness and favour towards the poor, the hungry, the humble and the helpless. That really is gospel – good news – for us all. It is precisely at our points of weakness, when our defences are down and we recognise how utterly dependent on God we are that he is able to break in and raise us up. In doing so he chooses and uses us – in other words, just like Mary, we are raised up to be his agents in the world.

We remember the littleness of Mary, "the slave-girl of the Lord"; God chose one who was, in her own words "humble and meek" to be the door through which he would himself enter this world and begin the new age. We remember Mary's own obedient response to the angel: "Behold, the handmaid of the Lord, be it unto me according to thy will."

Humility and obedience. It is important to understand these words properly. Humility does not mean self-contempt or being a doormat; it involves rather a realistic assessment of who and what we are; it also means recognising that it is through the poor and humble parts of our world, and of ourselves, that God can enter in. To be truly humble means to know that we are utterly dependent on God; it requires worship, which is both the cause and the result of humility.

Obedience does not mean reluctant, grim jawed dutifulness, it means joyful assent to the will of God. In order to obey we need first to hear; I have already spoken about the importance of worship in relation to humility, and part of worship is scripture, from which we know and celebrate God's mighty acts. The Magnificat, Mary's song during her visit to her cousin Elizabeth, is full of Old Testament echoes. Mary was steeped in the scriptures, as the expression of God's graciousness to his people. Mary's vocation was to bring the Word of God into the world. Her visit to Elizabeth is an expression of this, in anticipation of the birth of Jesus. In other words, Mary is called to be an evangelist and she hurries to share the good news with Elizabeth in obedience to God.

No wonder “all generations call her blessed”. Mary typifies two characteristics which are essential for every Christian: humility and obedience. Humility arises from worship, and prepares us for obedience. Obedience in its turn requires not only hearts humbled by worship, but also ears attuned by attention to scripture.

We must allow these characteristics to grow in us if we are to begin to share in the greatest of all the examples of Mary: intimacy with the Lord.

Tradition – keeping us going

by Tom Kennar – 10 October 2020

I wonder whether you heard Rowan Williams last week, on Radio 4's 'Start the Week' (28 Sept 2020). He was talking (in his usually fascinating way!) about his new book on the Rule of St Benedict. The whole programme is well worth listening to, but I was especially struck by the following nugget of history, which I'll paraphrase...

Williams said that St Benedict wrote his famous Rule, and established his Christian community, at a time when the Roman Empire was crumbling around them. All the old certainties were disappearing, but Benedict recognised that simple traditions and simple disciplines of living, would carry the Christian community through the tectonic shifts of the society around them. It would keep them anchored, and focused on the essential task of living together in loving service, praying regularly and with discipline.

It seemed to me that Williams (and through him, Benedict) was speaking directly to our time. We are facing economic and societal shifts beyond comparison, all across the world. Patterns of work, health-care, and social gathering are changing almost daily. The economy (of the whole world) is in free-fall, and the old certainties about our economic models are suddenly much less certain. The Climate Emergency and the COVID Pandemic are both causes and symptoms of the malaise of modern humanity.

Into this chaos, the traditions of our practice of faith speak out. They offer us a mast to which we can cling amid the storm. They give us a lens through which to view the chaos – a lens which reminds us of our place in both the Universe and in what theologians call 'the economy of God'. It is for this reason that, service-by-service throughout the pandemic, I have maintained the same pattern of worship, and why we've sung the old hymns, and prayed the old prayers. Tempting as it may be to use the tool of the internet to do something 'new and whacky', I have personally felt the need to hold fast to the traditions we have inherited. They have sustained our forebears, for generations before us. And I believe they are capable of sustaining us too.

Hope in sight?

by Tom Kennar – 12 November 2020

There has been a bit of hope in sight, during this last week, has there not? Those like me who have detested the bullying, narcissism of the present US President, have drawn hope from the recent US election. The whole world has drawn hope from the news that a vaccine may be on its way.

Hope is a constant theme of the Scriptures we love. The Hebrew Bible, and the New Testament, are full of hope—hope that God will transform darkness into light, death into resurrection. Example after example is laid out for us to contemplate. From the disaster of the Flood, Noah's family is offered a rainbow. From slavery in Egypt, the Hebrews are rescued. From Exile in Babylon, the Jews make their return. From the Cross of defeat, Jesus Christ rises from the dead.

But hope is hard to experience when you find yourself in the midst of a crisis—and even less so when you have lost loved ones. But our task, as followers of God, is to offer such hope, nevertheless. To the lonely, we offer companionship (even if it is only by telephone). To the homeless, we offer shelter, and to the hungry we offer food. To the bereaved, we offer comfort, and the promise of heaven.

This week, I was especially touched by the commitment of our choir, organist, flower artists, school children and bell ringers—and many others—to the task of offering a suitable Remembrance Service, despite the Lockdown. Some might have given up, and simply stood silently at the War Memorial. But not us. In a gesture of resolute hope, we offered music and ceremony, beautiful flowers and a hand-crafted wreath—and we tolled a single bell 161 times for each of the names on the Memorial.

My continuing prayer is that St Faith's should stand out as a beacon of hope in the troubles of the world. Many of our members are directly employed at the front-line of the crisis...doctors, nurses, food-sellers, carers. Others are constantly at work to bring comfort and hope to their neighbours—through phone calls, delivering the Chronicle, doing some shopping or dropping round a jigsaw. Others are singing, playing, stewarding, maintaining, building, donating what they can. Others are simply holding their neighbours and the entire world before God in prayer. Each of these (and many more examples) are signs of hope in a world confused and hurting. Long may we continue to offer such hope.

Despite the Lockdown, we still managed to pay tribute to the fallen of Havant and beyond. With a lunchtime concert on Armistice Day, a wreath from Bosmere pupils, a service with choir, organ, bugler, and dignitaries, two sermons, and a lot of video editing!

We are so grateful for the many warm and appreciative comments we have received. But we did it for them. We have remembered them.

Unity in diversity

by Tom Kennar – 19 November 2020

We have rarely lived in such divided times – at least not in this country since the Civil War. Brexit, in particular, has separated us from our neighbour, and opinions about each other's views are rarely kind. Opinions about the merits or otherwise of our Government's handling of the Pandemic are equally divided.

In 'the Colonies' across the 'Pond', our American cousins are even more divided, politically. Various forces, ranging from the malign to the simply ignorant are ranged against each other, and the whole nation is suffering from 'truth decay' (as former President Obama recently diagnosed).

Into this divided and perplexing arena, we find ourselves sandwiched, briefly between 'ordinary time' and 'Advent' – in a period colloquially referred to as 'Kingdom Season'. The Scriptures we are invited to ponder in these couple of weeks all push our vision towards a greater hope than the hope we place in our earthly leaders. We are confronted with images of the 'End of All Things', or 'the End of the Age' – a time which has been often predicted as imminent (even by some of the Bible's writers!), but which has yet to become a reality.

Nevertheless, the vision held before us by the Scriptures offers us an alternative route to follow, a different 'Way' (as Jesus called it). The Way of the Kingdom is the path of unity, in which all humanity comes together under the headship of the King of Kings. All petty squabbles are laid aside, because larger, wiser, deeper wisdom leads us onward. Every knee bows before the ethereal throne of the King, and in willing submission to his gentle, wise rule.

Who knows when such a Kingdom might be established? I certainly don't. But while we wait for the full coming of the Kingdom, we who call ourselves 'followers of the Way' are called to be lamp-bearers for it. By the way we live together, care for one another, love one another, and share that love with our neighbours, we exemplify the kind of unity which the Kingdom will make real for all human-kind.

So, as we ready ourselves for the coming of Advent, for hearing again the historic roots of our faith and preparing for the first coming of our Lord, we also hold fast to the promise of a Kingdom of Love – one which we already know, and long to share.

Tis the season to be jolly careful…

by Tom Kennar – 24 November 2020

Our Prime Minister did what he does best this week, and employed the English language to turn a memorable phrase. (What else he does – or does not do – well, I will leave for you to discern, individually). 'Tis the season to be jolly careful…', however, was a wonderful turn of phrase.

He's quite right, of course. I, for one, am facing the re-opening of our churches for socially distanced worship with a small amount of stress. Christmas at St Faith's just won't be the same without the 931 people who crammed into our building over 24 hours last year! But my trepidation comes from the caution that we must avoid 'snatching defeat from the jaws of victory' at this crucial moment in the vaccine timeline. We must each take responsibility for not being viral-spreaders...whether we are at home or in church. We do indeed need to be jolly careful – and not at all complacent.

We need to be jolly careful about other things too. We need to be jolly careful that the poorest in our society are not left behind as we celebrate the poor birth of our Saviour. We need to jolly carefully remember that the Good News of the life-changing arrival of Jesus should be good news for 'all humankind' – including those in refugee camps, domestic violence refuges, hostels and on the street.

We also need to be jolly careful to attend to our own spiritual and emotional health, at the end of a long and exhausting year. That means being jolly attentive to the things we know can make a difference to our ability to cope...not least, the power of prayer and prayerful contemplation of God and his message of hope.

I hope that our online offerings will help you to just that – especially for those of you who are unable (or understandably unwilling) to come to church itself. I was very touched indeed to receive a letter this week from a new parishioner, who commented about last Sunday's service with these words: 'All who watched and listened will want to watch again;

and some will become regular watchers and Christians!' I thank my correspondent for his warm words and timely encouragement.

So – be jolly careful, everyone! Look after yourself and look after your neighbour – both next door and far away. Keep encouraging one another. Be strong, be hopeful – in the certain hope that an end to our present challenges is now at least in sight!

Second Coming…or Third?

A reflection by Bishop John Hind – 17 December 2020

Advent means "coming" and "future". During the season of Advent, we look forward to celebrating Christ's first coming, his birth in Bethlehem, and we look forward to his second, as judge.

One problem about this rather simple account is that it is all about the past, which is over, and the future, which is yet to come. But we have to live in the present and need to know what Advent can mean for us here and now, while we both give thanks for the past and look forward to the future.

In a twelfth century Advent sermon, St Bernard of Clairvaux gave some thought to this question and described a third coming of Jesus: "a road leading from his first coming to the last."

"We know that the coming of the Lord is threefold: the third coming is between the other two and it is not visible in the way they are. At his first coming the Lord was seen on earth and lived among human beings, who saw him and hated him. At his last coming 'all flesh shall see the salvation of our God', and 'they shall look on him whom they have pierced.' In the middle, the hidden coming, only the chosen see him, and they see him within themselves; and so their souls are saved. The first coming was in flesh and weakness, the middle coming is in spirit and power, and the final coming will be in glory and majesty.

This middle coming is like a road that leads from the first coming to the last. At the first, Christ was our redemption; at the last, he will become manifest as our life; but in this middle way he is our rest and our consolation.

If it seems to anyone that I am inventing what I am saying about the middle coming, listen to the Lord himself: 'If anyone loves me, he will keep my words, and the Father will love him, and we shall come to him.'

Elsewhere I have read: 'Whoever fears the Lord does good things '– but I think that what was said about whoever loves him was more important, because whoever loves him will keep his words. Where are these words to be kept? In the heart certainly, as the Prophet says, 'I have hidden your sayings in my heart so that I do not sin against you.'

Keep the word of God in this way: Blessed are those who keep it. Let it penetrate deep into the core of your soul and then flow out again in your feelings and the way you behave. Feed on it well, and your soul delight in its rich nourishment. Do not forget to eat your bread, or your heart will dry up, but rather eat it up and your soul will be filled with abundance.

If you keep God's word like this, there is no doubt that it will keep you, for the Son will come to you with the Father: the great Prophet will come, who will renew Jerusalem, and he is the one who makes all things new. For this is what this coming will do: just as we have been shaped in the earthly image, so will we be shaped in the heavenly image. Just as the old Adam was poured into the whole man and took possession of him, so in turn will Christ possess our whole humanity – he who created everything, has redeemed everything, and will glorify everything."

History, Humour and Harmony

A collection of articles from parishioners and clergy
in which knowledge is shared,
or ideas advanced and discussed,
thanks expressed or inspiration and humour offered

"Now thank we all our God"

A reflection by Michael Laird

29 March 2020

We listened on the radio to the service this morning (22 March 2020) led by the Archbishop of Canterbury, which ended with the well-known hymn 'Now thank we all our God' – a great outpouring of thanks and praise. What is truly remarkable about this hymn is that it was composed in the midst of the Thirty Years' War, a disaster which ravaged the whole of central Europe to an extent not seen again until World War II, 300 years later. Some areas lost up to two-thirds of their population, from deaths in battle, massacres of civilians, epidemics, and starvation.

Martin Rinkhart, the author of the hymn, was a Lutheran pastor at Eilenburg, a small town in central Germany. By 1636-7 it was crammed with refugees, subject to assault by the invading Swedes, and to plague and famine – as a result of which he became the only surviving pastor, conducting 50 funerals per day. Rinkhart's ability to write this hymn under these terrible circumstances could be an inspiration to us all.

2020 Vision:
How do you educate the young during a pandemic?

By Clive Burnett.

29 March 2020

In 2009, just before my retirement as a civil servant attached to the Department for Education, I was asked to give a talk on the theme of what our education system might look like in ten years' time. I entitled it "2020 Vision". I was given full rein to indulge my wildest fantasies about what the coming of modern technology might mean for our schoolchildren. Over the last week or so, as the COVID 19 crisis has deepened and schools and businesses have closed, I've been reflecting on what I said at the time.

My starting point was to ask what was the point of schools when modern technology would be able to deliver lessons to children in the comfort of their own home. There seemed to be clear benefits in this, not least that children unable to come to school through, say, illness or transport disruption would be able to carry on with their learning. Over the last decade, many schools have developed quite sophisticated means of staying in touch with pupils when, for example, there's a school closure because of snow. Some of the wealthier (usually independent) secondary schools have gone further to develop on-line resources and methods of allowing pupils to communicate with their teachers, send in assignments and receive feedback. However, nearly all of these systems were predicated on the assumption that at most they would be required for a few days. Very few schools made provision for remote learning to take place for weeks on end.

Suddenly it has become necessary to put in place systems that enable lessons to be taught remotely. For most schools this means staff communicating with pupils by email or some other messaging application. For a privileged few, it means pupils logging into lessons and seeing their teacher as s/he teaches them. This raises some fundamental questions about the nature of teaching and the relationship of the teacher to their pupils. Suddenly, "the sage on the stage" has become "the guide by your side" and older teachers in particular, especially those lacking confidence in the use of the new technology, have found it difficult to adapt to the new reality.

For families of pupils being educated at home, there are some very real challenges especially if mum and dad are also working from home as a result of the pandemic. If the family doesn't own a laptop, how will parents and children keep in touch with school? If there's only one laptop in the family, who has first use? Will some lessons have to be downloaded at the start of the day? Who will supervise the youngest pupils when it comes to using the computer? Who will help the pupil with their work if it's not possible to contact the teacher? What provision will be made for key workers and vulnerable children who simply cannot be educated at home? Key subjects such as English and mathematics are no longer taught in the same way that they were when parents were at school so how are parents expected to help their children when they encounter difficulties with their learning?

Many of these issues are now beginning to emerge as parents and their children grapple with the reality of schools being closed for months on end. Maybe, at the end of this period, there will be a greater appreciation of the role that schools play in both educating and socialising the young.

Maybe, too, some parents will appreciate that the problem was not really the teacher after all!

Where is God in the COVID crisis?

An essay from the Rector, Tom Kennar. 15 April 2020

Many people, in recent days, have been asking this question. Our present challenges have brought the question to the forefront of minds – even though we are, of course, surrounded by suffering and death all the time. What follows is an attempt to offer a few thoughts in response to this important question – expressed in what I hope is accessible language.

The central question is 'where is God in human suffering?' Or, perhaps more urgently, the question is 'why doesn't God stop the virus?' The same question has, of course, been asked for centuries. This current plague is no different, in essence, to other crises that humanity has experienced before. Our ancestors tended either to see such events as either 'punishments' from an angry God, or, like us, they cried out, 'where is God?' Or, more painfully still, they cried with Jesus and the Psalmist, "My God, my God, why have you forsaken me?". (See Psalm 22)

The answer to the question rather depends on what the questioner means by the word 'God', itself. If the questioner's view of God is of a kindly, slightly deaf old man in the sky, who will only interfere in the world if the right number of people ask him loudly enough, then the answer to the question is quite simple: 'because you're not praying hard enough' or, worse still, 'you don't have enough faith!'. But that doesn't seem to me an adequate way of thinking of either God, or the important questions people are asking of God right now.

My picture of God is rather more complex than 'an old deaf guy', and with Good Friday in mind, it certainly includes the picture of a God who suffers and dies for us on a cross. The answer to the question 'where is God?' must therefore be rather more complex too.

The Vale of Soul-making

My general position is this: God has created a universe of infinite possibilities, in which we, his loved children, can grow to their full potential. That world has challenge built in – whether in the form of natural disasters (earthquakes, tsunamis, hurricanes – as well as viruses). How we respond to those challenges is the question. For it is through challenge that we grow, and develop. There are very few, if any, human accomplishments which have been achieved without the crucible of a 'problem to solve', or a challenge to overcome.

To use a simple example, imagine an aircraft about to crash due to engine failure. Imagine, then, a giant 'hand of God' reaching out of the clouds and putting the aircraft safely on the ground. What would be the effect? All aircraft engineers would be made redundant. No longer would we have to worry about health and safety. The aircraft manufacturers would realise that they are not needed. Nor would pilots need to be trained. People wishing to get to America would just step off Land's End and expect the hand of God to pick them up and take them to New York!

In such a world of divine intervention, we would be like toddlers, who expect mummy or daddy to catch us when we fall...never learning to stand on our own two feet. To extend the metaphor – how many parents have agonised over the pain they must cause their child to enable them to grow? (My Dad always said that you'll never learn to ride a bike until you've fallen off it half a dozen times.) I suggest that God loves us too much to interfere with the natural course of this, or any other virus. God's passion is for our eternal salvation not for the saving of our short lives on earth. Viewed from the Divine perspective, all life is temporary, anyway. God wants to save our souls. The healing of our bodies may not be the best way of achieving that ultimate end. This is, one might say, a 'vale of soul-making' (to quote John Keats).

You see, God wants us to grow in maturity of spirit...not just to have safety and good health. In fact, it is quite often in the midst of our suffering that God is able to do his greatest work. How many people don't even think about their eternal souls until they are confronted with the stark reality of their impending death? If the Cross means anything, it surely means that suffering (however much we might resist it!) has a place in God's plan for the world.

The Silent Watch-maker?

But this does not mean that God is silent – sitting back while we 'learn our lessons' and grow, watching us struggle and grow. No! I believe he is active and participating in all human suffering. God does not create our suffering; it arises out of the world, and out of human actions. Upon the cross, God suffers with us. God takes on human-caused suffering, and transforms it through resurrection.

Pushing God to the margins

We might also consider whether some of our suffering is in fact caused by the way we have systematically pushed God out of our lives. Almost every sphere of human life now carries on without God – he is largely absent from our schools, our workplaces, the way we spend our leisure-time, and even from our families. What this means is that when crises come (as they inevitably will) we humans have lost the language and the wisdom of faith. Like children, we cry out 'save us' to the God we have systematically ignored, but who we hope will hear us now – not realising that God is already with us, in the pit of our despair.

As I said in my sermon on Palm Sunday, the Kingdom of Heaven is at work every time a neighbour helps a neighbour, or a doctor or nurse cares for a patient.

So, is it worth even praying?

Does my thesis mean that we don't need to bother to pray? Absolutely not! But, I suggest, our prayers need to be focused rather less on asking God to 'please solve our problem', and rather more on asking God to 'grant us the wisdom and the serenity to be part of the solution'.

C.S. Lewis (the writer of the Narnia books) once said that prayer "doesn't change God. It changes me". I think he meant that we are not to imagine God as reluctant to act, or deaf to our pain. But rather that the task of prayer is to attune our spirits to the Holy Spirit. We should expect to spend far more time listening to God in prayer than speaking. Perhaps then God will be able to teach our deaf ears what we need to learn – how our society needs to be re-structured and re-formed, so that his Kingdom may truly be experienced 'on earth as it is in heaven'.

Listening to God in the Crisis

In respect of our current predicament, I don't think we have yet heard God speaking clearly – but perhaps we have heard some whispers. For example, in the face of a world economy which has so quickly collapsed, perhaps we are being asked to think about how we structure the economy in the future? In the face of a collapsing health service, (with thousands of vacant posts before the Crisis even started) what might God be saying about the political choices we have made (as a nation) in recent years?

The church is also listening to the whisper of God...what might God be saying to the church about what it means to BE the church? What role might the internet play in the future of the church – given the number of people who have re-connected to the church in recent days through that medium? What might it mean to be a 'people of God' who are liberated from bricks, stone and stained glass into being life-givers to their community?

Alleluia Christ is risen!

Reflections on an Orthodox Easter, from Eileen Norris.

22 April 2020

I heard this Greek cry of joy for the Resurrection in Crete one year. I had gone there after Easter for a holiday, only to live it once again because the Orthodox Church celebrates according to the cycles of the moon!

In the congregation we carried our candles up a hillside to the church, went to a very homely service where we all embraced each other with this cry of Christos Annesti (Christ is Risen!) before rolling our hard boiled painted eggs down the hillside!

Later we ate the Paschal Lamb (particularly delicious stew) and danced through the night! Unforgettable!

The Legacy of COVID-19 – Re-connecting with what's important?

An essay from Churchwarden, Colin Hedley.

22 April 2020

As a (sort of) farmer I have learnt to always try and look for the silver lining in every situation – no matter how dark or testing the times or how isolated one feels. Our society has become increasingly focused on retail, consumerism and debt, so perhaps the impact of COVID-19 will make us re-evaluate society and what is really important (including how we treat and reward those who deliver vital services, particularly the medical and caring professions).

Some scientists fear we are reaching the "tipping point" regarding irreversible climate change. So 2020 will be a good year for the World and may give us some much needed time to help deliver urgent mitigation. It's not too late for us to also take action to reduce our harm to the planet which sustains us. However, at a more local level, perhaps self-isolation and more local exercise will give many of us the opportunity to re-connect with nature. This can provide us with numerous experiences to enrich our lives at no cost.

The Government has been considering the direction of our new domestic farming and countryside policy. Farmers have been hearing more and more about the importance of the countryside for "relaxation, stress relief and spiritual health & well-being". Many get this, but it is ironic that those who manage the countryside often feel the opposite, but that's a topic for another article.

Occasionally I travel to London for work (remember that?) and one spring morning a few years ago the 7.04 morning train to Waterloo stopped near Godalming. The line, there, is on an embankment with a large lake close by on the right-hand side. Always keen to take advantage of a high vantage point to look over the countryside, I soon noticed that just about 50 yards away a pair of Great Crested Grebes were engaged in their exotic courtship display. This included them facing each other and going beak to beak so that their throats and necks gave the perfect heart shape outline for which they are famous. Marvellous. Superb. Free.

After a few moments, I averted my gaze and looked down the carriage. From what I could see no-one else was looking out the window; their attention was focused on papers, laptops, kindles, paperbacks and iPads. It seemed that the Grebe's performance was seen solely by me; and how honoured I was.

Our busy lives seem to be so driven and reactionary that real peace and engagement with the environment, and also spirituality, seems to be fleeting or even irrelevant for many. To an extent I am lucky; I am still able to see nature through some farm surveys and while rolling and harrowing my meadow in preparation for this summer's haymaking. But there is peace in our gardens and public spaces where the passing of traffic now seems an offensive intrusion rather than normality. How good is it to look at skies free of vapour trails, or to be able to hear the dawn chorus greeting the rising of yet another glorious sunrise?

Although there are genuine concerns about nature and the need for improved management there can be a surprising abundance all around. We have our gardens, our parks, trails such as the Billy Line and around the amazing Langstone and Chichester Harbours (which are of international wildlife importance, as well as stunning landscapes, and right on our doorsteps).

We shouldn't forget that our own churchyard at St Faith's has managed to increase the range of flowering plants and with native shrubs and new bird boxes. If we just take time to sit and look we will see and hear a multitude of wildlife all around, from red tailed bumble bees searching amongst early flowers to the energetic singing of chiff-chaffs newly arrived from Africa. Those moments are special and unique, to just those of us who catch that moment. They are gifts given freely; it's just up to us to make the time and unwrap the cluttered layers of our lives to open them.

‘Thank you to the Ringers’

By Carol Acworth – 30 April 2020

After living in France for fifteen years, one of the lovely things about England was to hear the church bells. No one rings like the English! The Tuesday evening practice which wafts over our way from St Faith’s on the evening air. Sunday morning presents a real blast of triumph to everyone going to the service, and inadvertently to all those drinking coffee nearby. When there is a funeral we hear that special peel when one side of each of the bell clappers is muffled. A moment to spare a thought for the people concerned. Several events in the year are commemorated with a ring, like the sinking of HMS Havant. A moment to spare a thought for the men who went down with her.

The real fun for me was to climb the tower (very steep little steps) and to come into this cosy room with all the bell ropes hanging down, and then to be completely blasted by the noise, watching the team as they each pull their bells at exactly the right moment in the peel.

Or even better, the midnight service on New Year’s Eve. Before midnight the bells are muffled (to mark the death of the old year). Then, sometime before midnight, a very game ringer climbs one floor higher to remove the muffles and the new year is rung with a full peel while the congregation belts out the hymns below. You almost feel the church shaking slightly as the tower bears the weight of these colossal bells turning round and round, and coming to rest upside down, delicately balancing their incredible weight on the old oak beams.

(I know of a church in the West Country with a full peel, but the church architect forbids ringing them because he does not trust the timber they hang on. Perhaps cross that one off your church visit list!)

Where did it all come from? Even in Rome, they can’t ring bells like us! It seems like a complete cacophony in other countries! Where does it come in the history of the church? Who designed such an extraordinary plan where the bells spend half their time balanced precariously upside down? And all the different patterns of ringing. Certainly even our oldest churches had them built in, and is that why we have a church tower? Which came first? The tower or the bells?

Perhaps hundreds of years ago, one medieval church architect said to another: ‘There’s a nice space up here where we are building a tower, shall we put a bell or two in there to tell the village it’s time for church?’ Or did he say ‘We must have a bell, or even several, to call the villagers to church, so we had better build a place for them, like a turret thing down one end'

Knowing nothing about how they came to be does not take anything from the enjoyment of them, so Thank You to the ringers, who brave freezing cold winter evenings, to practice on Tuesday. It is sorely missed. *(You can read much more about the background and history of our bells on the parish website at www.stfaith.com/st-faiths-bells/)*

A little bit of history

by Bill Jones – 30 April 2020

As you leave the Pallant Centre gate… if you turn right down the little road which leads into Beechworth Road you will pass, on your left two newish houses, 20 years old. These replaced The Red Cross Hall and centre, where they held dances and events, many of which I attended…several members of the St Faith's congregation were influential members of the Red Cross, including David Spittles former YCG member, he married Sheena and they went to live in New Zealand…

As you walk down this narrow little road, look at the wall. Still there on this wall you will see a number of circular marks. These were made by D Day Tanks as they made their way from hiding in the woods North of Havant and made their way off to France.

If you look right (over the wall) the car park is mostly made up of the original car park to Havant cinema, "The Empire," the front of which takes you into East Street (there is a newish block of flats there now).

As you make your way into Beechworth Road, number 11 is where Edna and Tom Gomersall, parents of John (Guitar) and June married to Ivan lived. Edna Gomersall founded the St Faith's Charity shop. Her Husband Tom worked for the Post Office then in Beechworth Road, he not only repaired all the Postman's red bikes, but also many items that were then sold in the charity shop.

Lastly for now, the original Post Office was for many years on the corner of Beechworth road. The building is still there on the left as you head to Meadowlands. It has a special place in local history… above the two doors is one of the very few ciphers from the short reign of King Edward VIII which lasted less than a year before he went off to marry Mrs Simpson. I think there are/were only 171 of his ciphers in the country mostly on post boxes: very few on buildings.

The Aftermath of World War II

by Michael Laird – 14 May 2020

Following rather muted celebrations of V.E. Day, our resident historian (and PCC Member) Michael Laird offered his reflections on the aftermath of the War in question...

World War I was supposed to be 'the war that ends wars', but this hope was soon disproved. However, the suffering and sacrifice incurred in World War II was not wasted: it has resulted in 75 years (and continuing) without a major war, at least in our continent of Europe.

Our good fortune is underlined by the fact that this is unprecedented in its history. A major theme in recent centuries was recurrent conflict between France and Germany, with Britain throwing its weight on one side or the other to maintain a balance. Thus from the mid-17th century Louis XIV and later Napoleon encroached upon Germany – then weak and disunited; subsequently a newly united and powerful Germany invaded France in 1870, 1914 and 1940.

We perhaps take it for granted now that things were bound to be different after World War II. But in 1945, the prospect was not promising. The humiliation of the German conquest, and the often atrocious behaviour of the Nazi occupiers, aroused feelings of hatred and vengeance in all the countries affected. And the degree of wartime loss and destruction made any quick recovery seem improbable – as Tony Judt wrote in his masterly work 'Postwar', the continent was 'scarred, embittered and impoverished'. Poland annexed Germany's eastern provinces, expelling their inhabitants (in compensation for losses to the Soviet Union); Czechoslovakia expelled its substantial German minority; France expected massive reparations and the detatchment of the Rhineland and the Saar; the German government ceased to exist, with the country occupied by the 4 victorious powers. But one day it would revive, with a real prospect of another round of suicidal warfare.

1947 brought a crisis: Europe could not afford to import enough from outside – mainly the USA – to proceed with reconstruction. This evoked an outstanding example of enlightened self-interest from the US, in the shape of Marshall Aid – including grants on a massive scale (to Britain as well as the continent); and conditional on cooperation between the European recipients. One reason for this was the apparent threat from Stalin's Soviet Union, which was imposing Communist dictatorships on the countries of east-central Europe – developing into the Cold War. 1948 saw a soviet attempt to take control of the western sectors of Berlin – frustrated only by an extraordinary air-lift of the necessary supplies. As a result, the Western powers – including now even France – were beginning to see the Germans as allies rather than enemies. And in 1949 NATO was established, linking the US and Canada with the countries of western Europe (including eventually the emergent West German state) as a deterrent to any possible Soviet adventures. And of course the Cold War never escalated into World War III, despite some dangerous moments: it was relatively well managed.

But with continuing worry about a German resurgence, the French Foreign Minister (Schuman) proposed in 1950 a plan to put west European coal and steel under a supra-national authority: the European Coal & Steel Community. Politically as well as economically this was a masterstroke: losing direct control over coal and steel meant that Germany and France could not go to war again. This became the kernel of the EEC (1958): Germany was European-ised. And in the early 1970s she was reconciled with her eastern neighbours also.

So as we give thanks for the sacrifices of those who fought to deliver us from the evils of Nazism and Fascism, let us also remember the statesmen – British, American, and west European – who took difficult and sometimes unpopular decisions to ensure that their victory was not wasted.

Venues ARE the Community

by Will Coulston, our General Manager – 14 May 2020

Nothing has been left untouched. The Corona Virus has affected all continents, communities, families, services and industries, directly or indirectly.

We are now relying on incomprehensible amounts of money, endless goodwill and limitless bravery to fight back.

It will continue to be tough but it will come to an end. A new dawn will present itself with fresh enthusiasm, and after much reflection. Entirely new ways of spending time with one another – be it through work, travel, family, friends, leisure and such like – will be born.

The ‘new normal’ will feel strange for a while. Just whilst we become accustomed to new social behaviours and expectations, but very quickly, it will simply be ‘normal’.

What will normal mean for communities that rely on venues to meet, socialise and catch up or simply to let their hair down? What does it mean for those venues that support those communities in return for their encouragement and love, often over decades? With next to zero income but still on-going costs, and often relying on charitable gifts/donations and a heavy reliance on volunteer effort, how do those venues recover?

I remain strong in the belief that people are generally good. We all act out of character at some point. When we are emotional or tested or simply do not hear or see what we wanted to hear or see. But when it comes down to it, we reach out in the hope that we can make a difference. That we can help repair bridges from both ends and meet happily in the middle whatever our differences and struggles.

Community venues have played a big part in this for hundreds or years and more so in the last century. Communities where families were torn apart by global conflict in particular. The people in those communities came together. They supported one another. They built a future through their gratitude of the present. They cried together, and laughed together. They felt pain and loss together and they celebrated when the moment was right.

Those communities are there to be served, and the halls and clubs and centres far and wide, are there to help make that togetherness last. They are there with beating hearts readying to make new and everlasting memories. For us all.

We'll meet again.

Soon.

“Jackanory”

by Colin Hedley

written for St Faith’s Variety Show –

shared on 14 May 2020

Written during the curacy of David and Vickie Morgan…

(Curtains open to reveal Louise Hedley sitting in armchair in centre of stage)

Now, are you all sitting comfortably on those cheap plastic chairs? I hope so, unless you've upset the organisers and they've given you the one with the crack in? So let's begin with today's story which is called Chicken Licken and the Day the Sky Started to Fall in.

One sunny morning, just outside the Church, Chicken Licken and the other curate, Henny Penny, we're having a swift fag out of sight of the security camera. Unbeknown to them a blackbird was investigating the new bat box just above their heads and as it did so a little piece of tile came away and dropped down onto Chicken Licken’s fair locks.

“Hells bells that hurt,” she said, “What was it?”

They looked around but couldn't see the little piece of tile which had bounced off into the wildflowers. Henny Penny looked up and said:

“Perhaps climate change is causing the sky to fall in?”

Most alarmed at this prospect they went to search for a church warden to ask their advice, although they made sure to put out their cigarettes first with a few sharp drags; what a nasty habit, uuugghhhh!!!!! Fortunately, one of the church wardens was there in church, hovering by the biscuit barrel and looking to see if the crunch cream he had hidden under the rich teas after Sunday service had remained undiscovered: It had!

“Wise Warden,” they chanted, “We were outside weeding (naughty curates) when a piece of the sky fell on us, what ever shall we do?” For a few seconds he thought carefully and then, once he had finished munching, he said, “I don't know. The intelligent church warden is away at the moment, so why don't you go and find Hector Rector, he’ll know what to do.”

“But wherever shall we find him?” asked the anxious acolytes and then the church warden showed his wise-ness. He put a finger to his lips so that they stopped talking and then put a cupped hand to his ear, indicating that they should listen. Instantly the lovely old church was silent and helped the curates for as soon as the church was quiet there was a distinct sound of snoring coming from the lady chapel. The wise warden simply pointed a finger and then returned to his foraging.

"Hector Rector, we fear the sky has started to fall in!"

"What's that, what's that?" Awakening from his short snooze, he dislodged the cassock he had been using as a pillow. "Angels' Delight has fallen at Goodwood. Blast I had a fiver on her to win!"

"No," they chorused. "The sky has started to fall in!"

"Phew, I thought it was important. I may be a font of knowledge on some matters, but the atmosphere is a complete mystery to me, you need to talk to someone even wiser."

"The Bishop?" Chicken Licken and Henny Penny said in unison.

"Good answer," said Hector Rector obviously impressed. "That will be 10 out of 10 for this week's assignment. But I was thinking of someone not quite that senior."

"Graham Norton?"

"Careful, you're becoming over excited now and I may have to dock some of those marks. No, I was thinking about Master Mayor at the Plaza, he'll know."

"How do we find his worshipfulness?" enquired Henny Penny, looking a little daunted.

"That's easy," replied the vicar, "Just go out of the north door and follow your nose." A bit bemused, off they trotted and were soon in north street.

"He's taking the St Michael," said Chicken Licken indignantly, "What's he mean; follow your nose?" But soon a waft of takeaway food came on the light breeze, and then another, and as they walked on so further smells came to their little nostrils until they had reached the railway station and there saw a bold sign for The Plaza. A short trot later and they were at the reception.

"Good morning, how can I help you?" said the stern lady behind the desk without smiling.

"Please madam we'd like to see the Master Mayor; we have some very important news."

"Which is?" asked the receptionist firmly, her eyes narrowing – giving away that she had only recently joined the Council from a Doctor's surgery.

"That the sky has started to fall in," said Chicken Licken earnestly.

"Is this true?" asked the receptionist

"Oh yes," confirmed Henny Penny, his head nodding so much his face appeared as a blur.

“You're lucky to see the sky, here in the north of the town we barely see it since the meridian centre was built. I expect it's due to climate change, everything's blamed on climate change now, it's the new Brexit. Anyways I'm afraid master mayor is out today at his second office, nudge, nudge, wink, wink and unless you have a decent five iron they won't let you in. You'll have to make an appointment for next month.”

“Next month!?” exclaimed the concerned curates, “That's way too late.”

“Sorry, force of habit,” said the lady, “How does tomorrow at 2 suit? Hang about, how do you know the sky is falling in?”

Chicken Licken replied. “We were standing outside the church, doing some weeding (Ahem) when a chunk of the sky fell on my head.”

“And you were right by the Church?”

“That’s correct,” confirmed Henny Penny.

“That wasn’t the sky. I’ve seen the state of your roof. I expect it was a piece of tile, you silly sausages.”

“Well, what can we do?” they enquired naively.

“Well, your Rector is a very busy chap, so why don’t you help him by sending a plan to Mr Fox, the cunning chair of the Diocesan Advisory Committee for permission to repair it?”

And that is what those young curates did. For two weeks they worked in secret, pulling it all together in a nice indexed folder. They made an appointment to see the cunning chairman of the Diocesan Advisory Committee. So on one sunny Wednesday morning they followed their noses again all the way to the railway station and caught the 11.15 to Portsmouth.

And Chicken Licken, Henny Penny and all their lovely plans were never, seen, again.

History they didn't teach you at school

by Clive Barnett – 21 May 2020

Why do brides carry bouquets of flowers?

In the 16th century, most people got married in June because they took their yearly bath in May and they still smelled pretty good by June. However, since they were starting to smell, brides carried a bouquet of flowers to hide the body odour. Hence the custom today of carrying a bouquet when getting married.

Beware of 'throwing the baby out with the bathwater'!

Baths consisted of a big tub filled with hot water. The man of the house had the privilege of the nice clean water. Then all the other sons and men, then the women and finally the children, last of all the babies. By then the water was so dirty you could actually lose someone in it. Hence the saying, "Don't throw the baby out with the bath water!"

It's raining cats and dogs!

Houses had thatched roofs – thick straw-piled high – with no wood underneath. It was the only place for animals to get warm, so all the cats and other small animals (mice, bugs etc) lived in the roof. When it rained it became slippery and sometimes the animals would slip and fall off the roof. Hence the saying "It's raining cats and dogs."

Why were four-poster beds invented?

There was nothing to stop things from falling into the house. This posed a real problem in the bedroom where bugs and other droppings could mess up your nice clean bed. Hence, a bed with big posts and a sheet hung over the top afforded some protection: that is how four-poster beds came into existence.

Why do we cross the threshold?

The floor was dirt. Only the wealthy had something other than dirt, hence the saying "Dirt poor." The wealthy had slate floors that would get slippery in the winter when wet so they spread thresh (straw) on the floor to help keep their footing. As the winter wore on, they added more thresh until – when you opened the door – it would all start slipping outside. A piece of wood was placed in the entranceway, hence a thresh hold.

Peas porridge hot, peas porridge cold

In those days, they cooked in the kitchen with a big kettle that always hung over the fire. Every day they lit the fire and added things to the pot. They ate mostly vegetables and did not get much meat. They would eat the stew for dinner, leaving leftovers in the pot to get cold overnight and then ate it the next day. Sometimes stew had food in it that had been there for quite a while, hence the rhyme:

"Peas porridge hot – peas porridge cold –
peas porridge in the pot nine days old."

Where did 'bringing home the bacon' come from?

Sometimes they could obtain pork which made them feel quite special. When visitors came over, they would hang up their bacon to show off. It was a sign of wealth that a man could – "bring home the bacon." They would cut off a little to share with guests and would all sit around and "chew the fat".

Beware of tomatoes!

Those with money had plates made of pewter. Food with high acid content caused some of the lead to leach onto the food thus causing death by lead poisoning. This happened most often with tomatoes and so, for the next 400 years or so, tomatoes were considered poisonous. (The Rector still suspects that they may be! Ed.)

Who were 'the upper crust'?

Bread was divided according to status, and bread was baked in open ovens with singed floors. Workers got the burnt bottom of the loaf, the family got the middle and guests got the top or "the upper crust".

Why do we hold a wake when someone dies?

Lead cups were used to drink ale or whisky. The combination would sometimes knock the imbibers out for a couple of days. Someone walking along the road would take them for dead and prepare them for burial. They were laid out on the kitchen table for a couple of days and the family would gather around and eat and drink and wait and see if they would wake up. Hence the custom of "holding a wake".

What about being 'saved by the bell'?

When cemeteries became too full, villagers would dig up the buried coffins, take the bones to a bone-house, and reuse the grave. When reopening these coffins, 1 in 25 coffins were found to have scratch marks on the inside and they realised they had been burying people alive. So, they would tie a string on the wrist of the corpse, lead it through the coffin and up through the ground and tie it to a bell. Someone would have to sit out in the graveyard all night ("the graveyard shift") to listen for the bell. Thus, someone could be "saved by the bell" or was considered to be "a dead ringer".

And finally (with apologies for the vulgarity...)

Where did "Piss Poor" come from?
They used to use urine to tan animal skins, so families used to all pee in a pot. And then once it was full it was taken and sold to the tannery. If you had to do this to survive you were "Piss Poor". But worse than that were the really poor folk who could not even afford to buy a pot. They "didn't have a pot to piss in" and were the lowest of the low.

What your teacher never taught you

by Clive Barnett – 4 June 2020

Shipshape and Bristol Fashion:

This means that all is in proper order, tidy and secure. The saying dates from the 1840s, when Bristol was the most prosperous port on the west-coast of Britain, its wealth coming from the Atlantic slave and sugar trades, and its ship chandleries were regarded as amongst the best in the country. In the 19th century, before changes were made to the harbour entrance, Bristol had an exceptionally high tidal range of 40-45 feet. As a result, at low tide, ships moored within the harbour would be aground and fall to one side. So, every item of equipment, luggage and cargo had to be properly stowed away or secured to prevent them falling – hence everything needed to be shipshape and Bristol fashion.

Cock Up

Cock originally meant stand up conspicuously, turn up at the edge, or bend at an angle. Thus, in the 17th and 18th centuries, we have the terms cock-up one's ears, cock-up one's nose, cock a snook and ladies were advised by milliners to cock-up their bonnets. There was also the cocking (or priming) of a gun, and a cocked hat (the brim of which was turned up). In time, the phrase came to be applied to things which, by mistake or otherwise, had been left sticking up: thus, there was the accidental leaving of the ends of ship's spars in a tilted or cocked position; the accidental putting up (into flight) of woodcocks during a hunt; the accidental leaving of the spigots (or cocks) on beer barrels; the incorrect placement of the cock-feather when loading a longbow; and the accidental misalignment of text in a line of type (the enlarged capital letters that used to be seen at the beginning of paragraphs were called cock-up letters).

Bob's Your Uncle

Bob's your uncle is an Irish phrase (one, incidentally, my father-in-law from Cashel in Tipperary often used) and means 'There it is', 'You're good to go', 'You're all set' etc. (Think of the French et voilà!). As a phrase it dates back to 1887, when the British Prime Minister Lord Salisbury (Robert Cecil) appointed Arthur Balfour to the highly sensitive post of Chief Secretary for Ireland. This was the time of mounting agitation for tenants' rights orchestrated by the Irish Land League (later to morph into the Irish National League); many in Ireland took exception to Balfour's appointment as an example of blatant nepotism because he was Salisbury's nephew, and was felt to lack the necessary qualifications and experience for the role.

Yellow Admiral

Most people have heard of the Yellow Admiral butterfly, which is native to Australia and New Zealand and has black and reddish-brown wings with distinctive yellow markings on the forewings. However, the term also has naval connotations, albeit ones that have fallen out of use: in the Royal Navy, it used to refer to a post captain promoted to the rank of rear admiral on retirement without having actually served at that rank.

Posh

Posh entered the English language early in the 1900s to mean any of the following: smart, stylish, upmarket, high-class, fashionable, chic and luxurious. Supposedly, Posh originated in the age of deluxe ocean-going travel between Britain and India when the most desirable cabins — the ones that did not get the afternoon heat — were on the port side going out and on the starboard side coming home. These luxury tickets were supposedly stamped with the letters P.O.S.H. However, we have no evidence to back up that story: no tickets stamped with POSH have been found and no magazine or newspaper articles have been identified which mention this fashionable mode of travel.

The Real McCoy

The real McCoy means the real thing or the genuine article. One explanation is that it is a corruption of the Scots The real MacKay, first recorded in 1856 as: "A drappie o' the real MacKay", which appeared in a poem entitled Deil's Hallowe'en published in Glasgow. A letter written by the Scottish author Robert Louis Stevenson in 1883 contains the phrase, "He's the real Mackay". Another possibility is that the expression is associated with an invention by Elijah McCoy's in 1872 for controlling oil-flow in locomotive engines. This was the great age of railway building in the USA and railroad engineers looking to avoid inferior copies would request it by name, inquiring if a locomotive was fitted with 'the real McCoy system'. Other possible explanations include a dispute between two branches of the Scots Clan Mackay over who was rightful leader; Joseph McCoy who was the mayor of Abilene, Kansas, in the late 19th century and who styled himself 'the real McCoy'; and the US boxer Kid McCoy.

Sold down the river

This term means a profound betrayal, cheating, deceit and originated in the southern slave states of the USA in the mid-19th century. The earliest reference is in a book entitled The Ohio Repository published in 1837. The river referred to is either the Mississippi or Ohio river. Slaves who caused trouble or who had become too expensive to keep were sold from the northern slave states into the much harsher conditions on the plantations in the lower Mississippi. Thus, they had been sold down the river. The figurative use of the phrase, meaning simply to deceive or cheat, began in the early 20th century and was used by PG Wodehouse among others.

Sweet Fanny Adams

Fanny Adams was an English girl who, aged just 8 years, was abducted and murdered by Frederick Baker, a solicitor's clerk, in Alton, Hampshire, on 24 August 1867. The murder itself was extraordinarily brutal and caused a national outcry. The expression Sweet Fanny Adams was coined in 1869 by sailors in the Royal Navy, whose macabre humour likened the contents of their tinned meat to Fanny's remains. From this it gradually became a euphemism for sweet nothing.

Tell it to the marines

Tell it to the Marines is not, as many people think, an American phrase referring to the US Marine Corps. Rather it refers to the Royal Marines and has been in use since the early 18th century. It means that the person addressed is not to be believed. The full phrase is Tell it to the marines because the sailors won't believe you, but only the first clause is usually used. The first marine corps was formed in 1664 by the Duke of York, who was the brother of King Charles II. The recruits were considered to be green and inexperienced and not on a par with hardened sailors; hence the implication that marines were naive enough to believe ridiculous tales about flying fish, for example, while that sailors were not.

And a bonus prompted by a recent discussion on 'Start the Week' on Radio 4:

Where does the term 'The Classics' come from?

The word Classics comes from the Latin adjective classicus, meaning "belonging to the highest class of citizens". The word derives in turn from the original Latin word for a trumpet-like instrument which was used to summon the citizens of Rome to gather together to be assessed for taxation purposes. Once summoned the citizenry was grouped together according to wealth and social standing. In time, the word came to be used to describe the members of the highest class. By the 2nd century AD, the word was also used to describe writers of the highest quality as opposed to the proletarius whose writing pandered to the lower classes. By the 6th century AD, the word had acquired a second meaning referring to the subject studied by pupils in school.

Reginald Heber

by Michael Laird – 4 June 2020

One of the hymns we often sing on Trinity Sunday – next Sunday – is 'Holy, holy, holy, Lord God Almighty', by Reginald Heber. This is just one of Heber's hymns which we still use – others include 'Brightest and Best of the Sons of the Morning', 'God that Madest Earth and Heaven', and 'From Greenland's Icy Mountains'. We might be curious to know something about writers of familiar hymns, and Heber was a most attractive personality whose life is perhaps of special interest.

Born in 1783, he became Rector of Hodnet in Shropshire, and emerged as a minor Romantic poet, friendly with Scott, Southey and Coleridge. In 1805-06 he had undertaken an unconventional Grand tour, travelling through Scandinavia into Russia and south as far as the Crimea, where he was delighted to encounter the Muslim Tartar community.

He came to see this as a foretaste of India, to which he went in 1823 as the second Bishop of Calcutta. Much of his time was taken up with travel, to visit the scattered Anglican communities throughout India and Ceylon. His most notable journey was of a length and difficulty unprecedented for a C.of E. bishop – across northern India from Calcutta to Bombay via Delhi, returning by sea via Ceylon to Calcutta. He kept a Journal, which was soon published and has been regarded as an exceptionally valuable description of India, by contemporaries and by modern historians alike. His interests included the economy, administration, education, culture, and the predicament of Indian princes. He shared the contemporary British distaste for Hinduism but not the prejudice against its followers. He considered British rule to be beneficial for India on balance, but criticised certain aspects of it.

Standing himself in the middle of the Anglican spectrum between Evangelicals and High Churchmen, he was notable for his friendliness – unusual at the time – towards representatives of other churches that he encountered – English Dissenters, Scottish Presbyterians, and the oriental churches. He was recognised as a man of good sense, charm and humanity which earned him widespread popularity. He died prematurely while on a tour of south India in April 1826.

'The Prophet'

by Tom Kennar – 18 June 2020

'The Prophet' is a book of 26 prose poetry fables written in English by the Lebanese-American poet and writer Kahlil Gibran. It is Gibran's best known work. The Prophet has been translated into over 100 different languages, making it one of the most translated books in history (next to the Bible), and it has never been out of print.

Synopsis: The prophet, Al Mustafa, has lived in the city of Orphalese for 12 years and is about to board a ship which will carry him home. He is stopped by a group of people, with whom he discusses topics such as life and the human condition. The book is divided into chapters dealing with love, marriage, children, giving, eating and drinking, work, joy and sorrow, houses, clothes, buying and selling, crime and punishment, laws, freedom, reason and passion, pain, self-knowledge, teaching, friendship, talking, time, good and evil, prayer, pleasure, beauty, religion, and death.

This beautiful poem, from the 'religion discourse' was suggested for the Corona Chronicle by Annelies Lewis de Lange…

I love you my brother, whoever you are -
whether you worship in your church,
kneel in your temple,
or pray in your mosque.
You and I are all children of one faith,
for the diverse paths of religion are fingers
of the one loving hand of one Supreme Being,
a hand extended to all,
offering completeness of spirit to all,
eager to receive all.

In former times, the publication in a church magazine of a poem from 'The Prophet' might have been considered scandalous. Our individual reactions to this text will be shaped by the ideas we have absorbed along the road of faith. Some will be content to believe that yes, indeed, all people are brothers and sisters, and that God offers 'completeness of spirit' to all - but only through the gift of his Son.

C.S. Lewis once spoke to this idea, by saying, in effect, that we know from Scripture that it is only through Christ that everyone can be saved. What we don't know (he went on) is whether it is necessary to commit to Christ in this life. Lewis opened up the possibility that those of other religions may well be welcomed into the open arms of Christ after death. Those who have honestly sought truth and love, along the paths of other religions, will surely run into the arms of Love Himself, when they meet him beyond the veil of death?

This is a classic intellectual compromise among those who work for ecumenism. Effectively, each religion says, "we can all agree on the existence of God but once we get to heaven, you'll see that I was right all along!". In many ways, this is a helpful rule to live by, ecumenically. It helps us to maintain our own commitment to our own faith, while being open to learning what we may from other practices.

Kahil Gibran, however, does not hold this compromised view. His poem invites us to take a further step into the mystery of God, and to allow for the notion that all religions are but fingers of the same one hand of God.

He does not deal specifically with what the effects of such a belief might be on the 'Cosmic Christ' – the Saviour of all – nor does he address our dogmas of atonement. But in stating his position so boldly, he invites us Christians to consider whether Christ might be present, perhaps unseen, in the deities of other religions too. Perhaps God who appears to us as our Saviour in the form of Christ also makes himself known, by his Spirit, by other names and other identities, in the teachings and experience of other religions? And perhaps 'salvation' is not only achieved, or possible, through the Cross, but by other means of God's grace as well?

What do you think?

Slavery and St Faith's

by Hilary Deadman – 18 June 2020

Churches, like other old buildings, can tell us a great deal about the lives and thoughts of the past generations. St Faith's is no exception.

There is evidence that the church is built on a Roman site. Roman bricks are to be seen in the walls and Roman coins were found when the tower was reconstructed in the nineteenth century. During the Roman Empire from 260 until 415 AD the slave population of the Empire has been shown at just under a million slaves. This represents between 10 and 15% of the population of 50 to 60 million inhabitants. We shall never know how many slaves were employed in this area but it is known that there are a number of villas around Havant and Langstone and that Havant was a through-road for troops and others going from north to south and to the east and west of the country.

Stronger evidence of the slave trade is to be found in the church itself. On the south wall of the Lady Chapel is a memorial to George Augustus Shawe and his family. He was born in Jamaica in 1782 and was a slave owner on the Whim Estate, St Dorothy. Following the abolition of the slave trade, he received £25,745.11s.6d in compensation. (In today's terms £20.000 equates to nearly £17m.) In 1834 the Shawe family were living at Lower Leigh, Havant, and by 1841 at Shawfield in Havant. During his time in Havant he was a judge and also a guardian of the Havant Union (the workhouse). He believed that people on Relief (those supported by the parish) should be taken off the support and made to look for work. He would arrange for the sons of the poor to get berths on board the king's ships and would obtain work for the young girls to get work in the local sacking factory. He died in 1850.

At the East end of the church above the high altar is a stained glass window in memory of Samuel Wilberforce. How many of us realise who he was? Known as 'Soapy Sam' because of his persuasive speech and manner, he was a great influencer. He was chaplain to the Prince Consort (Prince Albert), then became Bishop of Oxford in 1844 and then Bishop of Winchester in 1868. Undoubtedly his attitudes were shaped by his father who was William Wilberforce, philosopher and philanthropist, the leader of the movement to abolish the slave trade.

And now to the future: the Church of today recognises the evils of slavery and has written a comprehensive statement in accordance with the modern Slavery Act. This was issued in December 2019 and the first paragraph reads:

“Slavery is all around us, but we are too blind to see it. It is in our hands, and yet we are too insensitive to touch it. The enslaved are next to us in the streets, but we are too ignorant to walk alongside them. It must not be relegated to a footnote in history. It is still a living reality in all our communities, not because we think it is acceptable, but because our sin lies in blindness and ignorance.”

We cannot and should not destroy past history but should learn from it.

Never ignore our history…

(A supplementary thought to the previous article)
by Hilary Deadman – 25 June 2020

The American novelist Robert Heinlein said, ‘A generation which ignores history… has no part in the future’.

In St Faith’s Church through the ages there have been many faithful people who have recorded the past for future generations. Who has read Charles Longcroft’s ‘Hundred of Bosmere’? Published first in 1857, it is a fascinating, detailed book on the history of the area. It includes a large section about St Faith’s Church. Some of his arguments are not backed up from primary sources, such as suggesting that St Faith’s was once named St Barnabas’ Church. Neither does he include any index of his sources of information. However, a great deal can be learned from this comprehensive book.

In recent years our Church has had its own dedicated historians. Many long standing church members will remember Roger Bryant (about whose death we heard sadly this week. Ed) who wrote articles regularly in the parish magazine about many historical topics including the dignitaries memorialised in the Church. Before him was Ray Hawkins who was a major contributor to the church guide which is still available today.

Over the past five years the Church Recorders of the Arts Society Portsdown have been (and will continue to do so after lockdown) making a complete record of everything in the church building. This has been a mammoth task and last week’s article on slavery contained some of the research which Jenny Stewart and Pamela Davies, two of the members of the team, have contributed to the effort.

Thanks must go to everyone of previous times and of the present, who has given time and expertise to preserve the story of the past of our historic building for future generations.

The Pubs of Havant

by Clive Barnett – 18 June 2020

Pub names are used to identify and differentiate pubs. Many pubs are centuries old, from a time when their customers were often illiterate but could recognise pictorial signs. In Ireland, the names of pubs tend to be based on the name of the owner, or a former owner. However, in mainland Britain this is unusual, probably because pubs wanted names that could be related to an image on their pub sign, a key means of identifying them in an age of restricted literacy.

Pub names have a variety of origins, from random objects used as simple identification marks (e.g. The Boot, The Copper Kettle) to heraldry, especially the coats of arms of kings or local aristocrats and landowners (e.g. The Bear & Ragged Staff, The Blue Boar, The Red Lion).

Other names come from:

- animals (e.g. The Fox & Hounds, The Dog & Duck);
- the branding of pub chains (e.g. The Moon Under Water, commonly used by the JD Wetherspoon chain and inspired by George Orwell's 1946 essay in the Evening Standard);
- livery companies (e.g. The Three Tuns, The Three Horseshoes);
- local landowners (e.g. The Percy Arms, The Melbourne Arms);
- occupations and craftsmen's guilds (e.g. The Wheelwrights on Emsworth Road, The Bricklayer's Arms);
- historical events (e.g. The Trafalgar, The Alma Arms);
- literary references (e.g. The Hobbit, The Sherlock Holmes);
- myths and legends (e.g. The Black Horse, Fiddler's Green, the Green Man);
- paired names (e.g. The Shovel & Boot, The Crown & Anchor);
- personal names (e.g. The Duke of Cambridge, The Duke of Wellington); places (e.g. The Tavistock Inn, The Plymouth Inn);
- plants (e.g. The Pineapple, The Holly Bush);
- pub buildings (e.g. The Red House, The Crooked House);
- services provided by pubs (e.g. The Coach & Horses, The Horse & Groom); pub food and drink (e.g. The Barley Mow, The Haunch of Venison);
- religion (e.g. The Hope & Anchor, The Lamb & Flag);
- royalty (e.g. The King's Head, The Prince of Wales, The Crown);
- ships (e.g. The Victory, The Prospect of Whitby);

- sport and games (e.g. The Cricketers, The Bat & Ball);
- hunting (e.g. The Bird in Hand, The Greyhound);
- topography (e.g. The Half-Way House; The World's End);
- trades, tools and products (e.g. The Harrow, The Ship);
- and transport (e.g. The Ship at Hayling Island bridge, The Red Arrow, The Great Western and The Traveller's Rest).

However, my favourites are names derived from puns, jokes and corruptions (e.g. The Dew Drop Inn, The Hop Inn, The Dirty Duck, The Jolly Taxpayer), and political incorrectness (e.g. The Turk's Head, The Black Boy, The Labour in Vain).

Currently, the ten most popular pub names in Britain are (in order): The Red Lion, The Crown, The Royal Oak, The White Hart, The Swan, The Plough, The Bell, The Rose & Crown, The Queen's Head and The Railway Tavern.

The Lost Pubs of Havant

Havant, in common with most other towns in the country, used to have a large number of pubs, most of which have closed in the course of the last fifty years. All of them derive their names from the connections mentioned above. They include:
The Black Dog, which was in West Street and closed in 2002;
The Blue Anchor, South Street, 1914;
The Brown Jug, East Street, c1950;
The City Arms, Isambard Kingdom Brunel Road;
The Cobden Arms, West Street;
The Cricketers, Leigh Park, 2006;
The Curlew, Petersfield Road, c2000;
The Dolphin, West Street, 1958;
The Dolphin, Park Road South, 2004;
The Echo, West Street;
The Foresters' Arms, North Street, 1910;
The Fountain, West Street, 1913;
The Fox, Prospect Lane, 2012;
The George, West Street, 1960s;
The Greyhound, Park Parade, 2001;
The Hearts of Oak, West Street;
The Millers Arms, East Street, 1888;
The Perseverance, North Street 2012;
The Royal Oak, North Street, 2012;

The Sailors Home, Riders Lane, 1915;
Speed the Plough, South Street, 1960s;
The Star, North Street, 2011;
The Sun Inn, East Street, 1780;
The Warren, Strouden Court Precinct, 1999;
The Wheatsheaf, Botley Drive;
The White Bear, East Street;
The White Hart, East Street, 2014.
Here are the derivations of the names of some local pubs still in existence:

The Robin Hood (Havant)
This is a pub name that derives from legend. Robin Hood is sometimes partnered by his second-in-charge to form the name Robin Hood and Little John. These and similar Robin Hood names can be found throughout Nottinghamshire as well as in Havant town centre! Pubs built in the new estates of the 1960s by the Home Brewery of Daybrook, Nottinghamshire, include related names like The Arrow, Friar Tuck, Longbow, Maid Marian and Major Oak.

The Old House at Home (Havant)
Another pub name to be found in Havant, this derives from a literary reference, in this case a sentimental 19th century ballad written by Thomas Haynes Bayly which was subsequently put to music by Edward Loder. It first appeared in his operetta entitled Francis the First in 1838. The lyrics are a two-stanza poem about childhood and yearning for home:

Oh! the old house at home where my forefathers dwelt,
Where a child at the feet of my mother I knelt,
Where she taught me the pray'r, where she read me the page,
Which, if infancy lisps, is the solace of age;
My heart, 'mid all changes, wherever I roam,
Ne'er loses its love for the old house at home!

The Royal Oak (Langstone)
This is another pub name closely associated with this area. It was inspired by an historical event: after the Battle of Worcester (1651) following the English Civil War, the defeated Prince Charles escaped the scene with the Roundheads on his tail. He managed to reach Bishop’s Wood in Staffordshire, where he found an oak tree (now known as the Boscobel Oak near Boscobel House). He climbed the tree and hid in it for a day while his

obviously short-sighted pursuers strolled around under the tree looking for him. The hunters gave up; Prince Charles came down and escaped to France to become Charles II on the Restoration of the Monarchy in 1660. To celebrate this good fortune, 29 May (Charles' birthday) was declared Royal Oak Day and the pub name remembers this. The Royal Naval ship HMS Royal Oak gets its name from the same source. Early ships were built out of the heartwood of oak trees.

The Wheelwrights' Arms (Havant)
The original Ale House on this site was The Blacksmiths Arms, run by James & Mary Lipscomb and first recorded as a beer retailer in Havant in 1839. Blacksmiths and inns often ran side by side, providing sustenance and smithy work to stagecoaches travelling the length and breadth of the country. Many blacksmiths also provided wheel-making and repair services and the pub name later changed to reflect that booming business, carried out on this same site for many years.

Sandra flies the Flag

by Sandra Haggan (Lay Pastor & Reader) – 25 June 2020

I am often asked what I have been doing over the last few weeks. Well, one of things I do is to put up the Union flag at church.

June has been a particularly busy month and I seem to have been up and down to the roof of the tower many times. I am very patriotic and I like us to be flying the Union flag whenever we can.

When I was at work at 'The Shop' (U-Need-Us – sorry I always refer to it as The Shop), I used to dress a window for many of these occasions. I remember I did a special window for the Queen's 90th birthday. We took some photos and sent them off to Buckingham Palace – and it was very exciting to get a reply. It must be in the family, because when my grandfather started the shop, there was always a Union flag flying outside. Then, when we moved to the new shop in 1960, we had a flag pole to do the same thing.

Of course the most important thing is to put it up the right way…
Last month I gave our Union flag a treat and took it home to give it a wash, it had had a problem with some pigeons! It was lovely to see it on my washing line (the right way of course!).
Anyway back to this month...

Monday 1st June was the 80th anniversary of the sinking of HMS Havant.

Tuesday 2nd June was the anniversary of HM the Queen's coronation 67 years ago in 1953. (I had a dilemma here, I feel very strongly that flags should not be left up overnight but after consultation with a friend, I left it up between the 1st and 2nd. I hope you won't tell anyone!)

Wednesday 10th June was the Duke of Edinburgh's 99th birthday.

Saturday 13th June was the Queen's official birthday; it was low key event this year but we still needed to put up the flag.

Saturday 27th June is Armed Forces Day. It is very important to show our support for our armed forces.

We have to be mindful of our friend Health and Safety these days. So I send our Tower Captain (Bill Skilleter) a text when I am going up to the roof and then again when I am down!

There are some lovely views from the tower and I keep meaning to take my binoculars. But I never think about it until I am up there!

It's such a sight to see the Union flag flying from the church, definitely worth the climb up and down the stairs!

Being on furlough

by Will Coulston (General Manager) – 2 July 2020

What it's been like to be on furlough.

Having been on furlough for some time now, I can't deny I'm looking forward to getting back to some sense of normality. Whatever that might look like, as I've said before, we will simply refer to it as normal or not refer to it at all. It'll be a way of life. One that we will adapt to without giving it a second thought.

Being on furlough isn't what many expected or assumed or, to be honest, even heard of. Why would we? After all this is the stuff Hollywood movies are made of. The thickening plot. The complex storyline. The scenarios constantly outplaying one another. I don't recall any crisis or disaster film where 'furlough' was ever mentioned though. That said, given that it literally means 'grant leave of absence to…' I've no doubt many will have heard the word used at some point. Maybe the services?

Things soon became clearer and people understood that 'furlough' was now pretty much the short name for a scheme designed to help put people on leave and prevent mass redundancies and unemployment.

I for one have benefitted from the reassurance that 80% of my income was protected and furthermore that St Faith's PCC supported an approach that covers the remaining 20% shortfall. The immediate relief that such a scheme existed at all was one that reduced serious anxieties early on and allowed us to keep a clearer head moving forward. Never underestimate how much of an impact this has had. It keeps a roof over our heads. It keeps food on the table. It keeps a sense of purpose alive in us at all times.

So the obvious question: what do you do with that time? Those that know me know I'm not one to sit still but I've been far busier than I would have expected. Those awful flooding problems we had during the storms earlier in the year where we were bailing out 55 gallons in an hour to keep it from the threshold are now sorted. With a shovel and spade at arms and time on my hands we managed to protect our home and stand a better chance of defence should this happen again. Such a relief.

Any projects and wee DIY jobs that would have stayed on a cosmic list until they were forgotten have either been completed or started. It's been such a revelation to discover and rediscover skills and knowledge and experience. All God given gifts. Ones that I am more grateful for now than ever. I'd say when I called on Him during those moments of toil and test and reflection, He answered me well. I hope I can do the same.

Now here's a thing. I didn't expect to carry a sense of guilt. Feeling that others were suffering far more than we were. That I had the support of people that wanted to ensure my income wasn't affected during this torrid time. That I had this time to reflect and pray knowing that I hadn't made enough time previously and that others will be questioning their faith right now. That many will not see or hear anyone else for days and weeks. Literal isolation. That I had time to give and it wasn't in demand.

Sure, the team here have been marvellous reaching out to others and that's been reciprocated. Let me just add here that your calls to us too have really helped. I know from personal experience how much Trudie has valued those conversations. Other than those conversations and a socially distant VE Day fundraiser, she has only been in my company and one work colleague for 11 weeks. She finally got to see her parents in the garden last week. You made the difference.

So DIY pretty much done what else? Alarm clock still set for the same time each day – and still rising before it goes off. How annoying is that?! Start the day with exercise. Normally a run or a walk or cycling next to Mrs C when she runs as she's still very nervous about being out around people. Breakfast together as ever. Water the garden (oh the irony) then set about my day.

I've been really busy with meds/prescription and food deliveries on the motorbike and this last week doing odd jobs for people, like clearing gardens and mowing and external repairs. Seeing people again hasn't been difficult. I ensure at least 2m and often far more. It's funny, you wonder if you do these things because there's an altruistic element but what is lovely is that seeing these people has made me realise how much we need each other's company right now.

Dear ol' Charlie. Who always makes me a cuppa and leaves it at the gate with a note to keep well. I don't partake and it hasn't stopped him. He still leaves me a cuppa. Felicity who leaves me two paper bags of veg. One for Mrs C and I and one for anyone else we know who might need it. Mr & Mrs L who tell me how their latest Zoom meeting went with their granddaughter. Seeing little Miss, who has gone from struggling to pick her bike up to now being stabiliser free and riding her wee bike without fear.

I'm still taking the odd photograph and even starting to learn sign language now. Obviously, the grey matter continues to work on the future for us all at St Faith's too. Meetings have still gone ahead. Laptops and

PC's are still humming away and plans are still being discussed, but it's all about taking us all happily and safely into a fresh new chapter.

And that's furlough for me.

With my deepest gratitude for all that He provides and for the love and support around us all.

What's in a name – 'Orchard Road'

by Shelagh Legg – 2 July 2020

It really was an orchard. Perhaps not all of it but some of it was, as evidenced by looking at the walls made of handmade brick. Until recently there were old damson trees, apples trees and certainly a 'Perry' pear. The pear still stands; they can live up to two hundred years. In Victorian times "Champagne Perry" was very popular. It can no longer be called that because the French have patented the Champagne region of France so it has to be a sparkling pear wine. Until recently I had two damson trees and neighbours had apples trees which have all succumbed to old age.

Orchard Road was part of a pig farm which stretched from East Street into Langstone. There were allotments where the A27 now runs, the farmhouse is in Town Hall Road and neighbours in Grove Road can remember when that was just an unmade road leading into Grove Road and across to Orchard Road.

Remains of walls and or buildings can be seen under the tarmac pavements and by number 17a a farm bothy was altered to make a too small garage! The owners of number 11 believe their chalet bungalow was the first house built in Orchard Road about 1912 or so. My own house was built in 1914 being finished in a hurry when WWI began. It was built, as were others in the road, by a Mr. Jones from Emsworth with handmade bricks.

The road backs onto Lower Grove Road and a wall made of what are called 'garden bricks' separates us. It was probably the boundary wall for the Hayling Billy and may have belonged to the Marshall family who, when they needed money, sold off parcels of land. Until the A27 went through they farmed and harvested watercress on the Lymbourne Stream. I heard this from Betty Marshall. It is not marked on my house deeds or with the land registry and the previous owners had to sign a letter to say they had never been asked to maintain it. However, it was well-built wall.

There are no drains in the road and only three widely separated street lamps, however, when the A27 was built the gap between Orchard Road and the new road was filled in with new houses and there are drains and better lighting.

Like the TV programme 'A House Through Time' it would be interesting to know who the previous owners were and their occupations. That may have to wait until more census returns are available. One certainly had a cart, he cut out the bricks on the party wall to accommodate the axles.

Any information on the long garden wall between Lower Grove Road and Orchard Road would be appreciated.

The Gedge window

by Colin Carter – 2 July 2020

Many of the stained glass windows in St Faith's tell the stories of previous parishioners not only through inscriptions but from the iconography in the stained glass picture. At the West end of the North aisle of the church there is a single 'light' dedicated to Doctor Arthur Gedge, a general practitioner who died in 1927. This memorial window was paid for by subscriptions raised by the parish.

He was very well loved and respected by his patients and 300 people attended his funeral. He was active too in local affairs and a keen amateur archaeologist who played an important part in the discovery of the Roman Villa at Warblington.

The window is dedicated to St Luke, the Patron Saint of Physicians and Artisans which immediately indicates that Arthur Gedge was a doctor. The saint holds the wand of Asclepius with two twining serpents. This represents Asclepius, the son of Apollo, the god of healing, an appropriate symbol for Luke the Physician which is still used as a symbol of medicine to this day.

The background and frame to the white glass is richly decorated with medicinal plants, patterns and symbols. Mistletoe is shown as until the late 1980s a concoction of mistletoe was used as a treatment for epilepsy. Feverfew is to be seen in the lower half of the light. This can be a cure for migraine. On the right-hand side cherry is found. This is a strong narcotic. St Luke is standing on a carpet of ivy. This plant was once used as a cure for corns.

This memorial window was dedicated on 17 October in time for St Luke's Day to mark Doctor Gedge's special place in the Havant community.

Hakim – What's in a name?

by Alan Hakim – 20 July 2020

Having been sent to Bombay in 1964 by Thomas Cook at only three weeks' notice, I wondered who the staff there had expected to arrive from London. In the 1960s, there were very few Hakims in the UK, but plenty in the Middle East and India. In fact, my family came from Egypt, but nearly 200 years ago. We have lost the oriental look. My son Tim looks more like a Viking.

There were quite a number of Christians working in the office. Many of them had Portuguese names, but others came straight out of the Bible, such as Jacob or Peter. This had an unexpected benefit when going out on a cold sales call. We would send in our cards, Mr Hakim and perhaps Mr Matthew, and by the time everyone had sorted out which was the Indian and which the Englishman, the ice was always broken.

The Portuguese names were not very varied. I remember one day my phone rang, and a voice asked to speak to Mr da Souza. "Which one?" I said, "we have five." "Mr A da Souza." "Which one?" I said, "we have three." Eventually he revealed what he was ringing about, and I transferred him to Mr Aloysius da Souza, who dealt with Passports.

In England, Hakim is a difficult name, often misspelt (the best I have had is the Devon variant, Haycombe), but in India it is easy, unlike Smith or Jones. It has two possible pronunciations: "Hackeem", a medical man, or "Harkim", a judge. Both very respectable professions. I was surprised once when the counter clerk at my bank said the name itself was a medical qualification, almost like MB. "You could set up a dispensary in the evenings."

Cooks provided me with lessons in Hindi, but I made little progress. The Munshi, an elderly gentleman, would call at my flat to teach me after work, but I had a tendency to go to sleep and learned little vocabulary. At home, we had been the only Hakim in the phone book, but in Bombay I was one of many. So when the phone rang, I left it to Kalyan, my cook, to answer. Nearly always there followed a lively discussion in Hindi, ending with him slamming down the phone saying "Wrong number hai." So at least I know the Hindi for 'wrong number'.

Life in Myrtle Court

by Jackie Brookfield – 7 August 2020

Early in the season I sowed my vegetable seeds in the little plot allowed to me in the garden of the block of apartments in which I live. I was given some leek plants and these I planted carefully in deep holes. Next morning, I went out to inspect my plot only to find that where there should have been baby leeks there were, instead, small round holes. In fact, all the plot was devastated. Somebody seemed to have danced over my carefully prepared ground and disturbed all my carefully sown seeds. Who would do such a thing?

The following night the flower beds were attacked and newly planted flowers thrown in all directions. We have help with the garden, mowing the grass and keeping shrubs and trees in check, but the flower beds we do ourselves and I have a tiny vegetable plot. Next day the mystery was solved. One of the men was walking his dog for the last time that night when he met the culprit, well, culprits in fact. It was a family of fox cubs who had chosen our garden for a playground!

How to solve the problem? We found the hole under the fence which the foxes were using and one of the men blocked it up. Next morning there was more damage and a new hole under the fence. We asked the Manager to report this to the Council and we were told that somebody would deal with it if that was really what we wanted. The foxes would be shot. That was not what we wanted! Imagine, if you will, a peaceful community of elderly residents. A man arrives carrying a gun and waits for the baby foxes to come out to play...

The foxes are still with us. They have been known to sit with a resident while she dozed in the sun in the garden. They have invented a new game which is called 'running over cars and leaving muddy footmarks'. We don't feed them or encourage them, but they have become part of life in Myrtle Court. One resident, whom I shall call Graham, has a particularly shiny car which the foxes found very attractive, so he puts a cover right over it. One of the foxes finds it very comfortable and sleeps there regularly.

As a community we have been very fortunate throughout lock-down. We have our own tradition of meeting at 6pm, glass in hand, and enjoying an hour of chat. Our communal lounge is out of use for obvious reasons, but in good weather we can still gather in the garden, safely spaced out, and enjoy company for a while. A fox has been known to join us. When winter comes what will happen? I think there might be a revolution. We might demand to use our Lounge…who knows? Watch this space for more news from Myrtle Court.

World War II – in the Far East. Aftermath

by Michael Laird – 21 August 2020

Inevitably the War in the Far East and Pacific affected Britain much less than the European war – not for nothing was the 14th Army in Burma, with its British, Indian and some African units, known as 'the forgotten army'. But its consequences were huge, not just for the countries directly affected but for the whole world, and some of them remain as potential crisis-points to this day.

Perhaps the best known derives from the manner of its ending: the dropping of the two atomic bombs on Hiroshima and Nagasaki on 6 and 9 August 1945, which began the atomic era in warfare. The question of whether these were necessary to end the war has been much debated, given that Japan's defeat was inevitable by that time. The problem was that the military hard-liners who controlled Japan's government were resolved on a final – suicidal – defence of the home islands against the conventional invasion that was being planned, which would have cost many lives on both sides. Even after the two A-bombs had been dropped – and the Soviet Union had belatedly declared war – the extremists opposed surrender, and had to be over-ruled by the Emperor in a very rare personal intervention. In any case the death-toll was comparable to that from the devastating conventional bombing of Tokyo and other cities which had already taken place. And after the war, Japan was able to rebuild as a peaceable, stable and increasingly prosperous democracy.

But the Far Eastern war had really started in China, with a Sino-Japanese clash near Beijing in July 1937: some regard this as the real beginning of World War II. The Japanese soon overran most of eastern China, forcing the Nationalist (Kuomintang – KMT) government to withdraw to Chongqing, while the Communists preserved a redoubt in the north-west. After Japan's defeat, the Communists emerged in better shape that the corrupt and incompetent KMT and were able to win the inevitable civil war by 1949. The KMT retreated to Taiwan under the protection of the USA, but the Communist regime sees this 'renegade province' as unfinished business from the civil war, and it remains a potential flash-point. One can add that although China and Japan did eventually make peace after World War II, they have not achieved a level of reconciliation comparable to that of, say, France and Germany in Europe.

Another potential flash-point is divided Korea – also a legacy from the War. Previously a Japanese colony, as Japan surrendered the Soviets moved into the north and the Americans the south. Two mutually hostile regimes emerged, and in 1950 the Communist north invaded the south. With the USA and its allies, including Britain, bringing support to the south and Communist China the north, this soon became one of the dangerous crises of the Cold War. In fact, World War III was averted, but the Korean War ended in 1953 not with a peace treaty but just with an armistice, and the peace there continues to be somewhat fragile.

Moving to south-east Asia: in 1941-42 the Japanese took over the western powers' colonial territories, including British Malaya and Burma, French Indo-China (including Vietnam), and the Netherlands East Indies – Indonesia, the greatest prize of all. Although Japanese rule in these countries soon proved harsh and unpopular, their nationalist leaders seized the opportunity presented by the humiliating collapse of the colonial regimes to ensure that these could never be restored. A key figure who understood this better than most was Lord Mountbatten, Supreme Allied Commander for south-east Asia from 1943. He came to terms with Aung San, Burma's nationalist leader (and father of Aung San Suu Kyi), which paved the way for a peaceful transition to independence in 1947-48. He did his best to persuade the Dutch and French to recognise the inevitable with good grace – unavailingly, as both plunged into bitter, costly and unsuccessful conflicts with the nationalists. The Dutch were forced to withdraw from Indonesia in 1949 and the French from Indo-China in 1954.

As for India – it was not over-run by the Japanese, but it was already on the way towards independence and the War accelerated the process.

Prime Minister Attlee appointed Mountbatten in 1947 to oversee the final act, which he did in a way which ensured remarkable goodwill from the Indian leaders. The price was Partition, with the Muslim-majority regions forming Pakistan as demanded by the main Muslim political party. Unfortunately, India and Pakistan could not agree on the fate of Kashmir, which has bedevilled their relationship ever since – yet another legacy from the late 1940s, if only indirectly resultant from World War II.

Who was John Staples?

by Ann Griffiths – 3 September 2020

JOHN STAPLES 1835 to 1905
(to whom the Bell-ringers' pewter tea pot is dedicated).

John Staples was born in Kempsford, Gloucestershire in 1835 but the 1861 census shows him as a carpenter lodging in Bedhampton village. The following year he married Emma Dunn, daughter of a hawker, at St Faith's church and in the 1875 Post Office Directory John is listed as a carpenter and wheelwright of West Street, Havant. John and Emma had three children, Frank, Florence and Frederick but sadly, Emma died in 1888, aged 47.

In 1890 John married Mary Ann Platt and the 1891 census shows them at 80 West Street, with daughter Florence, a schoolmistress. By now John was described as a master builder and in the mid-1890s he built the beautiful chapel at Havant cemetery, which was designed by AE Stallard but tragically destroyed by fire sometime after 1950.

In 1897 the Hampshire Telegraph recorded that members of the Winchester Diocesan Guild of Bell Ringers had visited Havant and rung Arthur Knight's peal of "Treble Bob Major", consisting of 5,024 changes, in three hours four minutes. Afterwards they were entertained to tea by Mr J. Staples, conductor of the Havant section of the Winchester Guild.

John Staples died in Havant on 8th January 1905, aged 70. The Portsmouth News reported that "in connection with the funeral of the late Mr John Staples, which took place at Havant Cemetery, eight members of the Winchester Diocesan Guild of Change Ringers assembled at Havant belfry and rang a quarter peal of Grandsire Triples, 1,260 changes, in forty-five minutes. Mr Staples was a much respected member of the Guild and known as a good ringer".

Stuck in a rut?

by Clive Barnett

At a recent Zoom meeting of the Standing Committee, we were discussing the problem of people changing seats during a service and how we could encourage the congregation to remain in the same seat. Clive Barnett was reminded of some Hindu wisdom from many years ago...

At the height of the Raj, when Britain ruled most of India in the mid-nineteenth century, the Khyber Pass was the main commercial and strategic artery linking the North-West of India and Afghanistan.

In the days before asphalt roads, the track through the pass was liable to becoming nearly impassable at certain times of the year. A combination of slow-moving and heavy ox carts, torrential monsoon rains and blisteringly hot sun had the effect of baking the ruts created by the carts in the wet season until they were as solid as concrete. At such times, there were many tales of abandoned carts along the length of the Pass as a result of broken axles or the carcasses of oxen which had broken their legs on the ruts.

A wise Hindu merchant, who frequently used the Pass to transport merchandise, decided to warn unwary travellers of this danger and in so doing provided us with a touchstone against which we might live our lives. He placed a notice at the start of the trackway through the Pass which read:

'Choose your rut carefully; you will be in it for many, many miles'.

The Havant Fellowship Club

by Ann Griffiths

This may be of interest – discovered among historical papers in the Spring Museum's archives. It is difficult to find much in the newspapers about the club and I wonder if anyone else has any knowledge of it.

A certain Violet Beatrice Stevens was born in Havant in 1904 and christened at St Faith's church. In 1920, aged 16, she enrolled with the 'Havant Fellowship Club' and a copy of the paperwork is in the St Faith's files at The Spring. The 1939 register shows Violet as a glove packer at the local factory.

The president of the club was the Rector's wife, Mrs Harold Rodgers, and the committee members were the Marchioness of Tavistock, who lived at Warblington House, Miss Royds, Mrs Levick, Miss Bell and Miss Paxton.

The aims of the club were 1. 'Fellowship' in the true sense of the word and 2. That girls should be drawn together in a closer sisterhood. The club badge was a red and brown ribbon on a safety pin and the motto was 'Play the Game'. The club subscription was 1s 6d a year or 2d a night.

When Violet joined the Fellowship she was proposed by Dorothy Bright and seconded by Daisy Palmer. She had to promise always to be willing to help others and to 'Play the Game' at all times. She would have had to attend twice before becoming a member, and would then have been encouraged to take advantage of monthly meetings of the Communicants Guild, Bible Classes held at Warblington House, and meetings of the Girls' Friendly Society run by Miss Bell.

FELLOWSHIP SONG
(Written for the Club)

There's a Club beside the sea,
Dear to you and dear to me,
Dear to all our girls where e'er they roam –
For no matter where they are,
Friendship reaches near and far,
And draws them back again to home.
The deeds of kindness done,
And the laughter and the fun,
Make our hearts beat loud and fast.
Remembering what is meant,

Through the love that has been spent,
By the girls of the Fellowship-Club.

CHORUS
See – Havant girls united,
Loyal and staunch and true,
Kind-hearted, keen and merry,
"PLAYING THE GAME" right through.
Lightening another's burden,
Bearing ourselves the "rub,"
Do what we can,
That is our plan,
Girls of the "Fellowship-Club.

When there comes the hour of need,
On wings of love we'll speed,
To encourage and to cheer the hearts of all.
Be the danger what it may,
Ready now – as yesterday,
To answer to another's call.
For is it not our aim,
To make ourselves a name,
By holding out a helping hand.
It never shall be said,
That loving hearts are dead,
While there's a girl in the Fellowship-Club.

CHORUS

Progress

A reflection by Bill Jones

I was born in the middle of World War II (I know you didn't think I was that old). Anyway, I was told that during the war we had curfews and Wardens patrolling the streets, "Put that light out!" and "Careless talk costs lives!" Don't help the enemy!

78 years later, and I am told we have curfews and wardens patrolling the streets trying to help with Covid confusion, dispersing groups of more than six. It can only be a matter of time before… "Careless Covid cost's lives." Don't help the enemy! Still, that's progress?

Cpl Bill Jones. Farlington platoon

Count your blessings

A reflection by Sandra Haggan

While talking to a friend last night she told me of something that she started doing when lock down began:

She keeps a gratitude journal, and each day writes down three things that she is grateful for...they can be small things or big things. Then sometimes when the days don't feel so good, you can look back and remember the good things. All it takes is an ordinary notebook, it doesn't have to be anything fancy.

On Friday, while collecting some bits for our Harvest Festival along the Billy Line, I saw a robin and he was just sitting on the branch of a tree singing his beautiful song. I stopped and listened and had a little chat with him. I think I would write that in my gratitude journal.

Some days you will find lots to write but I am sure you will always be able to find three things.

The Church of England School in Brockhampton

by Ann Griffiths

At The Spring Arts and Heritage Centre, now reopened, I found a 1981 News article about Leslie Blanch, who was a pupil at the Church of England School in Brockhampton Lane from 1914 to 1921.

Leslie told the reporter that during the war the classroom was full of jam jars and old bottles, which were being collected to help fund the purchase of a special wickerwork wheelchair to help Ernest Deadman, a former pupil, who had suffered serious spinal injuries in France in 1916. The wheelchair was the idea of one of the teachers, Miss Hughes, who was a volunteer at the Red Cross auxiliary hospital at Langstone Towers. Leslie said that on his first outing Ernest was brought up to the school to thank them.

Ernest Deadman was born in Havant in 1894 and grew up at The Old Mill, Langstone, where his father was a cowman. During WWI, Gunner Deadman was an RFA driver. In 1917, while serving in France, he was shot in the face and leg and his spinal cord was fractured. He died of his wounds in 1920 and is remembered on the Havant war memorial.

Editor's note: Ernest Deadman is no relation to Hilary and David Deadman of this parish.

A company bids to buy the Church!

by Ann Griffiths

This was the headline of a News article in 1974, when a London development company wrote to the Reverend Derek Brown saying that a client of theirs was looking for sites to purchase in shopping areas. They were interested in buying St Faith's Church and there would be sufficient capital to pay for a new building on an alternative site in Havant.

The Rector said, 'There was no concern for the church at all. It was simply to be demolished. Before the church could be sold it would have to be declared redundant and a Private Member's Bill would have to be passed. Anyone can see that it is not dilapidated or unused. It is a ridiculous idea.'

The Rector had written to the company saying that he was very happy to tell them that the church was prospering and that they were thinking of building additional premises on a new housing area. 'because business is so good'. The Rector went on to say, 'With the upsurge of materialism people are realising that money can't buy everything and that includes the Parish Church of St Faith's. Your clients might well be interested in acquiring the site opposite the Dolphin and Anchor in Chichester on which stands the Cathedral but I am very doubtful whether the Cathedral authorities are at present considering the possibility of parting with their property.

'Greetings to your client and tell them the church is open all day and every day for worship and we will be pleased to see them, I enclose a copy of the parish magazine.'

Islamic Enlightenment

A reflection by Michael Laird

A lot of newspapers and some western politicians would have us believe that Islam is a backward-looking religion, which we in 'the West' should resist for fear of Sharia Law being established in British streets. How true is this, in fact? In this fascinating essay, our resident historian, Michael Laird, takes a look at the history of the 'Islamic Enlightenment'. Perhaps we need to see a bigger picture to gain a truer understanding? Ed.

I have recently caught up with an important book by the journalist and historian Christopher de Bellaigue entitled ‘The Islamic Enlightenment’. He takes issue with a view widespread in the West that Islam is hostile to ‘progress’ and modernity, and needs a Reformation and Enlightenment after the model of 16th-18th century Europe. Focussing on Turkey, Egypt and Iran as key centres of influence in the Islamic world, he points out how two centuries ago now, radical reform and modernisation did in fact start to take shape, largely under Western influences.

As of 1800, printing in these countries hardly existed; only about 3% of the population was literate; women were secluded in the harem; slaves were bought and sold; outbreaks of plague still occurred. But by then the once-formidable Ottoman-Turkish Empire had suffered humiliating defeats by European countries and its economy was in decline.

Awareness of this stimulated a programme of change and reform known as the Tanzimat. Books were translated from European languages; schools were established teaching modern subjects outside the control of the traditional Islamic authorities; new legal codes were introduced based on the French system, not the Sharia, and with Christians and Jews on an equal footing with Muslims; slavery was outlawed. Syria and Iraq were still provinces of the Ottoman Empire, so these reforms percolated there also.

It is true that reforming decrees from the top could not be rapidly or easily implemented across a still very traditional society. And nationalists among the Christian peoples of the empire, notably the Greeks, Serbs and Bulgarians, were not satisfied by these reforms and moved to break away as independent states. Nevertheless, the bare fact of these radical changes, introduced under the authority of the Sultan who was still recognised as the Caliph of the Islamic community, is a testament to the potential for change in Islam.

In Egypt, change was abruptly heralded by Napoleon's invasion in 1798: Nelson destroyed his fleet, but this did not stop the impact of European ideas. During the next 80 years its rulers pursued policies similar to the Ottomans. An unprecedented reception of European influences was symbolised by the opening of the Cairo Opera House in 1871; Khedive Ismail claimed 'we are now part of Europe!' Muslim scholars emerged to argue that the essentials of Islam were compatible with modern Western science and ideas, notably Muhammed Abduh, who was appointed Grand Mufti in 1899. He had no problem with Evolution; spoke out against polygamy; was friendly to people of other faiths; and used his position as head of the Sharia courts to give the most liberal interpretations of Islamic law. But if the 19th century saw an Islamic Enlightenment, de Bellaigue points out that the 20th brought something of a Counter-Enlightenment.

By 1914 the whole of north Africa was under French, British or Italian control – and after World War I the French and British expanded also into Iraq, Syria and Palestine following the defeat of the Ottoman Empire. People whose forebears had looked to European countries as inspirations for reform and rejuvenation now regarded them as imperialist interlopers. And the western-style liberal parliamentary systems which emerged in Egypt, Iraq and elsewhere came to be discredited as corrupt, ineffective and faction-ridden. This paved the way for military dictators: Nasser and his successors, Saddam Hussein, and the Assads: nationalists no doubt, but oppressive to their opponents and no friends to the pious. And whether parliamentary or dictatorial, these secular Arab regimes were humiliated by the emergent Israeli state in 1948 and 1967. Saudi Arabia, with its conservative Islamic regime, only emerged as a leading Arab state after the 1967 disaster.

Meanwhile in Turkey and Iran in the 1920s-30s Kemal Ataturk and Reza Shah had established strongly secularising, anti-clerical dictatorships. The backlash in Iran erupted with a vengeance in 1979 under Ayatollah Khomeini's leadership, and more gently under Erdogan in Turkey in recent years. Also in 1979 the Soviet Union invaded Afghanistan: resistance against this godless empire was galvanised under an Islamic banner. The Taliban emerged out of this conflict in the '90s – and allowed Al Qaida to establish a base; the even more virulent IS arose out of the turmoil in Syria and Iraq.

But such violent extremists, however news-worthy, are a small minority: despite apparent setbacks, the values which characterised the Islamic Enlightenment have been accepted in practice by many in what is now a world-wide community.

An interesting find...

by Ann Griffiths – 15 October 2020

In 1993, when workmen were giving St Faith's church hall a 'facelift', Canon Brown asked them to look behind a hatch in the hall 'out of pure curiosity'. Much to everyone's surprise they found two prayer books, dated 1806 and 1872, and a bible marked 1846. Apparently, the bible was a gift from the Rector, Thomas Goodwin Hatchard, who was at Havant from 1846 to 1856.

Canon Brown offered the books to Havant Museum and the library but I was told by Jennifer Redhouse that they were now in the Portsmouth History Centre and could be read ' with the permission of the incumbent'. Thomas Goodwin Hatchard was the son of Thomas Hatchard, the publisher, and some of his sermons can be read online. He also wrote 'The

Floweret Gathered. A Brief Memoir of Adelaide Charlotte Hatchard', who was born in Havant in 1849 but died aged eight, in Guildford. In 1868 her father was appointed to the Bishopric of Mauritius, only to die there 'of a fever' in February 1870, aged fifty-two.

Aunty Wyn

by Bill Jones – 15 October 2020

Rector Tom wrote a lovely piece in last week's Corona Chronicle about the death of our dear friend Wyn, or "Aunty Wyn" as she became known. As you read this edition, we are preparing to lay Wyn to rest on the 29th of the month. For many of us it will be a day of happy memories tinged with much sadness at the loss of such a good friend and founding member of "The Monday Club".

I would just like to add a few thoughts about my working partner, friend, and someone that I could share a thought and indeed a joke with. Wyn and I became partners on the Monday Stewarding team after the sad death of Mo Evans.

Wyn and I did not apply for the post or have to appear in front of a huge selection committee. It was more a matter of 'Can you do Monday mornings?'. So, we were thrown together as a partnership, with no one being really sure whether we would come to blows within a matter of weeks. But it soon became clear that we were going to be a good team with a blend of quiet and…not so quiet.

In our early days it was often just the two of us. We would chat about a wide range of subjects. Wyn would tell me of her early life in Westbourne, how she met her husband Cyril, of what life was like best part of a century ago and how they were married in the Village church.

Cyril, worked with nature, he was good at woodwork and spent many years in the nursery at Stansted House. Later when he became ill, Wyn was his fulltime carer. I always knew when an anniversary of their wedding or Cyril's Birthday came around, as Wyn was quieter than usual.

Mostly though, Monday mornings were fun and laughter all the way. I also admired the commitment Wyn had to St Faith's. Come rain or shine she would catch a bus from her home to Havant, and by the time I arrived (always five minutes late!), Wyn had the kettle steaming and I was greeted with 'Good afternoon Sir!'.

I have a theory why Monday morning in St Faith's became popular. When a visitor came into church, I would verbally accost them! Then, before they could catch their breath Wyn would arrive at my shoulder and with a welcoming smile, and shove a cup of tea and biscuit in their hand. The Monday Club was born!

A few years ago, Wyn began a series of hospital incarcerations, but the Monday Club team visited. Bob Crutchley, Martin and Pat would also supply a taxi service. When I took Wyn home and helped her out of my car there was always a cry of 'JCB required!', which made her hoot with laughter. We celebrated Wyn's 90th Birthday with cake and candles.

In the present crisis we have no idea when we will all be back together again. I really hope that day is not far away. But when it does arrive, for the Monday Club, I will look at an empty chair and think of the good times and good fun we shared with "Aunty Wyn".

God Bless You and thank you, my friend.

William John Duffin and the flagpole

by Ann Griffiths – 22 October 2020

According to a News article in The Spring archives, Bill Duffin came to Havant in 1901, aged 21, after spending fifteen months serving with the Bedfordshire Volunteers in South Africa. He had previously been employed as a skinner at the leather and parchment works in Potton, Bedfordshire and in the 1911 census he is in the same job at Havant parchment works. Bill was also the last man to leave when the parchment works at Homewell closed in 1936. He then obtained a job as a builder and when in his sixties, 'he made local history by shimmying up the St Faith's flagpole to replace a worn rope'.

Bill was a family man, loved gardening, and had a flock of twenty racing pigeons. His motto was, 'Plenty of work and never worry about anything'. He was living in Grove Road when he died in 1975, at the ripe old age of ninety-six.

St Christopher

by Sandra Haggan – 29 October 2020

We pass a carving of St Christopher every time we come in the North Door, have you ever stopped and read about him? I have read it several times lately, and thought that you might like to too.

St. Christopher July 25
Martyred c. A.D. 250

St. Christopher heard the voice of a Child which called him and said: 'Christopher, come out and bear me over.' Then he awoke and went out, but he found no man.

A second, and yet a third time was he called and came thither, and then he found a Child beside the rivage of the river, which prayed to him goodly to bear him over the water.

And then Christopher raised up the Child on his shoulder, and took his staff, and entered into the river for to pass. And the water of the river arose and swelled more and more: and the Child was heavy as lead, and always as he went the water increased and grew more and the Child more and more waxed heavy, insomuch that Christopher had great anguish and was afeared to be drowned.

And when he was escaped with great pain and passed the water and set the Child aground. He said to the Child, 'Child, Thou hast put me in great peril: Thou weighest almost as I had the world upon me, I might bear no greater burden.'

And the Child answered, 'Christopher, marvel thee nothing, for thou hast not only borne all the world up on thee, but thou hast borne Him that created and made all the world upon thy shoulders. I am JESUS CHRIST the King, to Whom thou servest in this work. And because that thou know that I say to be the truth, set thy staff in the earth by thy house, and thou shalt see to-morn that it shall bear flowers and fruit.'

Our portable Font

by Ann Griffiths – 29 October 2020

In 1974 a ship's bell, incorporated into a purpose made font, featured in a ceremony at St Faith's Church.

The bell, engraved 'RFA SPA 1941', came from a coastal water carrier. The ship was ordered in October 1939, was commissioned in April 1942 and between July 1942 and October 1944 she supplied fresh water to ships at Scapa Flow. In 1970 the ship was purchased by H.G. Pounds Shipowners and Shipbreakers Ltd of Portsmouth, for scrap but was resold to Haulbowline Industries Ltd of West Cork to be broken up.

An article in The News, dated 2 November1974, quotes the Rector as saying, 'With so many Naval families in the area I thought it was fitting that we should have the bell in our church.' First-year construction students at Highbury College were set the task of designing a font by Head of Department, Eric Hewitt, who was a member of the Parochial Church Council.

The chosen design was the work of Neil Pritchard of Fareham, aged 17, and Arthur Harrison, a senior technician at the college, made an oak plinth using wood supplied by the St Faith's Mothers' Union. The font was initially kept in the vestry for safety and brought out for baptisms. It can now be seen at St Nicholas' Chapel, Langstone.

Havant's Music Festival – 1791!

by Ann Griffiths – 5 November 2020

In the summer of 1791, the Hampshire Chronicle carried an announcement about Havant's Annual Music Festival when sacred music would be played in the parish church. The Messiah would be performed in the morning and in the evening, there would be 'a Grand Selection from the works of Handel'. Tickets at 4 shillings for the Messiah and 3 shillings for the evening performance could be purchased at all the principal inns. 'The whole band will consist of upwards of one hundred performers. No expense has been spared.'

Mr Printer, one of the principal vocalists of the Foundling Hospital, in London, would open the programme in the morning with an organ concerto (gratis). Mr Shaw, principal instrumentalist of the band at Drury Lane Theatre would be playing a concerto on the violin and choristers from London, Canterbury, Salisbury and Chichester would be attending.

On 4thJuly the Chronicle stated that 'By particular desire of several respectable families in Havant and Neighbourhood the Price of admittance is reduced to THREE SHILLINGS in the morning and HALF-A-CROWN in the evening. N.B. Admittance to the Rehearsal on the preceding evening is ONE SHILLING.'

There is quite a lot about John Printer online in Google Books and on the Foundling Museum website. He was apparently born with cataracts and was blind. He was admitted to the Foundling Hospital in London as a baby and baptised there in 1756. He was taught to play the organ when he was twelve. He was well paid as an organist for the Hospital and the parish church of St Katherine Coleman before being employed to teach singing in the Chapel. Interestingly, Handel had been a Governor of the Foundling Hospital, where the Messiah was performed each year in the Chapel, for the benefit of the charity, a tradition that continued until the 1770s.

Please stand

by Rex Plowman

I heard recently of a Parish in the South of England who were having financial problems. So on a Sunday morning at the regular service the Vicar felt that he must express his concern about the financial state of their Church. At a suitable time in the Service he wanted to express his concern that a serious shortfall of funds would affect every member of the Church and its future viability.

So grasping the nettle during the sermon, he said, "After all that I have said, would those of you who are willing to increase their monthly contribution to the Church funds, please stand up".

The organist immediately followed by playing the National Anthem.

Onward Christian Soldier – Basil Aston

by Ann Griffiths – 5 November 2020

Basil Aston was vicar of St. Mark's Portsea from 1933 to 1937 and Rector of St Faith's Church, Havant, from 1937 to 1943. (Our present Rector was also, previously, Rector of St Mark's, Portsea! Ed.) Aston was Rural Dean of Havant from 1938 to 1943.

He was born in 1880 at Fyfield, Berks, where his father was the vicar. He was educated at St. John's College, Oxford, and Wells Theological College, and in 1904 he was ordained Deacon. He held curacies in Somerset and Wiltshire before the outbreak of war in 1914. During the war he was a temporary chaplain to the Forces, was wounded, twice mentioned in despatches, and awarded the DSO for conspicuous gallantry during operations.

On 25 August 1916 The London Gazette published his citation. 'For two days and a night he worked incessantly, tending and clearing the wounded under shellfire. During the night after working for twelve hours he helped carry a wounded man to the dressing station through the trenches, blown in and deep in mud. He then immediately went back to rescue others.'

In 1924 Basil married Erica Bodington, a clergyman's daughter. She had worked at the YWCA Central Club in Boulogne from March 1918 to February 1919.

Canon Basil Aston was honorary chaplain to the Bishop of Salisbury from 1947 to 1951, and resigned his living in 1954. He died in Sherborne, Dorset, in 1957, aged seventy-six. The Times of 17 May 1957 carried an obituary by 'CP', who wrote,

'Canon Basil Aston was the most lovable man I have ever known. He was a strong man, a wise man possessed by a devastating common sense. He was a happy man enjoying the simple things of life. As I look back upon him he leaves a sense of continuing joy. There must be countless people who were the better for merely having seen the vicar as he walked the roads and streets of the parishes he served. He knew that Christianity was a life to be lived. He knew and understood the dogmas and profundities, but he also knew that it was not much use spending time talking about them. His ministry was a ministry to individual men and women. He brought peace with him. He was in the very best tradition of the English Parish Priest. He will be remembered by all who met him with gratitude and real affection.'

Havant War Memorial

by Ann Griffiths – 5 November 2020

In 1919 the Bishop of Winchester formed a small committee to advise with respect to parochial war memorials. One member of the committee was Sir Charles Archibald Nicholson Bart FRIBA, who together with Alfred Edwin Stallard FSI designed the Havant War Memorial. Sir Charles was a well-known ecclesiastical architect and Alfred Stallard was a well-respected Havant architect, who had designed a number of important local buildings. He was also surveyor to the Urban District Council for nearly thirty years.

The memorial, which is built of Portland stone and flint, was set in an alcove on what was church land at Havant's ancient crossroads. The appeal letter of February 1922 stated that it would be open and accessible to the public footway. Everyone with an interest in Havant was asked to contribute so that it would be a Memorial of the whole town. It was completed free of debt at a cost of £435. The stonemasons chosen for its construction were Henry G Wilkins and Sons of Portsmouth. Little did Henry Wilkins know that his own grandson, Flight Sergeant John Phillip Wilkins, (shown here) would be added to the memorial after he was shot down over Benghazi in 1941 while acting as a decoy for the rest of his squadron.

The unveiling of the cross took place at 3 p.m. on Saturday 30th September 1922. The service was conducted by Rev. Harold Rodgers, with the lesson being read by Rev. Edward Kirby of the Congregational Church. The Hampshire Telegraph reported on the impressive scenes at the dedication ceremony. Major-General Sir John Davidson KCMG DSO MP spoke of the courage and unselfishness of the men of Havant who had died for their country. Sir John unveiled the Memorial Cross and committed it into the care of the Local Authority. Frederick Leng, chairman of Havant Urban District Council, accepted the guardianship of the memorial on behalf of the council. Mr Leng and his wife had lost their son, Private Harold Leng, in September 1918 when he was killed in action while serving with the Hampshire Regiment in the Ypres sector. According to the Hampshire Telegraph Mrs Leng was the originator of the project for the erection of the Havant War Memorial. For seven years she was assisted by the Rector and collected from house to house for the funds. She later 'tended the memorial so that it was never without flowers for even a day'. Also, Alfred Stallard, joint architect, lost two young cousins, Albert Donald Stallard in 1915 and James Alan Stallard in 1918. The earliest local death recorded on the memorial is that of Lieutenant Lynton Woolmer White who died on 3rd September 1914. During September 1916 nine men died and 1918 was the worst year with thirty deaths. A further five men died after the end of the war.

Havant Borough Council owns the memorial and is responsible for maintaining it. It was Grade II listed in 2013 thanks to the efforts of several local historians. Recently some more names were added to commemorate those who had laid down their lives in the cause of freedom since the end of the second world war.

Adapted from the booklets by Ann Griffiths
http://thespring.co.uk/media/3463/22-the-great-war-of-1914-to-1918-3.pdf
http://thespring.co.uk/media/3006/36aa-havant-in-the-second-world-war.pdf

Shaken, not stirred

by Tom Kennar – 5 November 2020

From Tom Kennar: Following the sad news of the death of Sean Connery this week, I posted a wry message on Facebook. It simply said 'Kennar, Tom Kennar. Thank you, Sean". Hopefully, James Bond fans got the joke.

I was then contacted by Catherine Billam who informed me that in Icelandic, 'Kennar' means 'Teacher'. This was supplemented by Mike Skiffins, who pointed out that Iceland is close to Scotland (well, as he said, closer than Australia!) and that in the Celtic tongue to 'ken' something is to know something. So, in a single 24-hour period, my sense of my own name has gone from indifference to being 'The Teacher who Knows...'. Well, that's nice then, isn't it?

Your country still needs you!

by Bill Jones – 5 November 2020

Bill writes: 'This short piece came about when I noted several people who are anxious or have been in lockdown, or at home, and are feeling a bit fed up with life, or in one case had lost her husband two years ago and is still feeling a bit sorry for herself. Their statement "I am fed up with nothing to do today, or tomorrow" led me to think of all the lives and the ultimate sacrifice made by millions of service personal in numerous wars... so... that we have a tomorrow'.

I'm fed up!... I've got nothing to do again today! and I won't have tomorrow, I'm worried and lonely… I'm really fed up with life… (I hear you say). Don't ask how I know what you said, because… I'm dead. I left here a long time ago and sorry, I can't help you with what you're going do today or tomorrow… But… can I tell you what I am doing today… as it turned out my last day!

The Sergeant told us last night…'you're going over the top in the morning lads….' One of the chaps said afterwards 'we've lost a lot of blokes going over the top.' Don't know how he knows that…

I came out here with my two mates from back home, Chris Wheeler and Ralph Lenton. They went over the top yesterday. Come to think of it, I haven't seen them today! We decided to come out here after seeing that chap on the posters, he said, "Your Country Needs You", so we came. To be honest I don't really know where I am, except it's foreign. I'd never heard of this place. And now I'm here I can't even pronounce the name.

Another funny thing: the Sergeant said last night, 'when you go over the top, you need to be ready, because the enemy will want to kill you!' I was told I must kill him. Strange that ain't it! I have heard of the country he comes from, but I've never met anyone from there. I won't know him, and he won't know me. I don't suppose we will have time to say hello and even if we did we wouldn't understand each other's language. But the first time we set eyes on each other, we must shoot to kill. Funny that ain't it?

Most of us have been up all night writing, so I thought I would just add a line to you at home. Sorry I don't know what you are going to do today or even tomorrow! I just thought you would like to know what I am doing today.

Anyway, I have go now. I can see the Sergeant coming along the lines. Must be time to go over the top…

When you go home tell them this and say: for your tomorrow we gave our today…

Having a quiet week?

by Tom Kennar – 19 November 2020

Hopefully, we've all been having a quieter week, with Remembrance-tide behind us, and the evenings drawing in. But it wasn't a quieter week for poor Graham, our Director of Music. He bravely put on a one-man, live-streamed show of organ music (with Remembrance in mind), which raised a pleasant £90 to support local musicians and the church building.

What he didn't expect, however, was that half the organ would cease working just about in the middle of his concert! (It later turned out to be no more than a stuck magnet…these things happen even with newly refurbished mechanical beasties!). Graham courageously ploughed on though – much to the appreciation of those watching from home, and to the relieved Rector who was operating the camera over Graham's shoulder!

Well done Graham...for keeping going when your instrument was collapsing around you!

Well-being advice

by Sandra Haggan – 12 November 2020
with contributions from Penny Britt & Christopher Glassett

No sun — no moon!
No morn — no noon —
No dawn — no dusk — no proper time of day.
No warmth, no cheerfulness, no healthful ease,
No comfortable feel in any member —
No shade, no shine, no butterflies, no bees,
No fruits, no flowers, no leaves, no birds! —
November!

Thomas Hood 1799-1845

As we know November can be one of the bleakest months. This year, just as we get used to the shorter days we have Covid 19 to deal with too! This may leave many feeling worried, weighed down and very anxious. There are, of course, some things we can do to help ourselves if we are feeling like this:

Box breathing: This slows down our breathing and so helps to reduce anxiety. Give it a go: breathe in for a count of four, hold for a count of four and then breathe out for a count of four.

Have a routine for the day. Try to keep a morning and bed time routine. Plan things to keep you busy during the day, a walk or perhaps clearing out a wardrobe or staring a household task that you always have been meaning to do.

Take some exercise: Go for a walk, the best time for a walk at this time of the year is between eleven and three o'clock. The fresh air is good for us, and a walk gets everything going, getting the blood pumping around. Remember we are allowed to walk with one friend, so if you feel you are able, plan this into your week.

Enjoy your meals: If possible keep to a meal time routine and try to plan simple, healthy meals and snacks through the day. Look at including a rainbow of colours from fruit and vegetables. Think about trying out a new recipe or two or doing a bit of home baking.

Positive quotes: These are good for the morning; write a few on cards to look at when you need them.

Grounding: Diverting your mind, focus your eye on three things, concentrate on what you can see or hear.

Keep a gratitude/blessing journal: At the end of each day write down three things to be grateful for they can be simple things: the beautiful blue sky, the autumn colours, hearing the birds sing etc. Look back on these when, perhaps, it is a difficult day.

Jigsaws, colouring, crossword puzzles: Adult colouring books are quite inexpensive but are a way to distract the mind and relax. Concentrating on suduko or a crossword can also be a good way to take your mind off worries or concerns.

Give a friend a call: (If you haven't spoken to anyone). It's good to talk to people, why not try a video call if you can?

Give yourself a treat: And enjoy it!
Read the Bible: spend some time reading, if you do not usually read the Bible maybe start with the Gospels, Matthew, Mark, Luke and John or the psalms. Some words may speak to you.

Psalm 27:1 The Lord is my light and my salvation; whom shall I fear?

Psalm 46: Be still and know that I am God.

Psalm 139: That feeling that God knows us so well.

Matthew 6:34 So do not worry about tomorrow, for tomorrow will bring worries of its own. Today's trouble is enough for today.
A couple of other favourites of mine from other places in the Bible

The letter to the Philippians 1:6 I am confident of this, that the one who began a good work among you will bring it to completion by the day of Jesus Christ.

Isaiah 43: 1b, 4a Do not fear, for I have redeemed you; I have called you by name, you are mine. – Because you are precious in my sight, and honoured, and I love you.

Remember: everyone is anxious on occasions; anxiety is different for all people; it is OK not to be OK. We do have a team of people who make calls to congregation members if you feel that you would like a call or that you could help with this pleasant task, please do let me know. Likewise, to receive a letter in the post is a lovely surprise would you like to join in with this idea? We also have some resources from the Church of England which we can send or can be picked up from the Church.

Parish Magazine makeovers

by Ann Griffiths – 12 November 2020

The January 1970 edition of the parish magazine had a new format with a bright front cover depicting St Faith, who met her death by burning. A palm leaf can be seen in the flames, across the base of the picture. By tradition, St Faith's symbols are the palm and the grid iron upon which she is said to have been bound and burned. The February edition analysed the comments received about the new layout, as heard by a distributor.

"I thought it was a sales catalogue from 'Flairs', the dress shop" – No, we try to prepare the Soul for Heaven, not the body for a party!

"Is it free now there is no price on it?" – See this month's cover. (Now showing the cost to be 6d).

"Very striking cover but why the fire?" – Obviously you do not read the magazine thoroughly or know much about St Faith.

Several distributors calling for the annual subscription were thought to be Jehovah's Witnesses and the editor concluded the article by saying that he would be quite happy if they were thought to be as zealous as the Jehovah's Witnesses. "At least the new cover has made people think!"

However, after a while the format was modified and it was completely redesigned in 1975.

Kneeling for hymns...

by Mike Fairhurst – 12 November 2020

I was looking through the hymns in the latest Corona Chronicle and came across Eternal Father Strong to Save. I used to be in the Royal Navy and not surprisingly this was a special hymn to us.

I was particularly reminded that at the end of every service we used to sing just the last verse (while kneeling which everyone did in those days) as a prayer. It was always moving although I am not sure if it is still done.

I have never tried but I wonder if it works for other hymns....

High Altar destroyed by fire!

by Ann Griffiths – 19 November 2020

In the 'Parish News' of March 1976 the Rector thanked the police and fire brigade for their swift action in preventing St Faith's church from being badly damaged when the High Altar was set on fire. Canon Brown said that it was one of the most beautiful altars he had ever seen and he doubted that it could ever be replaced.

'The damage to the altar, the frontals, the cloths, carpets and kneelers fortunately is covered by the insurance but we will never be able to replace the beautiful carved altar. At present we have asked our architect to produce some plans for a replacement. In the meantime, we are using the altar from the Lady Chapel and I have the altar, which is for the Christchurch Centre, in the Lady Chapel.'

Damp Vestry

In 1976 the Rector also reported that a solution had been found which it was hoped would end the dampness in the Vestry. A solid concrete floor had replaced the suspended wood flooring and due to the generosity of Mr J Everett a wood block floor had been laid in the screed. The Rector said that it really did look very good and 'Miss Norkett will be pleased to see her polishing rewarded, to say nothing of the safety factor. She has already gone through a bit of the floor that had gone rotten.' [Unfortunately, it is believed the vestry was built over one of Havant's numerous springs.] It was to be hoped that in future the vestments and cassocks could be kept in the cupboards that were made for them, without the risk of mildew.

In 1929 Sir Dymoke White of Southleigh Park, a churchwarden, had put up the money for a Choir Vestry at St Faith's Church in memory of his son, Lieutenant Lynton Woolmer Rudolph White, who was fatally wounded in France on 1 September 1914. The plans were drawn up by the Diocesan Architect, Sir Charles Nicholson, and a plaque was erected at the entrance to the vestry. The Portsmouth News reported that the vestry was dedicated by the Bishop of Portsmouth in January 1930. 90 years later, it's still going strong!

Memories of Remembrance 2019

by Nick Pointer – 19 November 2020

I really can't believe it's a year since Carolyne and I attended our first remembrance service at St Faith's. We stood amongst the throng outside and were awed. Not afraid to admit I had tears in my eyes. I asked a uniformed policeman what he estimated the size of the crowd to be; I'd guessed 1000 but in his professional opinion it was 3000. And in this massive crowd you could have heard a pin drop during the 2-minute silence. And in the church afterwards Pam Ayers' beautiful "Down the Line" was read out. I love you guys.

Memories of Canon Duke-Baker

by Sandra Haggan with Mavis Floyd – 19 November 2020

Looking at the Corona Chronicle recently when we had had a long hymn, reminded Mavis Floyd of a time during Canon Duke-Baker's time with us (1943-1962).

Canon Duke-Baker liked processions and at Evensong there would often be a procession with him wearing beautifully embroidered robes and the choir following behind. They needed a long hymn to accommodate the procession. They would set off and stop at the end of the first verse, he would say a prayer and then they would continue with the next verse of the hymn and so on. Canon Duke-Baker was a flamboyant man much loved by all the congregation.

Mavis also remembers as a young communicant going carol singing. They would go to all the large houses and would often be given little edible treats as a seasonal thank you. One of the houses was Norfolk House which was knocked down many years ago and is now retirement housing. I wonder if they will be able to sing carols this year.

An up and coming group…

by Marion Porter – 24 November 2020

It is good to hear, and see, many of our choir singing so beautifully on Sunday mornings, artistically arranged behind Tom, supporting him and enhancing the very welcome live streamed services. Thank you to them and Graham.

During the singing of "When I Needed a Neighbour", last Sunday, a (rather irreverent) thought popped into my head.... "Tom and The Coronettes."

St Faith's High Altar

by Ann Griffiths - 24 November 2020

I found a photo on eBay, postally used in 1948, showing the old, carved altar at St Faith's, which was destroyed by fire in 1976. It was gifted to the church during the great restoration in the 1870s.

In October 1875 the Hampshire Telegraph included a report on the reopening of the church. In addressing the congregation, the Rector said that, 'beneath the east window there was the holy table, which was a special gift, and upon that table was a cloth, which was the gift of a pious lady of the parish. The service books, common plate, the lectern upon the altar, the ordinary lectern and the Holy Book which rested upon it, were also kind gifts'. In the Rector's opinion it would be difficult to find a Book that could compare with that in St Faith's Church, Havant.

In connection with the Victorian restoration a letter to the editor of the Hampshire Telegraph in June 1874 said that at the recent laying of the cornerstone of Havant parish church 'it was rumoured that a considerable sum of money had been offered to the restoration committee, by an influential member of the congregation, for the purpose of raising the level of the floor throughout'. It now appeared that the money might be used for another purpose and the author of the letter wanted the committee to ensure that the money was used as intended and that the base of the church be raised, as this was the only time when this could be satisfactorily accomplished. The letter was signed 'A SUBSCRIBER'.

On the subject of Altars burning...

A letter from Polly Chapman – 24 November 2020

Dear Tom

Last week's Corona Chronicle included an Ann Griffiths historical reference to the burning of the altar in St Faith's.

Not long afterwards, I found myself 'teaching' (it was more like social work, & we came to refer to what we did as 'therapeutic education) the young man responsible.

Like so many of our flock, he was very troubled. His older sister had been his protector in a home that was dangerous. He lost that protection when she got married, and the altar in the church where that ceremony had taken place felt the full force of his rage. This will not surprise you, I imagine.

Polly

A note in response from the Editor...

Thank you to Polly for her moving story. It helps us to remember that not all crime is committed by 'ne'er-do-wells' - but often by some really desperate people. Thank you, too, to Ann Griffiths, for unearthing a number of fascinating glimpses into the history of our parish. I was very amused by the 1874 discussions about the raising of the church floor - since that is something we have said we would like to do ourselves, in the next five years, funds permitting.

Mind you - as our Victorian fore-bears found (no doubt), its going to be a challenge. Thanks to the strangely sloping ground around the church, we have a flat entrance at the West Door, two steps down at the North door, and one step up at the Choir vestry door!

Canon Tom

Victorian Havant

by Ann Griffiths – 3 December 2020

The Soup Kitchen and Coal Fund

In January1875 the Hampshire Telegraph reported that due to the severity of the weather, 'it is proposed to begin the operations of these charities and the soup kitchen will open today, Saturday'. Those in need were invited to obtain tickets from the district visitors, though it was not clear how easily this could be achieved.

Pocket Picking in Church

In the 18th and 19th centuries thieves who removed men's wallets and cut the strings of ladies' pockets were known as 'pickpockets'. In April 1876 the Hampshire Advertiser reported that, 'Since the late confirmation service held in the parish of Havant, we have heard of several ladies who were unfortunate enough to lose their pockets and as none have since been recovered there can be no doubt that they were taken by practised hands'.

Church Railings

'The Churchwardens of the Parish decided to effect a much-needed improvement by not only repairing the fence on the south side of the churchyard but also by removing the wall of the north and east sides and replacing it with a handsome iron railing. The work has been entrusted to Mr Arter of this town.' (Hampshire Telegraph 6.1.1889).

In 1894, the News reported that due to the success of the recent bazaar, the Rector had been able to pay off the long-standing account for the railings round the church wall, the amount being £128 1s 6d.

In 1942 the railings were removed by order of the Ministry of Defence in aid of the war effort!

Thank you for the Angel…

a letter from Caroline Fisk (Bosmere School) – 17 December 2020

(following the placement of knitted angels all around the parish, inspired by Wyn Clinnick (RIP) prior to her death)

Hello Tom,

I just wanted to tell you about something special that happened today.

One little girl in my Year 3 class has been so upset as her little cat was run over. Mum collected her from school and had picked up one of your parishioners' knitted angels saying that it was a message from her cat. This was an instant source of support for this little girl.

I know these little angels will mean a lot to other people in our community as well – especially over this Christmas break. Please can you pass on my thanks to your group of knitters!

Have a lovely Christmas.

Caroline Fisk, Y3 teacher, Bosmere Junior School

Christmas Fun

by Sandra Haggan – 17 December 2020

Many of you will know that I used to work in U-Need-Us in Portsmouth until we closed in March 2019. One of the things that I did was to choose the jokes that went in with cracker kits. I always enjoyed choosing these as you may imagine. I thought I might share a few with you but cannot remember where I put them! I have come across a few though that would have been contenders:

A man walked into the doctor's surgery with a strawberry stuck in his ear. 'Don't worry' the doctor said 'I've got some cream for that.'

Q. What do Alexander the Great and Winnie the Pooh have in common?
A. The same middle name.

Q. How many tickles does it take to make an octopus laugh?
A. Ten-tickles

Q. What's yellow and scary?
A. Shark infested custard!

Q. How do Santa's helpers spell?
A. They use the elfa-bet!

This was a favourite that I can remember and did include many times:

Q. Where do policeman live?
A. 999, Lets be Avenue!

The Rector responds…

Thanks for making us groan, Sandra! Here's a contemporary one from me:
Q. Why couldn't Mary and Joseph make a conference call in Bethlehem?
A. Because there was no Zoom at the Inn!

The Bishop Mackenzie window
by Ann Griffiths – 10 December 2020

In St Faith's Church there is a window in the north transept dedicated to Bishop Charles Mackenzie, who died of a fever in Africa in 1862, aged 36. The window bears the inscription, 'Charles Frederick Mackenzie first Bishop of Central Africa and Anne his sister and companion'. The Clayton and Bell window was presented by John Mackenzie of Edinburgh.

After her brother's death Anne Mackenzie came to live at Woodfield, Langstone, with Anne Hinchcliff whose sister Katherine was the late Rev. George Mountain's wife. Between 1866 and 1877 Miss Mackenzie edited a magazine called 'The Net', for those interested in missionary work. Note the link to the first light in the Mackenzie window with the Miraculous Draught of Fishes being enclosed in the net. (Luke Ch.5)

The three ladies raised large amounts of money for missionary work in India, Canada and Africa, and in 1868 Katherine Mountain sent a small baptismal font (or 'basin') out to Natal for a new church. 'The Net' describes the font as being, 'a very pretty one sent out by Mrs Mountain, the widow of a late Rector of Havant, which had been used in the parish church until it was replaced by a very handsome one, given 22 years ago by the parishioners, as a memorial to their beloved Pastor'.

Rev. Derek Brown wrote that an observer of the stone-laying ceremony for the new organ chamber, in 1874, said that Mrs Mountain, who laid the stone, was 'a tall stately old lady; a friend to all in distress and a munificent supporter of the Church'. (Parish News October 1975)

Christmas at the Havant Workhouse 1891

by Ann Griffiths – 17 December 2020

'The poor people of Havant spent Christmas Day in the usual festive style. Roast beef, baked potatoes and plum pudding were served for dinner, the adults each having a pint of ale and the children milk. In the afternoon the men were served with tobacco, tea and sugar; the women had tea and sugar and the children were bountifully supplied with oranges, nuts and sweets. The various wards were tastefully decorated with mottoes, evergreens and flowers by Mr and Mrs Horril, the Master and Matron.'

Sir Frederick Fitzwygram sent a huge Christmas tree; Miss Hulbert of Stakes Hill House sent her usual present of 1lb tea and 2lb sugar for each adult with half of that for each of the children; Miss Deverell of Purbrook Park sent a parcel of Christmas cards and Miss Newman and Miss Watson sent a parcel of toys. Miss Hayes sent Christmas letters. 'A very pleasant day was brought to a close by hearty cheers for the donors, the Guardians and the Master and Matron.'

The 1891 census shows that there were 69 people living in the workhouse, about a third of whom were under the age of sixteen.

Christmas Market thanks…

A message from Sandra Haggan – 17 December 2020

We didn't know if it would happen but in the end, last Saturday, it did – and what a lovely day it was! Our Mayor, Cllr Prad Bains, came along and opened the Christmas Market for us and then stayed and chatted with lots of people. We had a few stalls for the church there were cakes and Jenny's jams of course and kiwi fruit from Beatrice's garden. Books, tombola, bric-a-brac, the bottle stall, Christmas gifts, the grand draw and our own charity shop. We were joined by local crafters, Endless Gifts, charities: Help Palestine, Tradecraft and two fairground organs all of which helped create a wonderful atmosphere and an excellent range of stalls.

We carefully monitored numbers and had hand sanitiser absolutely everywhere and people came and they came. We very much wanted it to be something with and for the community, a little bit of something 'normal' and from the many comments. I think we did that!

There is a list of grand draw prize winners on display in the church and the total raised was just over £3000, which is amazing! (Final amount subject to costs, when claimed).

So a huge thank you to everyone involved whether buying and selling raffle tickets, making donations, baking cakes, manning stalls, displaying posters, printing and laminating, providing items for the stalls, helping set up and tidying up, absolutely everything because all these things only work when we all do it together. Thank you!

And from Margaret Tait & Tim Wood

Tim and I were almost in control of the cake stall at the Christmas Fayre last Saturday. We would very much like to thank all the chefs and cooks who created such amazing donations. No sooner had we displayed them on the table than they were disappearing into shopping bags. Money rapidly filled our cash box and our entire stock was sold out by 13.45!

The jars of marmalade and jam proved very popular. More next time please! A number of people asked for savouries as they didn't want cakes.

We enjoyed our day and hope to do a re-run in the future.

Jigsaw Frustration

by Jackie Martin – 17 December 2020

Earlier this year my dear friend Wyn gave me a jigsaw for my birthday and it was of The Last Supper. During lock down I had enjoyed doing lots of jigsaws thanks to Sandra, especially when the weather was wet, and I could not get in the garden.

For the next few weeks, it was fine, so I was working in the garden. Talking to Wyn when she was in hospital she asked me how I was getting on with the puzzle and when I said I had not started it she replied "you will not get anything else from me" in the way she teased. So, I thought I had better make a start and I found it was very difficult.

I have always completed the outside edge of a puzzle first before starting on the picture. Well that was impossible as there were no straight pieces and very few interlocking pieces, also all the colours were very similar. I spent several frustrating weeks working on this puzzle and rang Wyn several times to tell her she was driving me to distraction to which she found very funny.

I eventually completed the picture and managed the outside which was very wriggly. Paul took a photo and took it show Wyn the weekend before she died. I am so glad I persevered as it is a very special jigsaw with a fantastic picture.

Sermons and Homilies

On the raising of Lazarus

By Tom Kennar
29 March 2020
Text: John 11.1-45

It is sometimes said, among theologians, that when we read Scripture, Scripture is also reading us. And we might wonder what that means. Theologians mean that Scripture has an uncanny way of speaking directly into our own situations and lives...almost as though the Scriptures were themselves a person, who could look the Reader, and then say 'this is what you need to hear. Here's a story, from which you can draw, right now'. Of course, Scripture isn't a person – but we believe it was inspired by God – the ultimate person. So, perhaps it shouldn't surprise us that this same God can continue to speak to us today through such inspired writings.

So what are the parallels we might see between the story of Lazurus, and our own stories? Well, first we observe Mary and Martha. They were distraught that Jesus had not come in time to save their brother. No doubt, while he lay dying, they were anxiously looking down the road to see whether Jesus was on his way. 'Where is he?' they would have said to each other.

Eventually Jesus does choose to arrive (and notice, it was Jesus' choice...he held back by two days before making the journey). Mary and Martha are decidedly cross. "If you had been here, our brother wouldn't have died!"

This is such a powerful phrase! It is full of all the confusion of tiny humanity, who cannot see God's purpose for the world. We want God to act when WE expect God to act. And when he doesn't appear to care, we feel resentful. We might even give up praying to him, or belonging to his church altogether.

But Mary and Martha's exclamation is also a sign of faith. They trusted that Jesus could save their brother...or how else can they say with such certainty that if he has come earlier, Lazurus would not have died?

Many people are desperately experimenting with prayer at the current time. Whether they are fearful of losing their jobs, or fearful of sickness, or even mourning the passing of a loved one. Each one is like Mary and Martha - wondering whether Jesus even cares. Can he hear their prayers? Are they saying the right prayers? Will he answer?

Jesus did answer Mary and Martha's prayer...he saved their brother. But not in the way that they expected. Rather than simply healing him, he raised him from death itself – foreshadowing his own Resurrection a short time later.

And I believe that God is answering our prayers now. But he is doing so in the way that will be best for all humanity. God knows what God is doing. As he once and for all redeemed the world through Jesus, he continues to redeem each moment of time. He is constantly at work in the minutiae of every day, seeking ways to bring blessing upon all humanity.

Now I need to be clear. This doesn't mean that I think God sent this particular plague upon us. I don't believe that God sends destruction. But when it comes – whether through human stupidity, or natural events, God works in the midst of it. He redeems it, by using each circumstance of life to challenge us, help us to grow, and move us onward – as individuals, and as a whole human race.

Perhaps we will only perceive God's blessing when we look back in time. Today's trials are often tomorrow's lessons. But perhaps God is teaching us, through our current difficulties, that it is possible for us to live differently. It is possible to consume less, to travel less, to party less, and yet still find contentment in our lives. Perhaps God is teaching us the preciousness of social connection, and making us more alert to the needs of those around us. Perhaps God is causing us to ask fundamental questions about the kind of economics we have adopted to run our world.

As he raised Lazurus from the dead, he said to Mary and Martha, 'Did I not tell you that if you believed you would see the glory of God?'. That is his challenge to us today. If you – and I – believe and trust...we will see the glory of God, even through the Corona Virus Crisis.
Amen.

Have a good argument!

By Tom Kennar – 5 April 2020

Text: John 8.31-42

One of the most interesting phenomena of recent days has been the exponential explosion in internet communication. Soon after the Prime Minister told us all to "stay home, save lives and protect the NHS", the message traffic on my phone exploded! Facebook, in particular, became a very busy place indeed. And there were lots of arguments! Accusations of a police state, or over-reaction were rife. On the other hand, hundreds of photos of "selfish people" ignoring the new rules were shared – to shame our neighbours.

I belong to a private Facebook group which is just for clergy. As soon as the new rules about closing churches were handed down, that group in particular erupted! There were lots of debate about the rights and wrongs of closing churches – I can tell you!

Today, we find Jesus in the middle of a debate with the teachers of the Jewish law. More than any other Gospel writer, John really loves a good debate – and he records some pretty intellectual tussles for us to enjoy. It's a fine old Jewish tradition, actually. Having a good argument. It's something that we British people don't do so easily. Even over such fundamental decision as the Brexit vote, most of us kept quiet and just muttered our opinions to one another. But Jesus, wasn't British! Jesus, the Jew, seemed to have enjoyed a good argument as much as any other Jew.

In today's reading, we are treated to just a small section of a much longer argument. It centres around Jesus' astonishing claim that whoever obeys his word will not see death. His debating opponents are furious at him for making such a claim. They argue back and forth over the fact that Abraham, Father of the Jewish nation, ultimately died. So was Jesus claiming to be superior to Abraham?

'Well, yes, actually,' claimed Jesus. 'You see, I am greater than Abraham. In fact, before Abraham was, I AM.'

Well that did it. The Jews were furious.

The phrase 'I am' was first used by God, to Moses at the burning bush. It's the name God gave himself, when Moses asked God who he was. 'I am who I am'. Or 'I will be who I will be'. It's a claim that God is the very essence of all things. Eternal: never beginning or ending. Just 'being'. By using that same phrase, in reference to himself, Jesus was claiming to BE God. To the Jewish teachers, this was blasphemy of the highest order. It was a crime punishable by death. So they picked up stones, and prepared to stone him…but Jesus slipped away.

Argument is a healthy thing to do. Societies in which argument is silenced quickly turn into mono-cultures. Argument helps us to refine our ideas: listening to different opinions is a good thing. Those who only listen to the words of people who agree with them are doomed to live inside an echo-chamber of opinion. Where ideas become stale, and healthy debate becomes a prisoner to the strongest voice in the room.

This is something I think the church needs to learn. For too long, churches have been divided over different ideas about the meaning of the Bible, and of the life and death of Jesus. Each denomination is essentially an echo-chamber of people who feel comforted by being with others whose ideas are more or less the same as theirs. But, as we've seen time and time again, such echo chambers are ultimately doomed to die. Without the continuous pressure of argument and debate, minds grow dull, and congregations dwindle.

Most people who walk up to St Faith's Pallant Centre from the centre of town don't realise that along that road, they pass a building which used to house a congregation of 'Dissenters'…those who 'dissented' from the Church of England round the corner. They are gone now. Their echo-chamber stopped reverberating.

One of the most divisive questions for Christians is the question of what Jesus' death on the cross really meant. Was it the payment for sins, loved by so many hymn writers? How did it 'redeem us from the Devil'? Or was it a great example of a man being willing to die for a beautiful idea? Wars have been fought over these questions – but the questions keep coming.

Next week, on Good Friday, I'm going to try to offer some meditative thoughts about some of the many different ways that the death of Jesus has been understood. I hope to give you something to ponder…and perhaps something to argue about afterwards online!

Pandemic Palm Sunday

By Tom Kennar – 5 April 2020

Text: Matthew 21.1-11

What strange times these are – when we can only imagine and visualise being in a massive crowd, waving our branches and shouting Hosanna!

Guidance from the Archbishops of the Church has even prevented me from sending out palm crosses to you by post – which I was proposing to do. The fear of infection from palms which have been created by many unknown hands is just too great.

Incidentally – the same prohibition stops me from sending you all an Easter Egg for next Sunday – so I suppose I'm just going to have to eat all those Easter eggs I bought by myself!

So we find ourselves on Palm Sunday, but without palms – except those that you might have kept from last year. I hope you'll wave them enthusiastically at your computer screen during the final hymn today!

But, actually, by a small play on words, we find that we DO in fact have palms we can contemplate on this day. Not palm branches – but the palms of our hands!

Our hands are a wonderful gift to us from our creator. Very few animals have them – just monkeys, and certain mammals (like the cunning squirrels of the Rectory garden). But hands are such useful things, for all those who would follow the King who rides on a donkey….and the king who was nailed to the cross by his own palms.

There are many ways of using our palms. We can use them to clap for the NHS and other frontline workers who are keeping our society going during this crisis.

We can put them together, and pray for God's peace and presence during the crisis.

We can use our Palms to carry hope and food to neighbours in need.

We can place them over our mouths and noses, when we pass people who are not abiding by the 2m rule.

We could, also wave our palms in the air and cry Hosanna – which is a word that is frequently understood. Many people confuse it with Halleluiah – a word that we are not supposed to say during Lent! But hosanna – the cry of the crowd on that first Palm Sunday – means 'Save us'. Hosanna in the highest' means 'save us, from the heavenly places'. To cry 'hosanna' is to acknowledge that we human beings can't save ourselves. For all our science, and all our cleverness, for all our technology and our cleverly-devised economic theories, the events of the present time show us just how fragile we really are.

To cry 'hosanna' – save us – is to acknowledge that we can't save ourselves. Our only real hope comes from heaven – and from the wisdom of heaven. The Kingdom of heaven is the only way of living that could ultimately save all humanity.

We see glimpses of the Kingdom, all around us. For the kingdom is rooted in self-sacrifice, generosity, the deliberate act of loving our neighbour and putting their needs above our own. So, when a nurse, or a doctor, puts their patients before their own safety – the Kingdom of heaven is at work. When billionaires open their bank accounts to feed the hungry, the Kingdom is at work. When we decide to self-isolate, to stop the spread of disease and death to our neighbours – the Kingdom of heaven is at work. Whenever we put others first – as Jesus did upon the cross – the Kingdom of heaven is at work.

So, let's use our God-given Palms today, to pray, to reach out and offer help, and to seek hosanna...the help from heaven we desperately need to save us all. Amen.

Easter in a pandemic

By Tom Kennar – 11 April 2020

Matthew 28. 1-10

We preachers are duty bound to help our listeners make connections between the stories we read in the Bible, and the stories of our own lives. Sometimes, that's quite hard – and we have to strain our congregation's credulity, just a little. Sometimes we end up resorting to silly jokes, like the oft-quoted mis-print of a parish newsletter which stated, deliciously, that on Easter Sunday, Mrs Smith of the Mother's Union, would lay an egg upon the Altar!

But this year, the task of making connections between the bible's stories and ours is not so hard. On Friday, the Roman Catholic Cardinal of Westminster sagely pointed out on the Today programme that Jesus' death on the cross has many resonances with the COVID-19 crisis. He pointed out that crucifixion brought about death by asphyxiation, as the lungs of the condemned mad filled up with fluid. Tragically, this is the main cause of death from COVID-19 too. There is therefore even more truth, this year, to the idea that Jesus has borne our sorrows.

And there continue to be surprising connections between the Easter story and ours too. For a start, the Disciples were hidden away in their room when Jesus rose from the tomb. They were in hiding from the threat of violence from the crowd, or the Roman soldiers. We too, are in hiding from a less violent, but nonetheless deadly threat.

Another connection – it is women who first go to the tomb, stepping out in courage despite the threat. In our time, according to the latest statistics, 77% of NHS staff are women too – stepping deliberately into the danger of infection. I say this not to undermine the equally fantastic work of our male medical staff, of course. I'm simply drawing a parallel. We rightly praise our mainly male soldiers for walking into danger on our behalf. But we're seeing more clearly what we've always known – that women are just as capable of unbelievable self-sacrifice, and of even laying down their lives for the sake of love.

Another connection...A little later in the post-Easter story, Jesus appears in the locked room of the Disciples – right there, in the middle of their private space. One of the more delicious things that I know is happening in some of your lives is the discovery that you can connect with God in your private space. I love our church building – and I can't wait to get back into it. But in the meantime, many of us are finding that God is just as present in our homes, or in one of our daily walks, as he is in the beautiful surroundings of the church.

The central story of Easter is of course a confident, hope-filled proclamation that God is alive! It's a message of re-assurance and promise, especially to those who are facing the prospect of death or mourning the passing of a loved one – especially in these difficult days.

The reality of Easter enables us to proclaim that Jesus is the 'first-born from the dead' – which is a rather theological phrase! It means that Jesus was the first human-being in history to be resurrected from the dead – not just resuscitated, as had happened in the past – to Lazurus, for example. Jesus wasn't resuscitated, but resurrected - given an entirely new body for the new future in which the Kingdom of heaven will finally come to earth, and all our tears will be wiped away.

(It was the fact of his new body which meant that even his closest friends failed to recognise him at first. Mary thought he was a gardener. The disciples on the road to Emmaus thought him a fellow-traveller.)

So, my friends, let us take heart this Easter day. Let us proudly and loudly proclaim the risen Lord, whose story always was, and continues to be, our story. A story of hope, a story which points to a better future. A story that drives us onwards, laughing in the face of death - for we know that death has ultimately been defeated, and love will always find its way! Amen.

Peace be with you

By Tom Kennar – 16 April 2020

Luke 24.35–48

So, how was Easter for you? A bit surreal, I bet. It was certainly a unique experience to not celebrate the rising of Christ together in one place – passing candles of light from person to person. I also missed hearing that tremendous shout of 'He is risen indeed! Alleluia!

There were two other things I especially missed. The first is that I normally give out Easter eggs at the church door, when the service is over. And there's usually quite a few left over! So I missed clearing up the left overs!

Secondly, I missed our Easter Bonnet competition! I was rather looking forward to seeing what John Burch, Paul Utting, Shirley Copper and Jude Caunter would come up with this year...having had such a fierce competition last year!

Many of you have been extremely kind about Sunday's online service – and I'm very grateful for your words of encouragement. It is very surreal for me to be standing here talking to a phone on a stick, instead of seeing your smiling faces (and the faces that are nodding off during the sermon!). But this is what we have, for now. And it must suffice.

Mind you, I have to tell you, I've been really pleased with the numbers of people who have been attending these services as 'virtual' congregation members. Last Sunday's service, for example, was watched by up to 91 people at one time...and just under 1,000 have engaged with it for at least a few minutes since. In fact, according to the statistics on my Facebook page, 156 hours of viewing has taken place.

This tells me that the live-streaming of services is proving very popular. I suspect that these services are giving an opportunity for people to put their toe into the water of worship – without fearing that they will be jumped on as soon as they enter the church, or signed up to the coffee rota! Perhaps that's true for some of you who are viewing this, right now. And if that's the case, I want to say that you are welcome here.

And believe me – I get it. I know what it's like to feel nervous about stepping into a large room full of people you don't know. Will I make a silly mistake? Will I sit in someone's favourite place? Will I know how to find the right words, or the right hymns? What's the correct procedure for going up to the Altar for communion? All these questions are very real...and even we vicars can feel nervous and out of place when we go to a different church!

So, if these services help you to worship without all those anxieties – then I for one am glad. I've been talking with my colleagues on the Standing Committee, and we've agreed that livestreaming should continue, even after we've started worshipping in church again.

Being anxious about faith is a very natural thing. The disciples were extremely anxious about theirs. There they were, locked into a room in Jerusalem...anxious, frightened, terrified even. By the time of today's Gospel story, they had heard the rumour that Jesus was alive...they'd seen the empty tomb for themselves. But they didn't know what to do next. And, they probably weren't even all that sure that the rumours were true.

And in the middle of their confusion and anxiety – suddenly Jesus is there. And what's the first thing he says to them: 'Peace be with you'. As he so often did, Jesus has the perfect words, and the perfect blessing for the occasion. In the midst of their anxiety, and their uncertainty, he offers them peace.

We need to hear these words for ourselves, right now. Many of us are anxious – anxious about stepping out of our front doors. Anxious about loved ones. Anxious about going shopping. Anxious about others getting too close. Anxious about whether we are doing this social distancing thing correctly. In some ways, just stepping out into the world has been a bit like stepping into an unknown church building for the first time.

We need to hear Jesus speaking to us all, right now. 'Peace be with you', he says. 'Come to me, all who are weary and heavy-laden – and I will give you rest'. Ultimately, this is about us all learning to trust God's promise that he will walk alongside us through every circumstance of life. We may be anxious, but he will bring peace. We may be sick, but he can bring healing. We may even die – and let's face it, we all will one day – but he will bring life everlasting.

Amen.

A sermon on St George's Day

By Tom Kennar – 23 April 2020

John 15. 18-31

Not much is actually known for certain about St George. Most of what we have was handed down by tradition – and like most traditions, it has gathered a lot of moss along the way!

George was probably a soldier living in in the Middle East at the beginning of the fourth century, probably born in modern day Turkey. We think he was martyred at Lydda – just north of Jerusalem – in about the year 304. He was one of the first to be martyred under the persecutions of Diocletian, and he became known throughout the East as 'The Great Martyr'. (Incidentally, these were the same persecutions that took the life of St Faith of Acquitaine.)

The story of George slaying the dragon may be due to his being mistaken in iconography for St Michael, who is usually depicted wearing armour. This icon is a very good example of the sort of images that crusader knights would have seen around the Middle East.

George replaced Edward the Confessor as patron saint of England following the Crusades, when returning soldiers brought back a renewed interest in his cult. Edward III made George patron of the Order of the Garter, which seems finally to have confirmed his position as England's patron saint.

So, it turns out, England's patron saint was a Turkish soldier, martyred in Palestine, who probably had little idea of where England was! But there was something about his character and his story which resonated with Edward III, especially. I wonder what those resonances might have been…

Perhaps Edward was drawn to the fact that George was both a soldier AND a Christian – as indeed many of our young men and women today find out. Being willing to offer one's life for a noble cause is a profoundly Christian idea. (The only question in Edward's case is whether the Crusades could ever have been considered a noble cause!)

Secondly, the rather dubious myth of the dragon-slaying was nevertheless a tale of helping the weak and defenceless. According the the 11th century legend, George slayed a dragon who was being fed by human sacrifices on the part of a terrified town.

These two qualities – sacrifice and charitable acts – are central to the Gospel which George lived out. And both sacrifice and charity are central to the character of the English people – at their best. Which is why

I am happy to celebrate St George's Day, and risk some of the accusations of patriotic jingoism that some of my more left-wing friends might hurl at me.

Patriotism, at is best, as a celebration of the finest aspects of any nation. I'm proud to be English when I learn that we are among the top 10 most charitable nations in the world. (We're actually number six in the world – so we could do better!). I'm proud to be English when I hear the stories of our armed services who lay themselves on the line in the cause of peace. In this Corona Crisis, I'm proud to be English when I see the way that our front-line workers, all across the country, are willing to lay themselves on the line, in service of their neighbours – though, to be fair, that is true of front-line workers in every nation right now.

There is a dark side to patriotism though. It is an ugly thing when it turns into nationalism – by which I mean any statement which suggests we are a better nation than any other. We are different, that's all. Patriotism is at its worst when nationalism tips over into xenophobia – that is, any kind of unfounded hatred or mistreatment of foreigners.

At the end of today's, I'm going to invite you to join me in singing a rousing chorus of Jerusalem – one of the greatest of all patriotic songs. At its heart is the notion that a new City of Peace – 'Jeru-shalom' could be established in England's green and pleasant land. A city of peace – like the vision of the New Jerusalem from the book of Revelation. A place where there will be no more mourning, or crying, or pain – because God himself will dwell with his people.

Now that's a vision that I think St George would have been very happy to fight for!

On the road to Emmaus

By Tom Kennar – 26 April 2020

Luke 24.13-35

There are times, I must confess, when this business of being a Christian is just a little exhausting, isn't it? I mean – all those meetings – services, concerts, fundraisers, committees! And having to wade through all that paperwork (I'm talking to PCC members now!). And all that charity that's expected of us! There are days, I must confess, when I feel like throwing in the towel. Just give it all up and have a quiet life.

I wonder whether those two Disciples who were walking along the road to Emmaus felt something similar. Not the pressure of admin, but of wondering whether the previous years of their lives had been in vain. They had left their homes and their families to follow the man they thought was the Messiah. But all their hopes and dreams for transforming their society appeared to have come to nothing; on a Cross erected at the Place of the Skull.

Oh sure, there were now rumours that Jesus had risen from the dead, but these Disciples hadn't seen him yet. And certainly there was no sign of the redemption of Israel that they had hoped for all these years. Perhaps it would be better if they just gave up and went home to the quiet solitude of Emmaus? Let someone else worry about the transformation of society for a change. Perhaps those Disciples, going home to Emmaus, will just hang up their sandals, sit in the sun, and let the world go on without them?

But see what happens next. In the midst of their despair, Jesus comes. He walks alongside them for a while, unrecognised at first. He explains that everything that happened in the previous week was all part of a much bigger plan; a divine plan for the redemption of the whole world. The Disciples are intrigued, and suddenly excited. Perhaps all their sacrifice has not been in vain after all. Perhaps God is still working to transform the world. Perhaps Jesus really was the Messiah after all. They want to know more, and they invite the stranger who has been teaching them to come and share a meal...and then, they discover who he really is, in the breaking of the bread.

Does Jesus walk alongside us too, perhaps even as unrecognised as he was to those Emmaus-Disciples? Does he still walk alongside disciples in despair at the apparent fruitlessness of their labours? I think he does. And if we will listen to his voice, I think he will unfold to us something of the divine plan in which we are involved – God’s mission for Havant.

For when we look at our parish's life through Jesus' eyes, and not our own, we can begin to glimpse the signs of the Kingdom that those Emmaus Disciples were looking for. Whenever a lonely life has been filled with companionship, the Kingdom is glimpsed. Whenever an addict says no to substances and yes to life, the Kingdom is glimpsed. Whenever someone's soul is lifted into profound worship at one of our services, inspired by our choir, the Kingdom is at hand. Whenever a hungry belly is filled because of our donation, the Kingdom is at hand.

Is that a plan worth straining every sinew for? Is that a plan worth committing our finances and time too? Is that a plan worth repairing and improving our buildings for? Is that a plan worth offering our lives to in every sense? I think it is. And I hope and pray that you do too.

And here's a final thought. For those Emmaus disciples, Jesus was finally made known to them in the breaking of the bread. Who can tell why this was? Whatever the reason, it was in a moment of brokenness that Jesus was finally and ultimately revealed...echoing the brokenness of his own body upon the Cross. We can find Jesus in our brokenness too.

May we each offer our brokenness to God, today – remaining open to what God is doing through us, and saying to us, in the midst of the Corona Crisis. I’m convinced that he has great plans ahead for us – as individuals, and as a parish. Let’s offer our brokenness, and receiving his wholeness. For that’s our only hope. Amen.

What should I believe?

By Tom Kennar – 30 April 2020

John 6.35–40

I'd like to focus on Jesus' phrase: 'Very truly, whoever believes has eternal life' (John 6. 47). That's a phrase which has tripped up many a Christian, for it immediately raises a question, doesn't it: 'whoever believes what?' In other words, 'what is it exactly that I'm supposed to believe to have eternal life'?

Must I, for example, believe that Jesus was born of a virgin? Must I believe that his death paid the price for my sins? Must I believe that he rose physically from the tomb? What if I can't believe these things, any more than I can believe in fairies at the bottom of the garden? What if these stories just sound like metaphors to me, or magical tales in an age of science?

Some Christians have tried to solve this conundrum by cutting and pasting different phrases from the Bible, to come up with a formula – a list of things you must believe to be true in order to be saved. The best examples of this are the various forms of Creed – which even today remain a source of debate between different Christian traditions and thinkers.

But I want to suggest caution. There are two quite different meanings of the word belief...and we need to be cautious about which one we use.

The first meaning of belief is the idea of 'intellectual agreement' to an idea which can't be proved by the scientific method. So, if I say that I believe Jesus rose from the dead, entire and whole in a newly created body, I'm saying that I hold that story to be literally and actually true – even though I didn't see it for myself, and there is no scientific proof that it ever happened.

But the second meaning of the word belief is something much closer to the word 'trust'. I trust, for example, that the sun will come up tomorrow morning, based on the evidence that it always has before. In much the same way, I trust the idea of God, because I've seen the difference that idea makes in my life and the life of those around me.

But trust is also a word we apply to relationships, isn't it? I trust that Clare isn't going to leave me for a better-looking bloke, because she hasn't done yet – even after a month of lockdown! Trust, within a relationship, is built on accumulating evidence of how the other person behaves.

And so, I come back to the idea, or the concept of believing – or trusting – in God. The evidence in my life is that trusting in God is a worthwhile endeavour. Studying and listening to the Scriptures makes a difference in my life. Praying and focusing my thoughts towards God makes my life more meaningful and hopeful. Living my life by God's principles of forgiveness, charity and sacrifice gives my life purpose and direction.

So, when I say that I believe in God, I am not saying that I believe things about God that other people tell me to believe – even other people who have written down their ideas in the collection of writings we now call the Bible. No. I'm saying that I trust the idea of God, and the transforming effect that idea has had in my own life, and the lives of other people I call my brothers and sisters in Christ.

But that leaves another question hanging in the air, does it not? The question is, what do I do, intellectually, with all the things people tell me I should hold to be true, even though I have no objective proof. What, for example, do I do with the claims about God that are made in the Creed?

My advice is this...hold those beliefs lightly and gently. They are just ideas: we cannot prove them objectively to be true or false. Instead, we can, if we wish, treat them as metaphors – pictures in our minds that are intended to lift our consciousness beyond the physical, provable world, and into the metaphysical world of imagination and story.

Stories have power, whether they are factually true or not. So far as I know, there never was a race between a tortoise and a hare...but we all understand the meaning of Aesop's fable. The same is true of the statements of the Creed. We can objectively prove very little of it. But all of its words, phrases and complex pictures have the power to lift our eyes beyond the physical horizon and into the world of heaven. Amen.

Matthias – the 13th Apostle

By Tom Kennar – 14 May 2020

Acts 1.15-26

Sadly, we don't know very much about the so-called 13th Apostle, other than the story we've just heard of how he came to be elected, after the death of Judas. From that story alone, we can deduce that he was one of the wider band of Jesus' disciples who had followed his ministry all around Judea, Galilee and Jerusalem. He had listened to Jesus teaching, and then made a decision to follow him, wherever he led.

Judas Iscariot had been on the same journey, and had been even closer to Jesus, as a member of his inner circle of 12. But he had taken his own road, and had betrayed his Lord. Quite how Judas died is rather a mystery. The account we've just heard from Act says that he fell headlong and burst himself open. Matthew, however, says that he hanged himself. Both accounts may, of course be differing versions of the same events. But they both stand as a word of caution to anyone who takes the Bible absolutely literally.

The fact is, though, that however it happened, Judas was dead. The Apostles needed to replace him, not least to make up the numbers to a nice even 12. 12 was an important number to them – it represented the 12 Tribes of Judah, and their sacred responsibility to lead the new Israel which Jesus had inaugurated.

After his appointment, however, the Scriptures tell us nothing more about Matthias. It's possible that Luke intended to fill in his story in the missing chapters of the Acts of the Apostles – but we'll probably never know. Various traditions tell us that Matthias went off to preach the Gospel in Cappadocia, part of modern day Turkey. Another tradition has him in the region of modern-day Georgia. His death is also rather a mystery. Either he died of old age, as some traditions have it. Or he was beheaded by a mob in Jerusalem.

Matthias' story – or rather the lack of it – reminds me of just how many faithful, Christian people have lived out their lives of service without recognition, and without fanfare. The lives of many saints can inspire us, with their miracles and wisdom. They become 'super-saints' – examples for us all to follow.

But most Christians are not called not to super-stardom. Rather, we care called to carrying out faithfully Jesus' command to love (so beautifully illustrated in our Gospel reading). The kind of Love which Jesus describes is the Love that is willing to die for others. It's the love that a friend bears for his friend. It's the love which bears fruit that will last.

So, I don't know much about Matthias the Apostle. But there is a Matthias that I do know, very well. Matthias Medadues-Bodohu (which is a name I've had to practice saying!). He is the Bishop of Ho, in Ghana – the bishop of one of the three Cathedrals I'm humbled to represent as a Canon. Many of you will have met Matthias, during one of his many visits to St Faith's. You might even remember that he was at my installation as Rector, five years ago. What most of you won't know, but which I will never forget, is that he came to my installation despite the fact that on the very same day he received the shattering news of his own brother's death.

Like Matthias the Apostle, Bishop Matthias' deeds often go unnoticed. Few people know how he cares for families all over his Diocese, helping with their school fees, and relieving their poverty wherever he can from his own tiny resources. Few people see his constant work to fundraise for the very small wages of his priests, and the basic costs of running his enormous, but poorly-equipped Diocese. Few see his faithfulness in prayer and intercession on behalf of all those for whom he cares. Few witness the hardship he experiences travelling all over his Diocese, which is the size of Ireland, but with dirt roads and ancient vehicles.

But like all Christians who are true to the name, that Matthias continues sharing God's love wherever he can, and with whoever he can, in season and out of season, in rain and in sun. In Corona Virus Lockdown, and in normal times.

So, today, I give thanks for both saints whose name is Matthias. They are both examples to us all of the calling of any Christian – to never give up the hard work of spreading and sharing love, in a society which prefers selfishness and revengeful-hatred. Even in a state of relative 'lockdown', there is much that we can do, to continuing spreading the love which lays itself down for others.

We can reach out to neighbours and friends, searching out the lost, and the lonely, and offering love.

We can use our resources to support God's work in far-less comfortable places than Havant, as well as in our own parish.

We can pray, steadfastly, for those for whom the current Crisis is anything but a slightly-annoying stay-cation from work.

We can give love to all those key workers who are the bedrock of our society and our community.

And so, I pray that we all might be given the strength to persevere, and to keep on sharing the love of God. Even when no-one knows that we're doing it! Amen.

Paul at the Areopagus

By Tom Kennar – 17 May 2020

Acts 17.22-31

To be honest with you, I'm not altogether sure how to pronounce the word Areopagus. But I'm quite sure that someone will send me an email to tell me. Probably Alan Hakim. And I look forward to it!

But however it is pronounced, the Areopagus was a rocky hill in Athens, where the senior leaders of the City gathered to make laws or conducts trials. Paul's sermon about the 'unknown God' was probably something between a trial and a guest-speaker slot for the 'great and the good' of the City. If he messed this up, he stood a good chance of not leaving Athens alive.

But Paul is typically canny. He has been in the city for some days, awaiting the arrival of his friends Silas and Timothy. He's been wandering around, looking at the various Greek temples to the various gods that he, himself, doesn't believe in. The Greeks, like the Romans, worshipped a multitude of gods – they had gods for everything, including war, love, poetry, music – and even beer. I quite like the sound of that particular god. A god of beer…hmmmm!

But the Greeks wanted to make sure that they didn't miss out a god by accident. Perhaps there was one they didn't know about – and he, or she, might be rather miffed if there wasn't a temple – or at least an altar – dedicated to them. Who knew what trouble that might cause? So, just to be on the safe side, the Greeks erected an altar to 'the unknown God'.

Paul seized his chance. "I have come to tell you about the unknown god", he says – and he proceeds to unfold an essentially Jewish understanding of who God is. He's the creator of the universe, who populated the whole planet through one single ancestor (namely Adam). This God is not far from us, as the Greeks supposed – but rather, he is so close that 'in him we live and move and have our being'. This idea is, of course echoed in today's Gospel, when Jesus assures us that he is in us, just as the Father is in him, and he is in the Father. God's Spirit binds us together, it enlivens us, it connects us – even when we are separated out of love for each other in this lockdown crisis.

More than that, Paul tells the Greeks that this God has a human face – the face of Jesus Christ, who was raised from the dead. Instead of a dead block of stone, Paul offers the Greeks, and us, a living, breathing likeness of God. This is someone we can get to know. He's a real person, whose teachings we can follow, and whose life we can live.

Before his death, as we heard in the Gospel reading, Jesus promised his disciples that 'in a little while the world will no longer see me. But YOU will see me. And because I live, you also will live.'

So the Jesus that Paul knows, and who he preaches to the Greeks, is a God who is the creator of all things, who gives us our life.

He is knowable, by us, through Jesus' life and teachings

And, by raising Jesus from the dead, God offers us all a life that goes on for ever.

This is all good news indeed. The Greeks had only known the gods of their own imaginations and stories. Never did they have a tangible, touchable, sense of God. This is a new idea to them – a god who actually speaks to his children. The leaders of Athens were intrigued. Some of them became Christians, straight away, and formed the first congregations of the Greek church which continues to this day.

But all of this is good news for us too. Across the whole world, we are battling a threat that we cannot see. But we serve a God who we DO see, and who we DO know, through the life and teachings of Jesus. Although we struggle with the effects of the virus we cannot see, we hold on to the God we CAN see. For we see him at work.

We see God at work in the faces of the caring professions, who continue to offer love and care even at the risks of their own life. That's God at work.

We see hear God in the conversations that take place over the phone, on the internet, and through the penpal letters some of you have been writing to children in lock-down. We hear him in the scriptures.

We experience God in the healing that does happen in the midst of this crisis, whether supernaturally, or through the application of wisdom through medicine. Never forget that something like 95% of sufferers actually recover from this virus.

And we experience God in our ongoing worship. For, in the words of our first hymn, this is a God who we have promised to serve until the end. And in the words of our last hymn, this God is our Shepherd, through all that life can challenge us with.

Even in the valley of the shadow of death. Amen.

Return to Sender
by Tom Kennar – 23 May 2020
Text: John 17.1-11

"You will be my witnesses, in Jerusalem, in all Judea and Samaria and to the end of the earth."

One of Elvis Presley's early hits went like this:

"I gave a letter to the postman, he put it in his sack,
But right and early next morning, he brought my letter back.
She wrote upon it: Return to Sender…."

I suppose that we've all been doing a lot of sending, recently. Whether it's the sending out of literally thousands of emails, or sending hard copies of the Corona Chronicle as Sandra and Pauline have been doing, or just sending cards and greetings to our loved ones, 'sending' is a way of us all keeping in touch during these trying times.

'Sending' is also something absolutely central to the Gospel. We worship a God who, whilst being separate from us, never stops sending-out to us. Throughout the pages of the Old Testament, we observe God sending angels and prophets...heavenly postmen, delivering instructions, or warnings, or encouragement, from God. Then, in the New Testament, we learn how God sent his own son. Not so much a postman, as a living, breathing, observable image of God himself. Jesus – with God – then sends the Holy Spirit to the world, through the church...to keep on teaching us. The Spirit's role is more like the internet than a letter. He's a living, constant connection to the Divine mind and the divine will – a source of power to which we can connect.

So, if God is all about sending, it should not surprise us to hear Jesus also sending his followers out into the world. In our reading from the Acts of the Apostles, we just heard Jesus saying to them that they would be his witnesses in Judea, in Samaria, and to the end of the earth.

It is this command, this sending out, which gives the Apostles their title. The Greek word is 'apostolos', which means 'one who is sent off'. Jesus gives his new messengers, his sent-ones, a command – that they shall be his witnesses.

And let's notice to whom he sends his new postmen. Not just to Jerusalem. Not just to Judea – the land of the people of Israel. No, he also sends them to Samaria, and to the ends of the world. We must not miss this detail.

First – Samaria. This is the land of the Samaritans – the sworn enemies of Israel. To the Jews, Samaritans were unclean, rogues and heretics. They wanted nothing to do with each other. Sending the new Apostles into Samaria would be like sending protestants into catholic territories, during the Irish troubles. Or sending Englishmen into Scotland during the Battle of Culloden.

This was dangerous stuff. Jesus was saying to his followers, that God's love, and his good news of salvation, is not just for our own little community. It's a message which needs to be taken to – and shared with – our enemies. It's a message designed to break-down the walls of bitterness and recrimination. It's a message of love, of healing and of wholeness for the whole world.

And that's precisely where Jesus sends his Apostles – to the ends of the earth. That means taking God's message of love to Rome, to the very people who crucified Jesus. It means taking it out to far-distant lands, with very different cultures and norms – which is why history tells us that some of those first Apostles ended up in far-flung places like Ethiopia, India, and even China.

And this act of sending has never been rescinded by Jesus. The God who sends his messengers, then his Son, then his Spirit, and then his Apostles, still sends his people today. You and I are being sent, every day – into our workplaces, into our hospitals, into our streets, into our families and communities – each of us carrying a letter of love from the King of Heaven.

In these days of lockdown, some of the ways we send God's love are different. For those of us who are shielding, perhaps we pick up a phone, or write an email, or post a card. For those Christians who are on the front-line of medicine, or caring, or food production, or food distribution, or education, or (now) building sites – we are sent carefully – and hopefully with appropriate PPE! But whatever our personal situation – never forget that you are being sent by the King of Kings. You are his postman, his herald, his messenger. It is his message of love, healing and wholeness for the whole work that you bring.

And your mission – and mine – is to help each and every person we encounter to open themselves up to the possibilities of a life in God. Yes...and you know this is coming, don't you...our aim is to help everyone we meet to…'Return to Sender'. Amen.

The War for God

by Tom Kennar

28 May 2020

Text: John 17.20-end

A war is underway. In fact, it always has been. Ever since the first human beings conceived of the very notion of forces outside of everyday life, they have argued, debated and fought with each other about what those forces are like. How do they impact on our lives? How should we respond to them? Much of this war is fought with words, thankfully. But all too often, the war has been fought with the actual weapons of the battlefield. The often-quoted trope: 'religion is the cause of all wars' has at least some truth in it (although economics, politics and plain old-fashioned greed have also played their part in most wars).

We think that ideas about external forces probably started with the most primitive humans. They would have noticed the changes in the world around them. They would have noticed that seeds sprouted after rain, and grew better in sunlight. But they also noticed that when sunlight or rain were absent, their plants didn't grow so well.

But early man couldn't control these forces. He could control some of the things in his life. But he couldn't make the sun shine, or the rain fall. So perhaps, he reasoned, there was a more powerful force – a bigger version of the man himself; up in the sky somewhere? Because the sky is where the sun was, and from where the rain fell, after all. Thus began, in all likelihood, the first stirrings of a human groping for an understanding of God.

But other early humans, in other caves, were also noticing these things…and arriving at different conclusions. Rather than a god they couldn't see controlling the Sun, perhaps the controlling-force for natural events was the Sun itself? Or, noticing that rain was made of water, perhaps the god they sought actually lived in the water, in the seas, or in the rivers?

These early thinkers about external forces talked to their friends and their families, around their ancient camp fires. Their listeners agreed that their ideas had merit. The people who came up with these ideas were obviously wise and fore-sighted, natural leaders and prophets. Their ideas were worth exploring – and then worth accepting as Truth.

Once that leap of faith was taken, all sorts of further questions needed to be answered. Like, how can I communicate with these gods? How can these gods be persuaded to make the rain fall, and the sun shine?

How can I please the gods, so that they will make things happen the way I want them to?

And, crucially, if my ideas about the gods are the correct ideas, how can I persuade the tribe down the road to do the same things as me? For surely, if we all think the same thoughts, and behave in the same, right way towards the gods, then those gods will listen to us? They will do what we ask of them. And so, the War for God began.

Both Jesus and Paul knew about this War. In fact, as we just heard in our first reading, Paul used the warring disagreement between the Pharisees and the Sadducees to get himself out of a pickle – by aligning himself with the Pharisee's belief in the Resurrection. Jesus, in our second reading, was so conscious of the division that religion can bring that he prayed that all his followers may be one. (John 17.21)

Jesus' prayer is the motto of the Young Men's Christian Association – which Clare and I served for about 15 years. The YMCA was founded on the belief that Christians from different churches and expressions of faith could combine their efforts for the good of all humanity. It was a trailblazer in that respect – and many other Christian Charities, like Christian Aid, for example, have followed the same path.

It is perhaps one of the ugliest facts about religion, that religious people are willing to hate one another, simply because they believe different things. Nothing could be further from the truth that all the religious teachers taught. The Prophet Mohammed envisaged a worldwide brotherhood of those who submitted to God. He would have hated the wars between Shi-ites and Sunni believers today. Jesus prayed that all his followers may be one – and he would hate the often vitriolic things that Christians say about each other. Debates rage in the church throughout the world – everything from the role of women, the place of Scripture, and the nature of human sexuality – to name but a few issues. Jesus would have wept – again!

What does this mean for us? Well, it means that we, who understand how religious ideas develop over time need to be patient – which is one of the nine fruits of the Spirit. God's Spirit of Truth is at work in the world – Jesus sent him after his Ascension, to be received at Pentecost. Jesus promised that the Spirit would lead us into all Truth – and that process, I believe, continues today.

200 years ago, the majority of Christians still believed that Slavery was a God-given structure of society. Now, none of us would say so. It was only in 1994 that 32 women were ordained as priests in the church of

England. It has only been 17 years since the first openly gay man was consecrated as a Bishop in the Anglican community.

God's spirit of Truth is alive in the world, and leading God's church into all Truth and into the Unity for which Jesus prayed. It won't happen overnight, because while God loves us, he doesn't force that love upon us. So, for now, we remain patient, and full of hope (another fruit of the spirit) – hopeful, for the full light of truth to dawn. Amen.

A little bit of heaven

by Tom Kennar
31 May 2020 (Pentecost)
Text: Acts 2.1-21

The last few days of glorious sunshine have been a little bit heavenly, haven't they. Unless, that is, you are allergic to heat, or to insect bites, or your skin got burned, or you didn't have the luxury of a garden, or you are REALLY missing your friends and family.

And that's the problem with trying to find a little taste of heaven! Heaven so often proves elusive for us, doesn't it? For me, heaven is sometimes a nice quiet evening at home, pizza in one hand, a bar of chocolate in the other...and a good movie on the box. That'll be heavenly, won't it? And then the phone rings and its Aunty Mabel; you know, the one who can't stop talking, and she wants to give you the latest instalment in her long-running bunion saga.

The problem is that we think of heaven is a place. We imagine that if only we can get all the circumstances right, we will find peace and harmony. Heaven, we imagine, is a place where the sun always shines, and where there are probably no screaming toddlers (at least, that's what my daughter thinks!).

But heaven is not a place. We can't find heaven by getting in a car. Yuri Gregarin, the first man in space, discovered that we don't find heaven by getting in a rocket either. Heaven is not up there. Heaven is in here. Heaven is not a place on earth. Heaven is a place of mind and spirit.

Jesus spoke about heaven quite a bit. When he first started out on his ministry, he declared that the Kingdom of heaven is 'at hand'. Another time he said 'the kingdom of heaven is among you'. Jesus declared that heaven is there, at hand, among us, ready for us to touch and experience.

That, I suggest, is what happened on the day of Pentecost. When God poured out his Spirit on the disciples, gathered in that upper room in fear and trembling, heaven broke through for a while. Filled with God's Spirit, they spilled out into the street in excitement. Some people in the street thought they were all drunk. But others found that they could understand what was being said by these excited, spirit-filled, heaven-touched people.

So let's see what the result of that taste of heaven was. What were the tangible signs that God was at work? And how can we recognise heaven for ourselves from this story? I'd like to draw out just two points.

First, there was a breaking down of national barriers. Luke uses the story-teller's technique of strange tongues being miraculously spoken. But what he is pointing to is that on that day, more than any other in biblical history, God's good news became good news for all the world. No longer was God to be seen as the small God of one small nation. Through whatever actually happened that day, God showed himself to be the God of the whole world...of all those nations who were gathered in Jerusalem, who could now hear Peter speaking in their own tongue.

This was, of course, a reversal of the much older story of the Tower of Babel. This was a God who was no longer to be understood as a partisan God of one tribe; but the Father (and Mother) of all humanity.

That means – and here's my second point – that heaven can be found when all nations lay aside their petty squabbles over resources and unite in the pursuit of justice. Heaven is found when all nations and peoples begin to work together for God's purposes of love and justice. Heaven is found when neighbour begins to truly love neighbour. Heaven is found when our love for God becomes greater than our love of profit.

The Bible's word for these kinds of actions is 'repentance'. On that first Pentecost, the crowd asked Peter and the other apostles "what, then, shall we do Brothers?" Let's take note of Peter's response. He replied, 'Repent and be baptised, every one of you...and you will receive the gift of the Holy Spirit.'

Those who repented on that first Pentecost very soon found themselves living in very different ways. According to the final verses of chapter two, they began living communally; sharing their goods and resources and giving to everyone as they had need. Luke paints a picture of a community who had put aside all notions of gain, of racism, of selfishness – and who had instead begun to live generous, sharing, joyful lives.

For a while, these people really began to get a little taste of heaven. As God's spirit flowed out through them, their response was a joyful self-giving; to one another, and to God. It didn't matter to these people what the weather was like. They could have been just as joyful in the rain or the sun, on the beach or in the country. Heaven, for them, was not a place, but a state of mind. It was a Spirit-filled, transformed state of mind in which generosity, love, forgiveness, and self-sacrifice were found to be the way that heaven comes to earth.

How I pray that our world, our country, our city, and our church could truly learn what it means to live that kind of spirit-filled, Pentecostal, heaven-touching life! Then we could really know what it means to pray 'thy kingdom come on earth as it is in heaven'. Amen.

The Golden Rule

by Tom Kennar – 4 June 2020

Text Mark 12.28-34

It sometimes comes as a surprise to learn that Jesus wasn't the only Rabbi who was teaching the people about God. According to Jewish tradition, there was another Rabbi doing the rounds at around the same time, whose name was Hillel.

One day, according to Jewish tradition, Rabbi Hillel was challenged to explain the Torah – the Laws of Moses – while standing on one leg. It's not altogether clear why he was challenged to do this – perhaps it was some kind of sponsored event! More likely, it was an attempt to get him to simplify his teaching. But anyway, Hillel agreed to the challenge, and lifted his leg off the ground. (If it wasn't for my cassock, you could see me do the same right now!). Hillel, then spoke:

"What is hateful to you, do not do to your fellow: this is the whole Torah; the rest is the explanation; go and learn."

With this one line, Hillel summed up the whole point of the law, as he saw it – which was that the Law was designed to stop us from hurting one another. He actually quoted what is known by philosophers as the 'Golden Rule' – essentially – "don't do to someone else what you wouldn't want them to do to you."

Evidence for the Golden Rule has been found in Confucian writings, from as far back as 500 years before Christ. It is common to Buddhism, Christianity, Hinduism, Judaism, Taoism, Zoroastrianism, and the rest of the world's major religions. In 1993, 143 leaders of the world's major faiths endorsed the Golden Rule as part of the "Declaration Toward a Global Ethic". It is essentially a concept that every religion and world philosophy shares, but belief in God is not necessary to endorse it.

Jesus also believed in the Golden Rule – but he expresses it in more positive terms. Rather than saying 'don't do what you wouldn't want done to you' (which is a rather self-protecting approach), Jesus expresses the Golden Rule more positively, in terms of Love. He says 'Love your neighbour as you love yourself'.

Ponder this, for a moment. Why does Jesus frame the golden rule in this way? Well, I think it's because loving one's neighbour as oneself requires a rather greater degree of commitment than the Golden Rule alone implies. I might very well be happy not to steal from my neighbour, on the grounds that I wouldn't want her to steal from me. But for me to love my neighbour as much as I love myself means that I should aim for the same amount of prosperity and comfort for my neighbour as I myself enjoy.

That's a pretty tall order, isn't it? Especially when we consider that Jesus also re-defined the very concept of neighbour itself. He taught it to mean not just the person next door, or in the next street – but all of humanity – even the people we might normally hate or fear. It means that I need to consider the starving child in Syria as my neighbour. It means the squatters in shanty-towns across the world. It means the homeless woman on the streets of the United Kingdom. In the context of this week's dramatic events in the USA, it certainly means the people of a different colour or ethnic background to me.

This is such a radical idea, that I don't think we have even begun to grasp what it really means. But Jesus raises the stakes even higher, by framing the Golden Rule within a love for God. Love God – and then love your neighbour as yourself. This is surely because Jesus knew that all love flows from God. If we cannot love God with all our hearts, soul, mind and strength – how can we begin to grasp the depth of what loving our neighbour means.

As the Apostle John said, in his first letter, in words we sometimes quote at the Offertory:

"Whoso hath this world's good, and seeth this brother have need, and shutteth up his compassion from him, how dwelleth the love of God in him?

In other words, how can I claim to love God, if I'm content to withhold my help from anyone I know to be in need. What good is it for us to sing hymns of praise to God, while we allow poor people to starve.

Or while we do nothing about protecting the downtrodden of our planet - yes, including those of ethnic minorities, whose 'black lives really do matter'.

Jesus calls us to a radical re-appraisal of all our choices in life. He asks us to act not out of fear – simply not doing things which would harm our neighbour, so that our neighbour won't do them to us. He calls us beyond the simple Golden Rule into lives of complete sacrifice...a sacrifice which pours itself out for all humanity, out of love for God, and love to neighbour. Amen.

The Trinity Conundrum

by Tom Kennar – 7 June 2020 (Trinity Sunday)
Text: Matthew 28.16-20

There's a saying which often circulates around social media for clergy at this time of the year. It goes: "Here's how to preach on the Trinity without blasphemy or heresy: don't bother! Show picture of cats instead!"

The reason for those cautionary words is that preaching on the Trinity is fraught with difficulty. After all, how can we individual human beings possibly grasp the notion of a God who is three persons, and yet also just one God.

Many attempts have been made. The classic illustration is the three-leaved clover – which manages to be one leaf with three distinctive bumps. But that illustration won't do – because it emphasises the three individual persons of the Trinity – the three bumps – whereas Jesus teaches that 'he and the Father are one'.

Another attempt is made on the St Faith's banner, in our church – which I've pointed out every Trinity Sunday since I've been your Rector. And there are many other attempts out there, including the image of an egg (shell, yoke and white, but all one egg).

But each of these metaphors are just pale shadows of the church's teaching on the true nature of the Trinity – which is why none of them really succeed and end up being essentially blasphemous. Blasphemous because they essentially tell a lie – or at least an untruth – about God.

Now I could start being all deeply theological on you right now. I could begin a biblical exegesis about all the places where the Trinity is either referred to, or implied. We could look at the beginning of John's Gospel (where Jesus was with God but also was God). Or we could examine Ezekiel's vision of angels crying 'Holy, Holy, Holy' – which we will repeat during the Eucharistic prayer., shortly. But I fear that those of you who are watching this service on catch-up will just skip forward if I try to get too deep!

So instead, let me just offer this thought. However we fail to grasp the reality of the Trinity, with our limited little brains, there is one thing we must not miss. And it's this…

The Trinity ultimately speaks to us of the absolute importance of community. The Father, Son and Spirit are locked to each other, with an unbreakable bond of love. Whilst they are one God, they are also three persons who live for each other, and serve one another, eternally.

Perhaps the reason we struggle to get our heads round this is because we are individuals. Even if we are married, or in a long-term relationship, and even though we preach that 'two become one', there's no escaping the fact that we remain, ultimately, a unique individual.

But God the Trinity teaches us that we can realise our best selves only in community with others. I know that's true for me. By being in community with each of you my life is enlarged, enhanced, and shaped by you. When you share with me your joys, or your sorrows, or your very silly jokes for the Corona Chronicle(!), I am lifted out of my individual self, and into the broader, deeper, wider life of the whole community. And that is always an enriching and rewarding experience

So let today's celebration of the Holy Trinity be a call for even greater efforts on all our parts to connect with one another, to be a community – even while we are socially distanced from one another. In fact, especially while we are socially distanced from one another. Ring up that friend you haven't talked to for weeks. Reply to that penpal letter. Email that story you've been thinking about for the Corona Chronicle...make the effort, today, to reach out and connect.

For in that act of connection, you will find yourself closer than ever to the Trinitarian heart of God. Amen.

Faith and Suffering

by Tom Kennar – 14 June 2020
Text: 2 Corinthians 13.11-13

Those who have had the inestimable fortitude to sit through my sermons in the past will know that I usually like to focus on the Gospel reading of the day. But today I'm going to break with that tradition. Today's passage of Paul's letter to the Romans seems to speak directly into our own situation so beautifully, that it would be a preaching crime to not contemplate it for a moment!

Paul's main theme is suffering – and the benefits that it can offer to the development of our character. But first, Paul places our suffering in the context of our faith. He reminds us that it is faith alone that provides for our salvation. None of us is holy enough, good enough, sinless enough to find our own way to heaven.

'Sin' is one of those words which are quite often mis-understood. The New Testament word which is translated as 'sin' was actually an archery term. To 'sin', if you were an archer, was to 'miss the target'. So for us, defining ourselves as a 'sinner' means we acknowledge that we all 'miss the target' of being as holy, holy, holy as God.

Human sin is a cause of great suffering in the world. Whether that's the sin of racism, which has provoked the campaign for Black lives to matter. Or the sin of destroying the fragile eco-system, so that viruses like Covid-19 move from animal to human populations. Or whether it's the sin of not sharing the wealth of the world, so that the poorest nations are suffering so badly from Covid's effects – in ways that we can only imagine in our nightmares.

Paul was probably talking about another kind of suffering – specifically the suffering from persecution because of faith. At the time he was writing, Christians were being systematically persecuted, in ways that would be quite familiar to Christians today, in places like Northern Nigeria, or in Syria, or in Palestine.

We are suffering too, albeit, mostly, in a very 'first world' kind of way. We are suffering the deprivation of rights we have enjoyed – the right to gather with our families, or indeed in our churches.

But Paul encourages us to look for God at work – right in the middle of all suffering. He even says that we might boast in our suffering, because...

- suffering produces endurance,
- and endurance produces character,

- and character produces hope.

This time of suffering for us – as a parish – has had many surprising benefits. Thanks to social media, emails, phone calls and the Corona Chronicle, I personally feel that I have become much more connected to many of you. New people have joined our common sharing of faith, through the miracle of live-streaming. I've seen SO many acts of kindness and generosity. And it is certain that, even when full church services are restored, nothing is ever going to be the same again.

This experience of suffering has enabled us to ask lots of questions about the priorities that we have given, in the past, to many aspects of church life. There are many things to which we will return joyfully and gratefully. But there are other things which will, I think, have changed quite dramatically. Our suffering has produced endurance. Our endurance has helped us focus on the character of our common life. Reflection on that character has produced hope: hope that God is very much alive among us, and teaching us to encounter God in many different ways.

So today, we give thanks to God for the teaching-value of suffering. We look forward expectantly to what else we have yet to learn. And we hold fast to the faith that gives us life. Amen.

The Lord's Prayer

by Tom Kennar – 18 June 2020

Texts: Isaiah 63.7-9 & Matthew 6.7-15

The version of the Lord's Prayer we have just heard has some different wording to the version we will say together a little later on. I am referring, of course, to two lines in particular:

'Forgive us our debts as we forgive our debtors,' *and*
'Do not bring us to the time of trial, but rescue us from the evil one.'

The reason that we have two competing versions of the Lord's prayer is quite simply because Greek scholars have never been able to agree precisely what was meant by the original Greek words. It's a problem – but it is also a salutary lesson to anyone who wants to take any phrase of the Bible and treat it literally.

The Bible is a text which needs careful study, at all times. It is not, as some suppose, a handbook from God, nor a letter from the Almighty, dictated word for word from the divine lips. Instead, it is a glorious mixture of story, myth, prophecy, poetry, history and the ancient laws of a nomadic people. Most of all, it is the record of one nation's attempt to understand something of who God is, and what God is like. Along the way, they made many errors.

No-one today, for example, could possibly believe in a God who gives permission for one group of humans to wage war on another group of humans, and to forcibly take their land from them. But that's what the writers of some of the Bible thought God was like.

No-one, today, could possibly believe that God thought slavery was a perfectly acceptable economic system – but some of the Bible's writers did. And when such writers thought such thoughts, they tended to imagine that God agreed with them!

So, our task is to approach the Bible thoughtfully, and carefully. We listen to the wisdom of the Scholars who understand the original languages of the bible – and then we weigh up their ideas against what the Holy Spirit teaches us about truth, and the actual reality of God.

Take for example this line from the Lord's prayer: 'Do not bring us to the time of trial.' Or, as the liturgical version has it: 'lead us not into temptation.' Both of these are attempts to grapple with the meaning of one Greek word in the original text. But both of them are problematic, when weighed against what we know about God.

They are problematic because they suggest that God himself might either lead us into a time of trial, or that God himself might lead us into temptation. But this doesn't sound right, does it? Why would God, who loves us so much, and who seeks only our good, actively lead us into either danger, or into temptation. It would be like a mother who leaves a bag of sweets on the kitchen counter, just so that she can take some kind of sick pleasure in telling off her children – when they steal one!

Pope Francis has wrestled with this line. As he said, in 2017, 'I am the one who falls (into temptation). It is not God pushing me into temptation to then see how far I have fallen'. As a consequence, most of the Roman Catholic world now uses a form of words which says 'Do not let me fall into temptation'. That's a prayer for strength to resist temptation, rather than a plea for God himself to stop tempting us!

So what can we take from this? Well, I suggest that the lesson for the day is that we need to be very careful about assuming we know anything about God at all. God is an infinite mystery, before whom we can only stand and wonder. It is the presence of God in our lives which lifts our hearts and inspires our actions...just as it was for Isaiah in this morning's lesson. As he said: It was no messenger or angel, but his presence that saved them. In other words, it was not words from heaven which saved the people, it was God's actual presence among them.

It is by seeking the presence of the Lord, that we begin to truly understand the Lord. All our human words, all the texts of the Bible, all the hymns and sermons in the world cannot actually teach us the ways of the Lord. We need to let go of what we think we know, and in silent adoration and awe, let the Holy Spirit truly teach us the ways of God.

Perhaps in these continuing quiet days of partial lockdown, we have no greater opportunity to lay aside the busy-ness of our monkey minds, and just dwell in the presence of the Lord. Amen.

Not peace, but a sword

by Tom Kennar – 21 June 2020

Matthew 10.24-39

Tough stuff this, isn't it? Verse 34-36: 'Do not think I have come to bring peace to the earth; I have not come to bring peace, but a sword. For I have come to set a man against his father, and a daughter against her mother, and a daughter-in-law against her mother in law; and one's foes will be members of one's own household!'

Jesus says that his followers may have to make some pretty tough decisions about where their allegiance lies. 'Whosever does not take up his cross, and follow me is not worthy of me...' and so on.

To us Western Christians, this speech seems rather odd, even a bit fanatical doesn't it? We have the freedom to worship wherever and whenever we like – except during a virus lockdown, of course. To us, Jesus' talk of persecution, poverty and martyrdom seems to represent another world altogether. But ask the Christians of Syria, or Iran, or Turkey, or Northern Nigeria, or Palestine whether persecution, poverty and martyrdom is a reality today.

Their often horrific stories force me to ask some pretty tough questions of myself. Could it be, for example, that we Western Christians have somehow tamed our faith? Have we re-fashioned it in our own image so that it no longer challenges our society at all? With our beautiful buildings, sublime music and art, our robes and our meticulous traditions, perhaps we have left behind us some of the more radical aspects of Jesus message.

Frankly, when church members start to worry more about when their church building can open than whether their church is doing enough to help the poor, we need to ask ourselves some hard questions.

Have we become so contaminated by the world around us, that the world no longer sees us as a threat to its selfish, violent, materialistic way of life? Could it be that we have become silent, when we should be upsetting the money-changers' tables?

The Christian faith, openly declared, is dangerous to the world. It is a way of life which stands in opposition to the way that many people chose to live. It is a way of peace, not war. It is a way of self-control, not pleasure-seeking. It is a way of poverty, simplicity and charity, not materialism and consumerism.

But what about these battles which Jesus predicts between family members? There is an old saying, that blood is thicker than water...which is sometimes used to justify all sorts of feuds between families. In some feuds, it doesn't matter who is right or wrong...it matters only that someone's family has been insulted. It's what the Mafia does. And, frankly, it's what some families do too.

I don't know about you...but I think that that way lies madness. If we all jump to the defence of someone who is clearly in the wrong, just because they were a member of our family – or our club – then pretty soon the whole of society would crumble into an endless battle.

The church has suffered from this temptation too. As we all know, only too painfully, the church is suffering from such bad publicity about its handling of sexual abuse, racism and homophobia. That's because churches, sometimes, have tended to put the church family above the need for justice and truth for victims of abuse, racism and homophobia. Sometimes, we've even hidden – or at least tolerated – abusers, or racists, or homophobes within our church family structures. We have failed to call them to a higher loyalty – the loyalty we all owe to God. The loyalty to truth and justice.

Now please don't get me wrong. I'm not saying that families – or indeed churches – are a bad thing. God loves families! God invented families. Families, and church families, are one of the most important structures in our whole society. The best families give us companionship and love, a place to feel secure, a place to make mistakes, and still be accepted.

But Jesus says to us, through this reading, that we have an even higher loyalty...a loyalty that only a God could claim...a loyalty to Him. And that, Jesus warns, will bring division even between members of the same family, and even a kind of metaphorical sword. Because God has an even higher claim on our loyalty than our families.... even if our families don't acknowledge him.

So when those around us choose not to follow the path of the Spirit, how do we respond? Perhaps they are our neighbours? Perhaps it's our Government, influenced by massive political donations to enact certain policies? Perhaps its companies founded on greed and materialism, and who use modern day slaves to produce their wonderfully cheap goods for Western consumers? Perhaps even members of our own family choose not to follow the path of the Spirit. How do we respond? Who is it who commands our loyalty?

May God give you the strength to stand up for Jesus, and for his radical call to a life of truth, justice, simplicity and charity. May you carry your cross, even when your family or neighbours tempt you to another path – an easier path, a path of least resistance. Be strong in the Lord. Carry your cross. And hold out for the reward of heaven. Amen.

Peering into the future

by Tom Kennar – 28 June 2020

Texts: Jeremiah 28. 5-9 & Matthew 10.40-42

Hands up if you want to know what the future holds. Well, I can't see your hands via my camera, but I'm willing to bet many of you put them up – at least in your heads. Most of us want to know the future. It's pretty much ingrained in our human nature. Farmers, when they plant their crops, would love to know whether they will succeed. Armies marching to war want to know if they will win. Investors in the stock market are obsessed by knowing what's going to happen – there's even an entire range of speculative stocks known as 'futures'.

People living through a pandemic really want to know. Especially parents, for whom home schooling has really lost its appeal. Or homeless people, who have been given a home during the pandemic, but now face real uncertainty. Or NHS staff who are desperately hoping that the hoards on our beaches in the last week won't trigger another pandemic wave.

I wish that I could see into the future, right now. Because then I would know how to advise the PCC about when the right time to open our church to the public would be.

This deep 'need to know' the future was no less real for our ancestors. And so, prophets and soothsayers who claimed they could see the future were given really high status in their communities. Kings consulted them, and religious leaders listened to them – sometimes.

Personally, I'm a little bit suspicious of anyone who tells me that they can see into the future, specifically and definitely. And I notice that even those biblical prophets who claimed they could see the future would describe in either very vague, or very metaphorical terms. Armies of scholars have argued for centuries about what Daniel meant by the 'Abomination of Desolation' standing in the temple. Or what John the Revelator meant by his lurid descriptions of the four horsemen of the apocalypse, the battle of Armageddon, or the Whore of Babylon. Even his glorious vision of a new Jerusalem, descending from heaven, feels rather more like poetry than factual description.

There are, essentially, two kinds of prophets. First there are the 'foretellers' – the ones who claim to have been given a specific vision or picture of what the future will be like, or of how specific events will unfold.

The second kind of prophet is the 'forth-teller' – that is, someone who tells-forth the teachings and wisdom of God into a given situation. They are the ones who warn the people of the consequences of their actions. “Listen up. If you carry on living the way that you are living, then bad things are going to happen”.

Some of the Hebrew Bible’s prophets went to some extreme lengths to get their forth-telling across to the people. I love the story of Hosea, for example, who deliberately married a sex worker to create a visual aid to the people. “Look,” he said, effectively, “I have married an unfaithful woman to show you that YOU have been unfaithful to God”. I wondered about trying a similar visual aid, for one of my sermons...but Clare wouldn’t let me!

Sometimes, the people would listen to the warnings of the prophets. Take Jonah for example. He did everything he could to avoid telling the people of Nineveh that they were sinful and about to be punished. But God insisted, and even sent a great fish to take him to Nineveh. Eventually, Jonah plucked up the courage to warn the people that they were all doomed. And guess what? They actually listened to him. The king put on sackcloth and ashes, the people repented, and the Lord decided not to wipe them from the earth.

Jonah was NOT happy. Having finally delivered his ‘end of the world’ warning, he wanted God to go through with it! But that’s a story for another day.

St Paul described prophecy as one of the greater gifts, and he advised the Corinthians to earnestly desire the gift of prophecy. And that’s because I think that be a really effective prophet, a great deal of wisdom is required. Today’s prophets are those like our climatologists, who predict an awful future for us if we don’t change the ways we live. Most pertinently right now, epidemiologists are another kind of wise prophet. Their years of study and accumulated wisdom enable them to forecast the effects of various social measures.

The prophets of the Bible times often struggled to make their voices heard by the decision-makers of their day. And we too have discovered that the dire warnings of scientists about COVID-19 are not always taken fully on-board by the politicians (who have a wider responsibility to the economy and the electorate).

The big task for the church, right now, is to prophecy about the future of our worship and community life. This is no easy task, for we must listen to the wise prophets of epidemiology, as well as the heart-felt desire of our parishioners to re-enter their church. What I think we can prophecy, fairly accurately, is that nothing will ever be quite the same again in our future. But that whatever our future holds, we know that God walks into it, with us, hand in hand. Amen.

The Gift of Doubt

by Tom Kennar – 2 July 2020
Text: John 20.24-29

Today, we are celebrating the Feast of the Apostle Thomas, transferred from tomorrow. This is mainly because I could hardly overlook the feast day of another man called Thomas! But it's also because the set readings for the feast offer us some inspiration in this time of crisis.

Saint Thomas is universally known as 'Doubting Thomas', quite simply because of this one occasion when he couldn't quite bring himself to believe that Jesus had risen from the dead. That 'moniker' he has had to live with stands as a badge of shame for just one small incident in what was otherwise an exemplary life. He was, for example, the first of the disciples to recognise Jesus as 'The Way'. He followed him Jesus diligently throughout his ministry, and unlike Peter, he did not deny his Lord. When confronted with the reality of his mistake about Jesus' resurrection, he immediately repented of his hasty words, and acknowledged Jesus as not just his Lord, but also his God...a word rarely used of Jesus by the other apostles.

Then, after Pentecost, the Church's tradition tells us that he went East, with great enthusiasm for the task of spreading the Gospel. He established not least the Church of India, which still functions today. But poor Thomas, everyone seems to forget all this wonderful stuff about him – they forget what a tremendous powerhouse for God that he was. They just dismiss him for one moment of doubt.

Actually, I think that doubt is a healthy thing. Doubt is a sign that the mind is working – weighing-up, critically and carefully, the information which it is being fed. I think we could all do with a little more doubt in our intellectual diet.

One area that we might exercise such doubt is in the way we interpret what our leaders, newspapers and social media try to tell us is true. We must all learn those critical tools of checking the sources of information, examining the evidence, and testing the veracity of what powerful voices say. In St Thomas' terms, we need to poke our fingers into some holes to find out for ourselves what is really true.

And, I have to say, within the field of religion, doubt is also no bad thing. We owe a huge debt to those who have gone before us in the faith, especially to the writers of the Scriptures. But if we accept everything they wrote without a little bit of doubt, we would, frankly, still be keeping slaves on Church of England-owned plantations in the Caribbean (because all the Bible writers shared a common belief that slavery was normal).

To borrow an idea from Rob Bell, we can picture faith as being rather like a trampoline. The central fabric – which holds us up – is the main meat of our faith, that is the very existence of God. But the fabric is held up by springs, which we can see as the various dogmas, theories, and claims of other people of faith throughout the centuries. Some of those springs are, I'm afraid, rather rusty. If we exercise the gift of doubt, intelligently, it is quite possible to take off one spring, without the whole trampoline collapsing. We can then examine that spring, that dogma or that idea, to see whether it needs polishing, or oiling, or perhaps even replacing altogether. But the rest of the trampoline still holds up.

Now here's a radical thought: I suggest there is a particular spring that we are being called to examine, right now. This COVID crisis has, among many things, asked us to question the weight of significance we place on church buildings. For centuries, we have unapologetically assumed that for the faith to flourish, we need magnificent buildings, dedicated to the glory of God. Whereas, for me at least, the reality of the last three months has been that without our lovely building, faith has been flourishing all around me. I've had more conversations about faith with parishioners in the last three months than I had in the whole five years of my ministry here prior to lockdown. Really. I have. And many more people have worshipped with us online than ever come into the church.

That's not the whole story – of course. For many, the deprivation of the church as a place to pray or meet others has been real and raw. Don't think, therefore, that I'm planning to bring in the bulldozers! I am looking forward with all my heart to the day when we get to sing God's praises in St Faith's again. What I am suggesting is that, from time to time, a little bit of doubt about things we've always just assumed to be true is a good thing. Perhaps there is more to faith than church buildings?

Perhaps St Thomas the Apostle deserves not to be mocked, but celebrated for the gift of doubt. Amen.

Come unto me…

by Tom Kennar – 16 July 2020

Matthew 11.28-end

Today, the lectionary invites us to contemplate the first of the phrases known as the 'comfortable words', which we will use later in our service. Come unto me, all ye that travail and are heavy laden...which I have to confess I prefer to the more prosaic version we've just heard from the New Revised Standard Version.

I like the old word 'travail' because it has its root in a Latin word for 'torture'. The word 'weary' just doesn't have the same energy about it. Does it?

Now I have to say that there is a tendency for us to over-sentimentalise these words of Jesus. We imagine that this is Jesus effectively mopping our brow, holding us to his bosom, and saying 'there, there...just come to Daddy, and everything will be alright'. But as I've often taught, context is everything. We need to understand the context in which Jesus speaks these words.

Jesus has been arguing – again – with the religious leaders of his day. They taught a form of religion which was packed full of rules. There were dire consequences at play for the failure to keep any one of such rules. After these words, Jesus has yet another debate, about the laws of the Sabbath.

The rabbis of the time had a phrase, which they often used, to describe the process of following the law, or the Torah. If you were a strict and observant Jew, then you had taken upon you 'the yoke of the Torah'. Like a horse fixed to a plough, you had put the heavy yoke of the law on your shoulders. The law was a burden to be borne.

In direct contrast, Jesus invites everyone to take up his yoke. His yoke is easy, and his burden is light. It's important to realise that Jesus himself was a recognised rabbi. When he used talk about yokes, his listeners would have known precisely what he was saying.

Jesus was inviting his followers not to worry about the strict letter of the laws of Moses. Whether you eat the right food, or wear the right clothes, whether you are ritually clean or unclean, how far you may walk or work on the Sabbath day – all these are distractions from the central, core, message of loving God and loving our neighbour.

Now I would fully understand if, by now, you're getting a bit fed up of me harping on about Jesus' message of loving God and loving neighbour. I freely acknowledge that it is often the point at which my sermons tend to arrive.

I'm reminded of the story of the Vicar who preached the same sermon two weeks running. Then on the third Sunday he preached it again. Then on the fourth Sunday, he preached it again! His churchwarden took him to one side and said, 'Father, do you realise you've preached the same sermon four times now?'

'Yes,' replied the priest. 'And when I see evidence among the congregation that my message has been heard, I'll move on to another one!'

This is not to say that I don't see signs among my congregation of love being expressed. Nothing could be further from my mind. I've been SO impressed by the love that our pastoral volunteers have been showing to lonely parishioners. I'm so grateful to those who have helped Sandra, Will and me to get the church open for visitors. I'm amazed by the loving generosity of so many donors to the parish, and to the Discretionary Fund, so that we can help some of the neediest of our neighbours. There has been a lot of love – for God and our neighbours – which this parish has shown in recent months.

But I do want to carry on encouraging each of us to take the two greatest commandments ever more seriously. I believe that we need to go deeper and deeper into what it truly means to love God with all our heart, mind, soul and strength. And what it really means to love our neighbours as ourselves.

It is not for me to work out what that challenge means for each one of you. I could offer a hundred examples of ways in which we could all love God and love our neighbour with greater depth. But actually, the task of working that out is yours. It's part of the yoke of Jesus to work out the implications of Jesus' radical message in your own life. How you spend your time, how you spend your money, where you direct your energies – all these choices are yours to make in the light of the two greatest commandments.

Jesus' yolk of love is indeed a light burden – compared to the yoke of the Torah it replaced. But it is still a yoke. It is still a call to a way of life which demands my soul, my life, and my all. For only then, when I have expended myself completely for the love of God and neighbour, only then will I truly find the rest for my soul that Jesus' yoke offers to all. Amen.

Weeds and flowers

by Tom Kennar – 19 July 2020
Text: Matthew 13.24-30, then 36-43

Unlike our Churchwarden, Colin Hedley, I'm not much of a farmer. Unlike many of the rest of you, I'm not much of a gardener, either…which is ironic since the Diocese has decreed that I should live in a house which has 200 yards of borders to maintain! I kid you not!

Fortunately, Clare knows a little bit more about gardening than me. Unfortunately, that means I can very quickly get in trouble for pulling up what I thought was a weed, but which she tells me was an expensive plant…lovingly nurtured from seed, and planted with infinite care by her green fingers.

The trouble is that weeds are not really weeds at all. They are actually just wild flowers which are growing in an inconvenient place. At least, that's how the Royal Horticultural Society labels them, I'm told. So, it turns out, the untrained eye finds it very difficult indeed to decide what is weed, and what is not. After all, they are both made of the same stuff. They are both green. Most weeds have some kind of flower.

This is something we've discovered to our great joy in St Faith's Churchyard in recent years. For many years, Ralph Hollins catalogued the many different plants which appear there. Then, an in depth biodiversity survey was undertaken a few years ago, kindly paid for by some members of our congregation. We discovered that our churchyard actually contained over 80 native British plants, some of which are quite rare. So much so that our churchyard is now a designated 'Site of Interest for Nature Conservation'. As you may know, we now routinely leave areas of the churchyard un-mowed, so that these plants have a chance to thrive and spread their seeds. Many of these plants would have been considered weeds, by our ancestors. But no longer, by us.

So, it seems, it's hard to tell weeds from plants in the real world. What about in the spiritual world, as described by Jesus in today's Gospel? Well, I have to tell you, after a lifetime of pastoring, it's not always easy to tell the difference among people, either.

Some people present themselves as magnificent flowers to the general population. They dress well, they say all the right words in all the right places. They donate generously to the church. They might sit on the right committees, or sing in the choir. But then, some event will take place, and all their fine words and actions get blown away in some awful action or horrible words. We find that underneath their beautiful plumage, beneath the gorgeous flower they displayed to the world, their roots were rotten.

And the opposite is also true. One of the great joys of St Faith's, for me, is that we attract people from all walks of life. And, let's be honest, some of the people who walk through our doors are not normally our kind of people. In any other part of life, we would probably not even speak to them. They don't play our kind of game. Or they don't dress in our kind of costume. Or they don't eat in our kinds of restaurant. But, when you get to know these apparent weeds, these odd plants which don't appear to be in the right place, we so often find that they are, in fact, beautiful flowers.

So, if weeds can turn out to be flowers, and flowers can turn out to be weeds, how are we to tell the difference? How shall we react to them? Well, to this question, Scripture offers us an answer. The Bible's unambiguous message is that Love must be our watch-word.

To the apparent flower whose roots turn out to be rotten, we offer Love. Perhaps with the balm of love, their roots can be strengthened, in the good soil of the church; so that their flower can bloom again.

To the apparent weed, whose manners and untidy appearance initially perplexes us, we offer Love; in the hope that in the good soil of the church, they will find their own flower, and learn to bloom, gloriously.

That's all that God requires of us. Love, love, love. We feed, we water, we prune where necessary. We love.

But, wait a minute. What's that you say? What about the weeds who will always be weeds? What about the weeds who cannot stop strangling the life out of the flowers around them? Well, yes, they are a problem. There will always be those stubborn weeds which choke the life out of the flowers. They are the Japanese Knot-weeds, which just refuse to go away, and which wreak destruction on all around them.

Well, Jesus, tells us in today's Gospel, 'leave them to the Angels'. It is not for us to judge, for judgement is the preserve of God alone. There are indeed some unfortunate souls who will always be weeds. We cannot know what life has thrown at them. We cannot know what poor soil they grew up in, or the harsh environment which made them what they are. Like any gardener, we are wise if we protect the rest of the flowers from their influence. But what their ultimate destination might be – that's in the hands of the angels. Whether they will one day end up at the flower show, or on the compost heap, is something we leave in the hands of God.

In the end, for us, the command is to Love. We keep on watering. We keep on feeding. We keep on loving, trusting that God has the future safely and securely in his hands. Amen.

The power of stories

by Tom Kennar - 23 July, 2020

Text: Matthew 13. 10-17

I wonder how many of us remember the late, lamented crooner, Max Bygraves. He had one of those catch-phrases, which impressionists would copy, so that everyone knew, straight away, who they were impersonating. For Max Byrgraves, it was 'I wanna tell you a story'.

Then, old Max would start to sing – all sorts of wonderful, imaginary stories. There was the question 'What noise annoys an oyster?'. There was that song about the imaginary tiny house, by a tiny sea, in Gillegilleosenfefacatsanellenbogan-by the sea. And then there was my favourite – 'You're a pink toothbrush' – the story of a romance between a pink dental hygiene instrument, and a blue one!

The genius of Max Byrgraves, like so many before him, was that he realised human beings are hard-wired for stories. We love them. From Homer's Iliad, and the story of Noah's Ark, to the latest movies on our screen, or the novels on our shelves, there's nothing we enjoy more than losing ourselves in a good story.

Stories have power you see. We see ourselves, and our lives, reflected back at us in stories. We identify ourselves, or at least our aspirations of who we would like to be, in the lines of stories. Romantic stories wake up our emotions, and help us to find the romance in our own lives. Heroic tales of 'daring do' enable us to imagine ourselves as the hero of the story. They lift our eyes and our hearts to bigger, greater horizons.

Stories in the Bible are no exception. The stories of the Hebrew Bible are often centred around a 'great hero' who, by obeying God's command carries out a great a mighty deed. Noah, Abraham, Moses, Joshua, David, Daniel - they are all heroes, made of heroic stuff, which inspire us to also seek God's will and to become heroes ourselves.

Jesus understood the power of story. Which is why he told so many parables. But when his disciples asked him why he used so many parables, his reply – as we just heard – was enigmatic, to say the least.

We don't have the time for a line-by-line examination of the Gospel text. But what I think Jesus was pointing to was this: he noticed that the people had become deaf to the wisdom of God, especially as it was taught to them by the religious leaders of the day. They taught the people rules and regulations, dogmas to be believed and followed. But the result, as Jesus says, was that "seeing they do not perceive, and hearing they do not listen, nor do they understand."

Jesus attempted to break through the log-jam, by re-imagining the faith in terms of stories. These were stories about fishermen and bakers, farmers and home-makers – ordinary people, in fact. He invited his listeners to see themselves in these stories, just as story-tellers have always done. He sought to awaken their imaginations, and by doing so to re-awaken their hearts to receive the message of God's love.

We too are invited to do the same. When we read the Scriptures, we are invited not to get too bogged down in the questions of the theologians – the detailed questions about whether this event or that really happened exactly as it was recorded. Or whether this or that story is provable by modern archaeology. We are invited, instead, to ask what this story says to our heart. How does it lift our imaginations beyond the humdrum, every day nature of our existence? How does it inspire us to go further, go deeper, be braver, more loving, more steadfast?

So when you read the Creation story, don't worry about how many days it was completed in. Ask yourself, instead, how you can be involved in God's ongoing act of creation.

When you read the story of Moses crossing the Red Sea, don't get caught up in questions of how likely or unlikely the story is. Rather, focus on what barriers are in your life, and how you might begin to cross them.

When you read of tiny David defeating gigantic Goliath, don't get caught up in the questions about who the Philistines were and still are today. Instead, take courage that even you, with your small skills, can make a difference in the world.

Let the power of these stories, and the parables of Jesus seep into your heart. Let them challenge and encourage you, to ever greater works for the Kingdom of Heaven. Amen.

The search for wisdom

by Tom Kennar - 26 July, 2020

Texts: 1 Kings 3. 5-12 & Matthew 13. 31-33 & 44-52

Today's readings invite us to consider the quest for Wisdom. First, we encountered King Solomon, who rather than ask for wealth or power first asked God for wisdom. God was pleased with this request, and in what is, frankly, rather a Trumpian response, told Solomon that he would be given a 'wise and discerning mind; no one like you has been before you and no one like you shall arise after you'. Very Donald Trump!

Then, in our Gospel reading, after a series of short parables about the diligent search for the Kingdom, Jesus teaches his disciples with a rather enigmatic phrase. He says, 'every scribe who has been trained for the kingdom of heaven is like the master of a household who brings out of his treasure what is new and what is old'. Jesus is telling his disciples that the wise teacher of faith will use the best of the old knowledge, and combine it with the new, in the task of bringing the Kingdom to pass. Wisdom requires the acquisition and then the wise use of knowledge.

A key theme of Matthew's Gospel is that Jesus is the living, breathing personification of Divine Wisdom. The Hebrew Bible often sings hymns of praise to Divine Wisdom, and, often, wisdom is given a personality. Take for example, these lines from the first chapter of the book of Proverbs:

'Wisdom cries out in the street;
in the squares she raises her voice - {…}
'How long, O simple ones, will you love being simple?
How long will scoffers delight in their scoffing
and fools hate knowledge?'

I find these lines encouraging. They remind me that teachers and writers throughout the ages have always despaired of how the mind of the common man seems to work. Just like I do. Human beings have always been subject to spin, fake news, and they have always acted on instinct, rather than fact. Fools have always hated knowledge. And they have always scoffed at those who do put in the hard work to find out what is true and good and right. 'What do these scientists know?'. 'Theologians? Pah!'

Four and a half centuries before Jesus, there was a famous man in Greece, called Plato. He was a philosopher – a word made up of two Greek words, 'philia', meaning love; and 'sofia' meaning wisdom. A philosopher, then, is simply someone who loves wisdom. Plato had a tremendous impact on his time, and in the centuries afterwards. His thinking was widely known, and often quoted. I would be extremely surprised if Jesus had never heard of him.

Plato offered the world a simple metaphor for the accumulation of wisdom…the metaphor of a cave. Imagine, he said, that you were born in a cave, facing the wall. And that this is the only life you had ever known. On the wall of the cave in front of you were shadows of things which you believed were real. Trees, houses, people. This was your whole life. A tree was just a shadow of a tree. A house was just a shadow of a house.

Imagine, then, said Plato, that one day something made you turn around. To your surprise, you found that there are people standing behind you, who are holding up wooden silhouettes of the trees, the houses, and the people. Suddenly, your eyes have been opened. You realise that there is a cause of the shadows. Your whole world-view has shifted.

Then, said Plato, imagine that you notice the daylight, shining behind the people with the silhouettes. Your enquiring mind has been awakened…and so you make your way to the entrance of the cave. And then, stepping into the sunlight, you find our exactly what a real tree looks like, and a real house, and real people.

You might be interested to know that Plato's cave is the reason why many Nativity scenes are shown in a cave. Jesus is shown as the Divine Light, the Divine Wisdom, emerging from the Cave of human ignorance and lazy thinking.

The Cave, suggested Plato, is a metaphor for the quest for Wisdom on which we are all invited. It is a way of life, which anyone can follow, just like the Way of Jesus. And it is a prize worth selling everything you own to possess – just like the pearl of great price, or the treasure hidden in the field of Jesus' parables.

But isn't Jesus talking about the Kingdom of Heaven, not wisdom per se? Well, yes. But, the Kingdom of Heaven is first and foremost a place in which Divine Wisdom reigns supreme.

It is Divine Wisdom, for example, which teaches us that in giving things away, we accumulate great wealth. Or as I said a few weeks ago in the Corona Chronicle, 'true wealth is what you find you have left when all your possessions have been taken away'. (You might want to think about that one, for a moment.)

- It is Divine Wisdom which teaches us that forgiveness is the only way to deal with hatred.

- It is Divine Wisdom which teaches us that God's voice is best heard in silence.
- It is Divine Wisdom which teaches us that servants make the best leaders.
- It is Divine Wisdom which gives us a King who has a Cross as his throne.

The Kingdom of Heaven is an upside -down place. There is almost nothing in the Kingdom which feels normal to a society which values hatred, greed, fake news, celebrity, and worldly power. That's why it is such a hard message to communicate to the world.

'Wisdom cries out in the street;
in the squares she raises her voice - {…}
'How long, O simple ones, will you love being simple?
How long will scoffers delight in their scoffing
and fools hate knowledge?'

Amen.

Black lives matter

by Tom Kennar – 30 July 2020

Texts: Galatians 3.26–end; 4.6, 7 and Luke 4.16–21

Today, (30 July) the Church of England remembers William Wilberforce. He was born in 1759 in Hull. Having been converted to an Evangelical piety within the Church of England, Wilberforce decided to serve the faith in Parliament instead of being ordained. He became a Member of Parliament at the age of twenty-one. He was a supporter of various missionary initiatives and he helped to found The Bible Society.

He eventually settled in Clapham in London – which we used to call 'Cla'am' when I lived there! Wilberforce became a leader of the reforming group of Evangelicals known as the 'Clapham Sect'. Of all the causes for which he fought, he is remembered best for his crusade against slavery. After years of effort, the trade in slaves was made illegal in the British Empire in 1807 and Wilberforce lived to see the complete abolition of slavery by Britain, just before his death on this day in 1833.

Some of you may not know that one of the Canonries I hold is for the Cathedral of Cape Coast, in Ghana. The Cathedral is an old garrison church for the English soldiers who once protected slave merchants at the next-door castle. On the day I was made a Canon there, I had the strange experience of preaching to a congregation of entirely African faces, in the building which would once have had only English faces looking back at me. I was struck, really forcibly, by the irony of that moment. One of the most disturbing things I learned in Cape Coast was that the first Anglican church in Ghana was actually built over the entrance to the pits in which slaves were kept before being shipped off.

But largely thanks to Anglican William Wilberforce, Britain was the first major economy to abolish slavery, at a time when the rest of the world still considered it a normal practice. Led by an Anglican Christian. For me, there is hope in that statement.

There is no doubt that the Anglican Church, like many British institutions of the time, benefitted from the slave trade. Around these walls there are memorials to men who undoubtedly had stocks and shares in the slave trade – at the very least. I very much expect that some of the stones from which this ancient church was built were purchased with slave trader's profits.

But it was also an Anglican, William Wilberforce, who caused the church, and the Nation, to wake up from its collective evil and folly. It was an Anglican, inspired by Christ, who proclaimed release to the captives, and who knew in his bones that in Christ there is no longer slave or free. That we are all, black and white, one in Jesus Christ.

Now, I doubt very much that such an intelligent audience (as I know you all to be) would need me to outline the horrors of slavery. But I do want you to ponder, just for a moment, some of lasting effects of that abhorrent practice.

Some of those effects include the fact that slavery is still very much alive and well in our world today. It is no longer state sponsored, in any significant sense. But it carries on, all around the world, largely underground. Wealthy people in wealthy nations are able to acquire other people to carry out the menial tasks they don't want to do, giving them nothing in return save basic food and shelter. Such people are supplied by people traffickers, and modern-day slave owners. Children are taken from their families, and sold to wealthy families, or car washing gangs, or prostitution networks, all over the world. And unless someone steps in, there is no escape for such people. And more people are said to be in slavery today than at the height of the Atlantic slave trade by the great economic powers.

Another lasting effect of slavery has been the way that we still, as a society, instinctively treat non-white citizens as somehow different, or less important. Why is it, for example, that the awful case of Madeleine McCann still grabs newspaper headlines, while tens of thousands of abducted non-white children around the world rarely get a mention?

It is said that people from non-white backgrounds are statistically more likely to be infected with COVID-19. Could that be because statistically, non-white people are more likely to be working on the frontline of our communities, in our hospitals, driving our trains and buses, and living in over-crowded housing?

All lives matter. But the events of recent weeks have reminded us that Black Lives Matter at least as much as white lives. Until we have created a society in which all slavery is vanquished, and where non-white people have all the same economic, educational and healthcare opportunities as white people, we need to keep on reminding ourselves that Black Lives matter too.

Perhaps we Anglicans, drawing from the heritage of William Wilberforce, still have a role to play. Perhaps we need to raise our voices, as he raised his, to challenge our society, and speak the truth, that Jesus commanded us to 'let the oppressed go free', and to proclaim that this is the year of the Lord's favour.
Amen.

Getting and keeping. Or giving and sharing?

(The Feeding of the Five Thousand)
by Tom Kennar – 02 August 2020
Text: Matthew 14:13-21

Last week our gospel reading was all about metaphors...pictures to help us envision the Kingdom of Heaven is like. A mustard seed, yeast, treasure, a pearl of great price – and so on. In other words, we were being asked to think about just what a life-changing idea the Kingdom is.

This week – the focus changes, to a real-life example of the Kingdom being worked out. It's story of the Feeding of Five Thousand. I'm afraid I can't think of this story without remembering a Sunday School song that has stayed in my head for about 45 years! Do you remember it?

Two little fishes, five loaves of bread.
Five thousand people by Jesus were fed.
This is what happened when one little lad
Gladly gave Jesus all that he had.
All that I have, all that I have
I will give Jesus all that I have.

It's basically a simple story. Jesus has been pursued by a great crowd. When evening falls, the disciples ask Jesus "Shouldn't we send these folks away to buy some food?". But Jesus takes a few loaves and fishes, he blesses them, and commands them to be distributed among the crowd. The food somehow multiplies - so much so that there are 12 baskets left over.

Was this a miracle of multiplication? Was Jesus showing off his divine power? Or did something else take place – something much more radical, and much more important than a divine conjuring trick?

Could it be that people had, in fact, brought food with them? After all, not many people would go out to a deserted place – miles from home – without packing a few sandwiches for journey. So perhaps, when Jesus started to distribute all that he had, people started to open their picnics up - and began to share with each other. You can be sure that most people had packed far more in their picnic than they would need! But until Jesus showed them how to share, they were keeping their sandwiches hidden away…

Here's another important point to note. In response to the disciples' question about sending people away, Jesus replies, "They need not go away...YOU give them something to eat". Then, a few lines later, after he has blessed the food, in verse 19, Jesus gives the food to the disciples, for THEM to pass it on to the crowd.

God gives the task of sharing the wealth of the world to US, his friends and followers. The disciples could have taken the blessed food, and disappeared behind a bush to eat it all themselves. But Jesus commands them to share what they have. There's a really important Kingdom principle at work here: the Kingdom of Heaven is not about getting and keeping, it's about giving and sharing.

We live in a time when getting and keeping have become such a normal pattern of life. We live in the time of 'consumerism' – when getting and then keeping as much stuff as we can has become the norm – perfectly acceptable to most people.

This pandemic is showing us, starkly, just how much of our Western economy is based on the consumption of stuff…and on so called 'entertainment'. I feel very sorry for the for the staff of shops who sell plastic rubbish, meaningless birthday presents and fashionable clothing. Their sales have taken a huge hit, and their livelihoods are desperately threatened.

And I feel sorry for staff of pubs, cinemas, and theme parks.

And the airline crews.

And the cruise-ship crews.

And the car factory workers.

And the eyebrow-waxing salons.

But, honestly, is this really the way we want to live? Is this all we are? Consumers of stuff, wholesale burners of fossil fuels, obsessed with foreign holidays and the appearance of our eyebrows and nails?

It is an uncomfortable fact that consumerism as the new religion. Temples, mosques and churches have been replaced by shopping arcades. The priests of this new religion are the marketing managers, who tell us what will make us happy. "Buy more stuff!" they cry, and find fulfilment.

The collection plate, once used to maintain the church and bless the poor of the community, has been replaced by the cash register.

Icons and spiritual imagery has been replaced by advertising posters.

Hymns and spiritual songs have been replaced by jingles and advertisements.

But Jesus still calls to us across the centuries. "You fool!" he says, to the man who has stored up great wealth for himself. "Do not store up for yourself treasure on earth, where it will only rot and decay. Instead, store up treasure in heaven, where it will last for eternity". "Stop hoarding and learn the power of giving!" Live simply, start sharing, and actually you'll find there's plenty to go round.

The feeding of the five thousand is the only story that is common to all four Gospels. It demands that we radically re-appraise the way we live. Much more than the story of a God who can magically multiply fish and bread, it's a call to all humanity to dig deep, bring out the wealth from our pockets, and share the wealth of all creation.

Amen.

Too much heaven on their minds?

by Tom Kennar – 06 August 2020

Text: Luke 9.28-36

The story of the Transfiguration is told in the Gospels of Matthew, Mark and Luke. Peter also refers to it in his second epistle. So what's it all about? All these shining faces, and visits from long-dead prophets? The main purposes of the story are two-fold:

First – the story is intended to re-assure us that Jesus is the continuation and culmination of the past. He builds on the great Teacher of the Law, Moses, and he fulfils the predictions of the great prophets, represented by Elijah. Remember that the first readers of the Gospels would have been mainly Jewish, or at least people mightily interested in Jewish ideas. They would have been grappling with the question of who Jesus was. Through this dramatic, mountain-top story, they were being encouraged not to doubt for a moment that Jesus is the Messiah, the one whose coming was foretold.

Secondly – at the climax of the story, we hear the voice from heaven saying 'This is my Son, the Chosen; listen to him. The first readers of these Gospels, and indeed we ourselves, are being encouraged to take Jesus seriously – and specially to take his teachings to heart.

This is a moment of high meaning, and of high significance. Peter doesn't want it to end, does he? He wants to build dwellings for Jesus, Moses and Elijah. He wants to capture the moment, and tie it down. Which is a very human thing to want to do.

Our beautiful churches are a bit like that. God sometimes feels a bit distant, doesn't he? We get glimpses of him, in the world, in our imaginations, in those sparks of sudden insight which we all experience from time to time. You know – those moments when the things we've learned about God drop into place. "Ah! I get it," we say. But those moments are fleeting. They are incredibly precious. But fleeting. Because our little brains can't hold on to the enormous reality of God for very long.

So like Peter, we feel a deep, human need to construct something in which to preserve our sense of those precious moments. We build it with great care. We fill it with the work of craftsmen; stained glass and beautiful ornaments. We place it in the heart of our community, as an ongoing sign of those precious moments of connection with our Maker. And we visit it – as so many have done since our doors re-opened – to search, once again, for that feeling of connection.

But, just as Peter, James, John and Jesus himself had to do, we have to move on from those moments. Life should, and often does, contain moments of spiritual ecstasy. But, real life, the daily task of becoming more like God, that goes on once the moment of ecstasy is passed. In simple terms, 'you have to come down from the mountain'. For Jesus, that meant a dark and dangerous journey to Jerusalem, and to his death.

But what does it mean for you and for me? It certainly means realising that we can't remain on the mountaintop all the time. If you keep your head in the clouds, you'll quickly become 'so heavenly minded that you're of no earthly use'.

Will, our General Manager, has been teasing me this week. He's been grabbing – and then publishing! – pictures of me caught in practical action…fixing noticeboards and pressure-washing pigeon muck off the bell-tower staircase. It's all been jolly good fun. But it's also been a reminder that the work of serving God doesn't just happen in the Sanctuary, or here at the Altar. We have to come down from the mountain, with our sleeves rolled up, and our hands ready work, and our mouths ready to speak the words of Jesus.

So let me ask you this.

What can YOU get your hands into this week?

To whom could YOU speak Jesus' words?

You, who believe that Jesus is indeed the Messiah, continuation of the faith of ages past. How can you come down from the mountain, and be his hands, feet and mouth to a dying world in need?

Whom can you bless with your charity?

Whom can you help along the road?

Whom can you help to heal, or house or feed?

In response to your faith in the Chosen One, whose words you are commanded to heed…what are YOU going to do?

Amen.

Doing what Jesus is doing...

by Tom Kennar - 09 August 2020

Text: Matthew 14. 22-33 – Jesus and Peter walk on the water

Those of you who have enjoyed the Corona Chronicle will be aware that a small crisis took place at the Rectory during the darkest days of the Lockdown. The Rector's wife suddenly started digging a great big hole on the Rectory lawn. This, I have to tell you, was no mean feat. After getting through 8 inches of top soil, Clare was confronted by a solid concrete slab, and a buried gate post, made of reinforced concrete. But she was determined – and for many days she hacked and bashed and gradually made progress into the hole.

I watched all this activity with some bemusement. I had just had an operation on my ticker, so I was forbidden from doing any heavy work. So I watched the hole gradually enlarging from a distance through the lounge window.

What really worried me was the size. It was about six feet long…and the way she was going; it was going to be six feet deep as well. Could it be that Clare had finally had enough of living under lockdown with me? Was this hole meant for a dark and sinister purpose?

When she had finally reached her required depth, Clare set about filling the hole with water. Perhaps, I thought, she doesn't intend to bury me there. Perhaps she simply intends to drown me? 'Well!' I thought 'I'll show her. This will be an excellent time to try out the notion of walking on water!'

The stories of Jesus walking on the water – across three of the Gospels - come out of a long Jewish tradition. In the ancient Scriptures, water is often seen as a metaphor for chaos and death. 'In the beginning', says the writer of Genesis, 'the earth was formless and void…and the Spirit of God brooded upon the face of the deep'. Into that chaos and formlessness, God speaks his words of creation – words of life and hope and potential.

So, through these stories of Jesus walking on the water, or stilling the storm, the Gospel writers wanted us to understand that God, and his Way, brings order to chaos, it brings life over death, and hope over fear. Those of you who are interested in biblical literature in general might be interested to know that the ability to 'walk on water' was ascribed to other great leaders, before Jesus, such as the great King Xerxes and to Alexander the Great.

It is only in Matthew's Gospel, however, that we have a delicious detail added to the story…and that's the detail of how Peter got out of the boat to also walk on the water. He then got scared, and Jesus had to raise him back to the surface, while ticking Peter off for his lack of faith. The most obvious point of this story is, clearly, an encouragement to have faith. The Gospel writers want us to put our trust in God, and to keep it there…never wavering, even when we get scared or confused by what is going on around us. The waves may crash and roll, but Jesus always reaches out his hand to us, to steady us against the storms of life.

There's something else too. Something I think we shouldn't miss. And that is that the question of why Peter steps out of the boat in the first place. I think the answer to that question is that Peter sees what Jesus is doing…and then he wants to do it to.

Throughout the Gospels, Peter is depicted as 'Everyman'. He is the archetypal human being, who yearns to be a better man, but who often fails and gets things wrong. Peter is you and me. He dreams and hopes, he's often a 'man of action', but he also gets things wrong – like when he denies Jesus, or cuts off a soldier's ear, fails to understand why Jesus is washing feet, or fails to actually walk on the water.

But through all his failings, Peter consistently tries to do what he sees Jesus doing. And whilst he fails, time and again, eventually he rises above his nature, and becomes the premier voice for God in the years following Jesus' ascension. He finds he has the power to heal, the power to speak powerfully, and the power to shape and lead the entire movement called Christianity. With all his failings, he becomes the Rock – the Petros – on which Jesus builds his church.

But he only achieves this by first watching what Jesus does, and then doing it, himself. He lives alongside Jesus as Jesus heals the sick and preaches powerfully, and sets up the basic structures of the church. Then, after Jesus ascends, Peter copies Jesus. He does the same things. He becomes the healing hands, the preaching voice, and the organising force for God's mission on earth.

And, if Peter is an archetypal Everyman (and woman) – this is our task too. We, like Peter, are called to see what Jesus does, and then to do that. We must not be deflected by the priorities of the world around us, but rather we must focus our entire energies on doing what Jesus did.

This, ultimately, is what it means to be a Christian – or a 'Christ-ian'. A follower of Jesus. We are called to bring healing to the world. We are called to preach as powerfully as we can, each in our own way, the good news of the coming Kingdom. And we are called to organise ourselves to be God's hands and voice to a dying world.

It's scary, sometimes. We have to be prepared to step out of the boat and into the chaos. But Jesus offers his steadying hand to all who have the courage to follow him…and to do what Jesus does.

Amen.

As we forgive those who trespass against us...

by Tom Kennar – 11 August 2020
Texts: Ezekiel 12: 1-12 & Matthew 18.21–19.1

I can't help but wish that I had the time to explore both of this morning's readings with you. The first is a marvellous tale of how Ezekiel, prophet of God, acted out a little cameo of carrying his baggage. He did this to make people wonder, and so that they would ask him what he was doing…so that he could warn them that unless they mended their ways, they too would be carrying their baggage out of the promised land.

It's a delicious little story, and it makes me wonder what dramatic cameos we could act out, as a warning to the people that we are called to serve in God's name. Perhaps a cameo of me drowning in a bath-tub might warn people of rising sea-levels. Or perhaps putting Sandra in a hospital bed outside the front of the church would encourage more people to pay attention to COVID restrictions!

But, as I say, there isn't time to do justice to both of these readings. And the Gospel reading for today is SO important, that we really mustn't skip over it. It deals with the topic of forgiveness, of course.

As a priest, who has heard many a confession or life-story, I know that forgiveness is one of the hardest callings of the Christian faith. How can someone be expected to forgive another who has abused them, or stolen from them, or falsely accused them, or hurt them in a myriad of ways? How can we forgive the negligent parent whose drunkenness marred our childhood? How can we forgive the internet scammer who took all our savings?

And yet Jesus calls us to forgive those who trespass against us…as much as seventy times seven, he says metaphorically to Peter. He is talking, on this occasion, in the context of a church fellowship. Note that

Peter's original question is 'if a member of the church sins against me, how many times should I forgive him?'. And this is because Jesus knows that a lack of forgiveness can completely wreck a church fellowship.

I'm sure all of us have come across those tragic stories of how a person has left a church – or stopped going to church altogether – because of a thoughtless word or action on the part of another church member. Some of these occasions can seem trivial to us. For some reason, the more trivial stories always seem to revolve around flower ladies who have been slighted by the Vicar, or choir masters who go to war with the PCC! Arguments over pedestal arrangements or the volume at which hymns are played can quickly build into deep and abiding resentments…until one side or the other bursts, and resigns.

The trouble is, it's usually the person who walks off in a huff who suffers the most. They are left with their seething resentment, however justified, whilst the rest of the community usually heaves a sigh of relief that the situation has been resolved. The church moves on to the next challenge…but the person who resigned is left feeling hurt and angry, and possibly never darkens the door of any church ever again. And they lose out on all the potential for spiritual, intellectual and moral growth that membership of the church would have offered them.

And that is why forgiveness is so important. To forgive someone is, quite literally, to give up one's right to feel aggrieved or hurt by another. When we do that, we deny the person who has wronged us any power over our own emotions. We take away their ability to hurt us, or damage us in the longer term. Altogether.

In fact, true forgiveness means giving up the right to feel hurt before the hurt even has a chance to take root in one's soul. To forgive is to give up the hurt before it can take hold.

But does this mean that the person being forgiven gets away with whatever they have done wrong? Well, perhaps – especially for the little things…the annoying word, the careless insult. By forgiving someone for that, we rise above them. We see them for what they are…symptoms only of that most common of diseases…the disease of being a failing human being.

But what about the really big things…the systematic abusers, the scammers, the murderers? Well, for such people, Jesus offers further advice. In Matthew chapter 10 he advises that we need to be 'as wise as serpents and as gentle as doves'. If I know that someone has the potential to cause great harm to another, I have a duty and a responsibility to do all I can to prevent that harm. So it is only right that I must, and should, involve the appropriate authorities in stopping them. But never out of revenge. The gentle dove releases the hatred. But the wise serpent makes sure – as sure as they can – that the wrongdoer is prevented from causing further harm to anyone else, and suitably punished for the wrongdoing they've already wrought.

This is why we have a justice system, after all. Having forgiven the wrong-doer, so that they no longer have the power to hurt us, we hand over the responsibility for punishment and correction to the society in which we live. There, appropriate punishment is meted out, without passion, without hatred. Just punishment is handed down, but not by the person who was harmed. Not least so that the harmed person is not further damaged by committing some act of violence or retribution themselves.

So, may you find the strength to let go of the hurt that others have done to you. May you release your heart from the resentments it holds onto, so that your heart may fly free, and straight into the heart of the forgiving God of Love.

Father, forgive us our trespasses as we forgive those who trespass against us. Amen.

Reflections on VJ Day 75

by Tom Kennar – 15 August 2020

Sermon on the 75th Anniversary Commemoration of VJ Day

War is, without doubt, the most destructive force on our planet. Forget earthquakes, hurricanes and volcanoes. Their destructive power – though often immense for a few hours – pales into insignificance against the destructive power of war. The destruction of cities, the millions of victims of any world-wide conflict, the destruction of whole economies and entire races of human beings – these are just some of the effects of war.

Nuclear war cranks up the destructive potential to an even greater height. It was Albert Einstein, reflecting on the pure destructive potential of the weapon he helped to create who said, "I know not with what weapons World War III will be fought, but World War IV will be fought with sticks and stones." He understood that a worldwide nuclear war had the potential to push the human race back into the Stone Age.

And yet, War is an inevitable and, it seems, ever-present aspect of human nature. So, what can we learn from the wars of the past (let alone the wars of today)? On this 75th anniversary of the surrender of Japan, perhaps it is worth a look at the causes of that particular conflict.

Between 1928 and 1932, Japan faced domestic crisis. The Great Depression – across the whole world – led to spiralling prices, economic collapse, mass unemployment, falling exports and social unrest. In November 1930, the Prime Minister of Japan was shot by an ultra-nationalist. In 1932, the army tried to assassinate the next Prime Minister, and ultimately the military seized control of the country. Between 1932 and 1936, admirals ruled Japan. Confident and arrogant, they believed that the whole of Asia should be ruled by them – as a way out of economic collapse. China was invaded, and in response, in 1941, the United States announced a punitive oil embargo. For the Japanese leaders, that move was a perfect pretext for war, unleashed in December 1941 with the Pearl Harbour attack.

The rest, as they say, is history – including the history that some of neighbours in Havant lived through in all its horror. In our Monthly Information sheet for this month is a compelling and harrowing tale of what it was like to serve in the Far East in the 1940s – penned by a recently deceased member of St Faith's, Govan Easton.

But it is the history behind the history from which we need to learn. The conditions which prompted the rise of the Japanese military machine are similar to those that led to the rise of Hitler, half a world away. Market forces in crisis, spiralling debt, unemployment and poverty – however caused. It is when economies go bad that people look to extremist leaders for solutions. Given our current economic woes, throughout the world, not least as a result of COVID-19, we need to be on our guard against this tendency. We must not let populist fear-mongers rise again. We must not let fear drive us to more war.

War is what happens when language fails, and when we focus our angst, our fears, our problems on some other easily identified group. For the Nazis, it was the Jews. For the Japanese, it was the 'evil Americans' and their allies. Today, for billions of people throughout the world, the West is still perceived as 'the great Satan'. And many in the West, following populist leaders, are blaming immigrants and 'others' of all races for the problems we face.

To imagine that the Second World War was the last Great War is to be naïve in the extreme. There has never been a 'war to end all wars'. And there never will be – for as long as human beings choose violence over talking, self-preservation over sharing, hatred of the 'other' over love of neighbour.

British Troops have been involved in wars all over the planet – since 1945. Many of you will remember such wars – some of you have even fought in them. Greece, Malaya, Korea, Eqypt, Kenya, Cyprus, Indonesia, Dhofar, Aden, Nigeria, Northern Ireland, the Falklands, Lebanon, the Gulf War, Bosnia, Iraq, Kosovo, Sierra Leonie, Afghanistan, Iraq (again), Libya, and Syria.

But there is another way. Writing around 2,700 years ago, the Jewish prophet Micah dreamed of a day when all the peoples of the earth would 'learn the ways of God'. "He will teach us his ways", said Micah, "so that we will walk in his paths". "He will settle the disputes between peoples, and they will beat their swords into ploughshares, and their spears into pruning hooks. Everyone will sit in peace under their own vine, and no-one will make them afraid".

This peace will only come about when the peoples of the earth finally accept the rule and governorship of God, when they take seriously what God meant when he told us to love our neighbours as ourselves. That's a message repeated again and again through the Jewish & Hebrew Scriptures, and the Scriptures of all the great religions. It's a message that was taken up with vigour by Jesus of Nazareth. Only when we stop keeping the best stuff for ourselves, being content to watch our neighbours in other lands starve and die, will the world ever find the peace for which we all yearn.

If we will let him, the Lord will indeed be our Shepherd. If we will follow his ways, he will indeed lead us beside still waters. Our cups will indeed overflow.

But how will this be achieved? There is no other way but the way of changing one person at a time. To quote Mahatma Ghandi, 'if you change yourself, you will change your world'.

So today, we give thanks for the 75 years of relative peace we have enjoyed here in Britain, not forgetting the Manchester and London bombings, Novichok poisoning and other terrorist outrages. We remember, once again, those who gave their lives – or who were forced to give up their lives – for our peace. Today we especially pay tribute to those who endured the horror of the Death Railway and the Far East prisons. We remember, too, the innocent children of Hiroshima and Nagasaki – those who never raised a weapon against any one of us. We remember them, and all those who have sacrificed themselves, or who were sacrificed, in the vast number of conflicts ever since.

But let us not simply remember them. Let us honour their sacrifice with a sacrifice of our own. Let us, each one, commit ourselves to living differently from today. Let us put aside the lure of wealth, and the pettiness of nationality, and realise that we are all, each one, children of the same God. Let us learn from him, and follow his ways…so that perhaps, one day, such commemorations as this will no longer be necessary. Amen.

Racism in the Bible?

by Tom Kennar Sunday, August 16, 2020
Isaiah 56. 1,6-8 and Matthew 15. 10-28

I'm going to say something shocking, now…perhaps to some of you. It's this: the Bible contains rather a lot of racism.

This should not surprise us. The Scriptures we have inherited from our ancestors inevitably reflect the mind-set of the people when they wrote them. In particular, the Jews believed that they were the 'chosen people' – a special people who were set apart from all other nations, through which the salvation of all humanity would come. In a sense, this of course was true. Jesus was a Jew – and therefore, through Him, salvation for all the world did indeed come through the Jews.

But this truth bred some pretty uncomfortable ideas in the minds of certain Jewish leaders over the centuries. Despite all the awful things that happened to them as a people – all the conquests and defeats, the carrying-off into exile - they felt a deep sense of being special to God. And for some leaders, that special status drove them to believe that they were in some sense superior to other nations. They were the nation through whom God has chosen to reveal himself to humanity, after all. Didn't that make them super-superior? And therefore, other nations were just not as special. They were less than the Jewish people. Inferior. And that the Jewish nation must remain 'pure'.

A very good example of this mind-set can be found in the books of Nehemiah and Ezra. After returning 70 years in exile, in Babylon, Nehemiah, the returned Governor, rebuilt the walls and the temple of Jerusalem. Many of the common people of Israel had not gone into exile. It was only the leaders who were carried off. The common people stayed behind and carried on their lives as best as they could under Babylonian rule.

But after rebuilding the walls and the temple, the high priest, Ezra, also newly returned to Jerusalem, stood up to pronounce to the common people that God now commanded them to separate themselves entirely from the nations around them. He sharply condemned them for having 'mingled the holy race with the peoples around them' (Ezra 9.2). Men who had married Canaanite women, for example, were commanded to divorce them and send them away.

Not all leaders believed this was what God wanted. Whilst Nehemiah and Ezra were battling for racial purity, many, like Isaiah and Jeremiah argued that their special status was a calling to servant-hood, not domination of others. The famous picture of the 'suffering servant' in Isaiah is a key passage, which encourages the Jews to see themselves as servants to all humanity, being prepared to die in the attempt. Jesus embodied this idea, which is why the suffering servant passages are often seen (especially by Christians!) as a foretelling of his story.

And in this morning's reading, also from Isaiah, we hear a call for all foreigners to be welcomed into the house of faith. 'These foreigners', says Yahweh, 'will I bring to my holy mountain, and make them joyful in the house of prayer….'. Jeremiah had a similar vision, in which the people of all nations would be welcome onto the Holy Mountain of God.

And so, you see, racism was as much a live issue for the people of Bible-times as it remains for us today. Its pages are full of the clash of civilizations, competing endlessly with each other for dominance, and always claiming that their God was on their side. There have always been people who consider themselves essentially superior to everyone else. It's part of fallen humanity's nature to look down on, to ridicule, and to fear 'the other'.

It was this inbuilt racism to which Jesus was referring when he spoke sharply to the Canaanite woman who was seeking healing for her child. We find him ministering in a foreign part of the area in which he lived. Canaanites, a conquered people, lived there. Jesus has chosen to expand his ministry beyond the Jews, beyond Galilee, Nazareth and Jerusalem, and into the heartland of foreigners.

And when one of them asks for his help, he sees an opportunity to prick at what he knew all Jews of the time would have been thinking. He clearly senses – or divinely knows – that this woman is someone with the capacity to teach the Jews all gathered around him. So he fences words with her. "It is not fair to take the children's food and throw it to the dogs". In other words, he boldly states that his mission is only to the children of Israel, not to the 'dogs' of other nations. But this woman has courage, and a quick intelligence. "Ah," she replies, "yet even the dogs eat the crumbs from their master's table".

I like to visualise Jesus laughing out loud at that reply! Yes! This is what he needs! Someone who can show by their wit, intelligence and their faith that they are just as good as any Jew, and just as deserving of God's love. This fits entirely with the rest of his teaching – including the parable of the Good Samaritan, and his encounter with the Samaritan woman at the well. Jesus wants the whole world, every nation and tongue, to know of God's love. And that's what he commands his disciples to tell, in the Great Commandment at the end of his time on earth. "Go," he tells them, "and make disciples of all nations".

And this, is what he commands of us too. There is no room for racism in Biblical Christianity. No nation is superior to another – whatever great things some of their individual people have achieved. God's love cries out to every nation and every people…Come. Come up to the mountain of the Lord. Amen.

The Wedding Robe
by Tom Kennar – 20 August 2020
Text: Matthew 22.1-14

In Africa, and especially in West Africa, there is a wonderful tradition for big events, like weddings and even funerals. It's a tradition of printing a huge bale of cloth, and then making garments from that bale – so that everyone wears the same cloth to the event.

I've seen this particularly in the Diocese of Ho, where I was present for the 10th Anniversary of the founding of the Diocese, a few years back. Bishop Matthias had commissioned the cloth, and he gave me a stole made from it. It happened to have pictures of Mary on the cloth, as well as a picture of the Bishop himself. And the stole he gave me ended up with the Bishop's picture right over my heart!

The parable we've just heard is about such a wedding feast – as a lens through which to understand the Kingdom of Heaven. It is essentially a history of salvation. God is, of course, the King who throws the party. The slaves he sends out to invite the guests are his prophets and priests. The wedding guests are the Jewish people – at first – who, according to the parable, fail to turn up to the wedding. In our first reading today from Ezekiel, we are reminded of all the times God's people turned from God's way, worshipping other idols, their hearts turning to stone.

In other words, many whom God invites never quite sit down and eat from the table of God's Kingdom.

So the King invites everyone else in. These are the Gentiles…the rest of humanity. The parable is teaching us that whilst our faith has Jewish roots, it is a faith meant for all the world.

But then there's a sting in the tail. Among the guests, the King spots a man who is not wearing a wedding robe. He doesn't have one of the pieces of special cloth produced for the occasion. He has obviously decided that he wants to be in the party, but he doesn't want to live by the rules of the host.

Who is this parable pointing to?

One day, when I was out driving with Bishop Matthias, he pointed up to a mansion on a hill. It was a fine mansion indeed…with high walls, vast gardens, security fencing and many many rooms. 'Who do you think lives there?', the Bishop asked me. 'I don't know', I replied. 'A pop star? A chief? A banker?'. 'No,' replied the Bishop, 'that mansion is owned by the self-styled Apostle of one of the TV churches. He gets people to send him money via his TV channel, promising to do the work of God – and then he builds himself that mansion to live in!'

The man without a robe is anyone who comes to the party, but who doesn't want to play by the party's rules. He is any church member – or church leader – whose lifestyle, beliefs, and choices and not Kingdom lifestyle, beliefs and choices. He is the church member, or church leader, whose heart has remained cold to the preaching and teaching of the Kingdom. And who uses the church for his own gain.

The man without a robe is the kind of so-called Christian who promises healing in return for donations. Or the kind that assures you that if you just make a generous donation to the church, the Lord will shower you with blessings in return. He is the charlatan, who finds other guests at the wedding feast, and then gets them under his spell and influence. Or worse still, perhaps, he is the kind of so-called Christian who joins a church, and pretends his faith, just so that he can abuse children, or steal from the church's coffers.

There are some politicians who try this on too. They make a pretence of their piety – going to church, or, perhaps, standing outside a church brandishing a Bible, when in their heart they are full of hatred for others, and greed for themselves. Some people have suggested that a certain American president has these characteristics.

But of course, it's easy to point the finger at others. Whenever we point our finger at others, we have three fingers pointing back at us. The Bible always invites us to consider whether we are the villain in the story.

That's a question each of us can only answer for ourselves. But if we are the kind of Christian who puts on our religion when we leave the house, but who never practices their faith at home…

And if we are the kind of Christian who prays about forgiveness, but who actually nurses and feeds the hatred in our heart…

And if we are the kind of Christian who offers himself publicly as a living sacrifice, but then makes no sacrifice at all…

…then we should be wary. The King may decide to deal especially harshly with such a one. The outer darkness may await.

The Kingdom of God is a place of welcome for all. Go out into the streets, and say 'Everyone is welcome here. Jew and Gentile, rich and poor, black and white, male and female…and every other description you can think of!' God's gift of life is freely given, and lavishly provided. But let no-one take such generosity for granted. And let no-one use it for his own gain. Amen.

An Address for the funeral of the Reverend Douglas Bean
by Tom Kennar – 22 August 2020
Texts: Luke 6. 27-38 & Philippians 4. 4-8 & Psalm 139

I'm very sorry indeed that I only had the chance of meeting Douglas, briefly, on one occasion – and that, I think, was at the end of a Christmas service here at St Faith's, when I customarily get to shake about 400 hands. Not really the best time to make someone's acquaintance.

But from what I've heard about Douglas from Teresa and Alan over the past few weeks, I have no doubt at all that I would have enjoyed his company immensely. It seems we had quite a few things in common – not least a love of music, and of encouraging others to play music in ecclesiastical spaces. It was ironic, to me, that just as I was beginning to think about re-starting our lunchtime concerts season here, I heard about Douglas' efforts as a musical impresario at St Paul's.

What I am not going to do, however, is try to do justice to Douglas long life and ministry – his two primary ministries of being both a priest, and a family man. I don't know about you, but I usually find myself rather dissatisfied at any eulogy by a minister who never really knew the deceased. The rather more interesting question for me, as a priest, is to ask what Douglas wanted you, his family, to remember him by. The answer to that question is found in the choices that he made about the readings and hymns we are using in this service.

Many such choices, made for funerals, are frankly usually pretty arbitrary. They tend to consist of distantly remembered childhood hymns (which is why 'The Lord's my shepherd' remains so popular). Scriptures chosen tend to be either those suggested by the church, or again, dimly remembered passages about 'my father's house has many mansions'. But the choices of a priest, who has lived and breathed these Scriptures and these hymns throughout his life, are choices worth contemplating. What messages might Douglas have wanted to convey, through these Scriptures, and through these words?

The first hymn he chose, of which we only heard the tune, reminds us of the sacrifices of the Saviour, on a green hill far away – clearly the foundation of Douglas' hope and life. The second hymn asks for the guidance of the Great Redeemer to every pilgrim through the barren land of world in which God's Kingdom is yet to be fully established. It asks for nourishment along the journey, through the Bread of Heaven.

The first reading, is a long discourse on forgiveness. Perhaps there have been people in Douglas' life who he found it hard to forgive. Perhaps he guessed that others struggled to forgive him. I know that I frequently have to ask my own family for forgiveness, especially for those times when I let my ministry as a priest take precedence over my ministry as a husband, father and grandfather. Perhaps Douglas asked for your forgiveness too, through this reading?

Then, through the reading from Paul's letter to the Philippians, Douglas offers us advice. Rejoice! Rejoice in everything that life throws at you. And always focus your thoughts and intentions on things that are true, lovely, honest, just and pure. Perhaps in these days when our television sets are filled with half-truths, false news, dishonesty and impurity, these are words we do well to heed as we live the rest of our lives?

Then comes the psalm. Psalm 139 – a deep and penetrating sense of God's deep and penetrating knowledge of each of us. For some, this notion can be discomforting. For those with secret sins, or blackened hearts, it can be an arresting notion to realise that God knows us intimately, and has known us since we were formed in our mother's womb. But for Douglas, after a life lived in search of God, I suspect there was joy in the invitation to "Search me out, O God, and know my heart".

The "Battle Hymn of the Republic" is the colloquial name for the last hymn we shall sing today. But I suspect that for Douglas, it held before him a glorious vision of the end of all things, when the Son of Man returns to earth, when the Kingdom is fully established, and when all humanity can sing together 'Glory, glory, halleluiah!'.

And all these thoughts, and all this depth, is summed up in Douglas' last hymn choice – the tune of which we will hear as we finish our service. Written by Sydney Carter, whom I suspect was Douglas' friend, 'the Lord of the Dance' reminds us that in Jesus Christ, all things hold together. He is the dashing dancing-partner, who invites us to take his hand on the dance-floor of life.

Through all the ugliness of the cross on a green hill far away, for all the barren land through which we need the guidance of our Great Redeemer, through all the lies and impurity of our messy human lives, Christ invites us to dance with him. "I'll live in you if you'll live in me…I am the Lord of the dance, says he".

You will all have your own memories of Douglas, of Dad, of Grandad. And I hope you'll enjoy sharing them which each other today. But let me encourage you not to miss his final words of encouragement and hope to you – mediated through the choice of these hymns, and these readings, today. Amen.

Who do you say that I am?

by Tom Kennar – 23 August 2020

Text: Matthew 16. 13-20

Who do you say that I am? That's the question that Jesus asks Simon. And it's an important question – because identity matters.

If I asked you the same question, I imagine that many of you would reply 'You are the Rector'. But that's only because you know me primarily in this role, at this time in my life. In other places, and in other times, I've been a youth worker, a housing officer, and a charity chief executive. I've been a government advisor and a shop-floor salesman of microwaves and stereos. I've been a passport writer, a singer, a piano-player and a trumpeter. I've been a student, and a roller-skate rink attendant. I've been an ice-cream seller, a burger-flipper and a farm labourer. I still am a priest, and a deacon, and a Canon, a teacher, and a social entrepreneur.

In my private life, I have been (and am) many things too. I'm a husband, a dad and a son. I'm a brother, an uncle and a best friend. Now I'm a grandad.

But there are other things about my identity which could be used to describe me. I'm tall. I'm big. I'm hairy around the chin. I'm Caucasian (or white), I'm straight. I'm middle aged – just, and I'm a cardiac patient!

All of these words and all of these descriptions are summed up in the one word…Tom. But all these words, all these descriptions, only scratch at the surface of who I really am. Because I know the secret 'me'. I know the internal conflicts I live with. I know the thoughts that rage through my monkey mind. I know the temptations I have to fight. I know the things that give me pleasure, and the things that stress me out. They are all part of me too. They are what I'd have to try to describe if you really wanted to understand who I am.

SO imagine, the panic that must have crossed Simon's mind when Jesus asked him the same question! 'Who do you say that I am?' What answer could Peter give which would sum up succinctly all that he already knew about this man. He could have said, 'You're Jesus of Nazareth, the son of Mary and Joseph the carpenter. You're the brother of James and Joses and your other siblings. You're the teacher, the wanderer, the story-teller of our time. You're the preacher, the prophet, the man of wisdom'. But Simon used none of these descriptions of Jesus.

'You are the Messiah. The son of the living God'.

Messiah – Saviour. The one whose coming has been long-expected. The one who would offer the path of salvation to the Jews and to the whole world. And the very son of God.

Jesus was delighted. I imagine him throwing back his head and laughing! 'Blessed are you Simon, son of Jonah! You've got it! You've understood the essence of who I am. And that's a revelation that could only have come from God!'.

'And you, Simon, you are a rock! That's what I'm going to call you from now on…Rocky. Petros. Peter. Because you, with all your mistakes and gaffs, are open to what God teaches you. And it's on that kind of openness, and attentiveness to God that I'm going to build my church. Alright? Rocky!'

You see, Simon wasn't all that his description said he was. Any more than the word Messiah described all that Jesus was. It was a nickname. An epithet. A way of getting a handle on Simon Peter. It said nothing about his failures. Nothing about the times he completely got things wrong, like denying Christ, or lopping off the ear of a High Priest's guard. Or that time when he thought he should build some shelters for Jesus, Moses and Elijah on the mountain.

Simon, as I said a week or two ago, is 'everyman' (and woman). He's you and me. With all his failures, he sticks straight to the path of faith. He is determined, and he wants with all his heart to follow where Jesus leads.

But his nickname doesn't say all there is to say. Nor does 'Messiah' say all there is to say about Jesus. Nor does 'Rector' say all there is to say about me.

It's supposed to be a Native American saying, that you should never criticise another, until you've walked a mile in their shoes. Simon Peter had walked more than a mile in Jesus' shoes. He'd lived alongside him, got to know him, heard him, listened to him – and at the end of that experience, he found that he could after all, describe him in a single, powerful adjective: Messiah.

Jesus had walked a mile or two in Simon's shoes too. He'd sat with him, listened to him, laughed with him, eaten with him, watched him fail, watched him grow. And at the end of all that, he had a an adjective – a nickname – for Simon too. Rocky! He was going to call him Rocky.

Here's a final question to ponder…

How do you think others would describe you? What nickname would you like be given by someone who has walked a mile in your shoes with you? Gentle one? Courageous one? Prayerful one? Faithful one? Generous one? Resourceful one?

How would you like to be summed up in one word?

And how can you live in such a way, that such a nickname becomes yours?

Amen.

Sermon for the Feast of St Monica

by Bishop John Hind – 27 August 2020

(On the day of Commemoration of St Monica)

Today we commemorate St Monica, a fourth century African saint and mother of St Augustine, one of the greatest teachers in the history of the Church.

We only know about Monica from her son and in particular from his famous Confessions in which he tells about his turbulent journey towards Christian faith and her role in it.

North Africa at the time, like the rest of the Roman Empire was a kind of religious supermarket – just too much choice. Monica was a devout Christian, but her husband, Patricius, was a pagan, and the young Augustine did the rounds of the different religious options – except when he was pursuing his main interests which seem to have been sex and hanging out with his friends.

All this was pain and grief to Monica, who never ceased to pray for her wayward son and for her husband. There must have been times when she was tempted, humanly speaking to give up, but, being told by a wise bishop she consulted that "the child of those tears shall never perish", she stuck at it. Her persistence paid off, and eventually Augustine, by now a successful teacher and scholar in Milan, converted to Christianity, as too, shortly before his death, did Patricius.

With Augustine's conversion, Monica, who had followed him to Milan felt that her life's work was complete. "I don't know why I am still alive, she said to him, there's only one thing I wanted, to see you a Catholic Christian before I died." Shortly afterwards just as they were about to go back home to Africa, she fell terminally ill and told her son to bury her where she died in Italy. Augustine's brother, who was also with them said he hoped she would not die so far from home but in her own country.

"What silly talk!" said Monica, "Lay this body anywhere, and take no trouble over it. One thing only do I ask of you, that you remember me at the altar of the Lord wherever you may be". Augustine therefore returned to Africa without his mother and was quickly ordained. The rest, as they say, is history.

What can we learn from this moving story of a mother's love and persistent prayer?

Above all, I think, it is the responsibility we all have to pray for all those for whom we have a care that they might come to know the love of God revealed in Jesus Christ and put their trust in him. Everyone has their own unique journey of faith, but the influence of other people has a very important part to play and we all can and should do the best we can to encourage and support them in it.

Intercession, praying for others, is a permanent obligation for every Christian, as St Paul so often insists. As it likely that we shall all continue to spend more time in isolation as the threat of Covid-19 continues, this is a particularly good time to reassess our pattern of intercession. We may not all be mothers, but we can all exercise a mother's prayerful care for each other. What shall we pray for? Of course, everyone has so many needs which we should hold in our hearts before God, but surely nothing could be more important than that they should come to realise the eternal dignity for which they have been created.

Our own times are every bit as religiously confusing as the fourth century Roman Empire. Just too much choice: with the added complication that so many people now grow up with no sense at that their lives ultimately matter – ultimately that is, to the very end and beyond it.

This is why persistence in prayer is so important. Don't give up even if nothing seems to be happening. The status of every soul is God's secret, as too is how God will answer our prayers. It is just for us to keep going. Remember the advice given to Monica: "the child of those tears shall never perish."

Take up thy cross...

by Tom Kennar – 30 August 2020

Text: Matthew 16.21-28

SPIRITUAL HEALTH WARNING…the first three paragraphs are a parody…to be read in a phoney American accent!

I have great pleasure in announcing last night, I had a vision! The Lord God Almighty spoke to me. He said to me..."Pastor", he said, "Pastor - I have good news for you! I want to shower you and your congregation with abundant blessings. (Praise the Lord!) I am going to make yours a church of millionaires! You are going to become so wealthy, so full of miracles, so full of powerful acts of God Almighty, that the whole of Havant will flock to your doors!

All your congregation has to do is to show that they trust me. They simply have to sign over the deeds to their houses to the church. Then I will know that they trust me. Then I will bless them with riches from heaven. Then they all will become millionaires, and all their problems will disappear". (Praise the Lord!)

So, my brothers and sisters, our Treasurer, Sister Shelley, will be standing by, at the ready, with forms for you to sign at the end of our service. Just sign over the deeds of your house to the church, and the Lord God Almighty, in the glorious name of Jesus, will give you your heart's desire! A-men, brothers and sisters. A-men!

It's a bit frightening to think that there really are churches like that in the world. They feed on people's misery. They create an image of the world which is so pumped up with future hope, that gullible people really do believe that God is in the business of making them wealthy...but they are tricked into making their preachers wealthy instead. Remember that TV Evangelist I talked about last week – with his massive house on a hill. Hmmm…perhaps I'm in the wrong branch of the church?

According to today's Gospel text, modern-day prosperity preachers are not the first people to have got the wrong end of the stick. Verse 21: "From that time on, Jesus began to show his disciples that he must go to Jerusalem and undergo great suffering at the hands of the elders and chief priests and scribes, and be killed,"

You can just imagine Peter's reaction can't you? He has just confessed Jesus as the Messiah (as we heard last week). He's just been told that on him – Mr Rocky – Jesus was going to build his church. And now…Jesus is talking about having to suffer and die. Peter probably thinks that Jesus has gone nuts. Perhaps the Messiah has been working too hard? "Never, Lord" he said. "This shall never happen to you!" (Matt 16:22)

But Jesus is adamant. He tells Peter off with really startling words: "Get behind me, Satan!" Pretty stern stuff. And then Jesus goes on, in verse 23: "You are setting your mind not on divine things, but on human things". In other words, "You are thinking like a man, but by now you should be starting to think as God thinks...to see things from God's perspective".

And then – here comes the 'drop the mike' line: "If any want to become my followers, let them deny themselves and take up their cross and follow me" (verse 24).

So what does it mean to embrace suffering as part of the Christian life?

Let me introduce you to my friend Lucy (not her real name). She had spent all her life serving others through the church. She had been at coffee mornings and fundraisers, and served on the PCC, and made endless cups of tea. She had truly denied herself for others. And yet, Lucy now found herself bed-bound, and unable to serve others anymore. She even had to rely on others to help her to the bathroom.

Lucy's body was failing her but not her mind. She said to me, "perhaps God is teaching me that there was still a bit of pride in me. I'm learning that I need to let others serve me for a change. Perhaps I'm learning that in the end, we all must rely on God, and on other people. That none of us can exist in isolation."

I was intensely moved by what Lucy said. After a life-time of faith God was teaching her something deep, something profound, about our need for each other, and for God. There was, for Lucy at least, a purpose in her suffering. She learned to gladly take up her cross, for what it would teach her and others, even as she neared the end of her life.

This does not, of course, explain all suffering. To even begin to explore the place of suffering in God's plan would take a lot more time than I have today! And it does little to explain the awful and apparently senseless suffering of so many. But I suggest to you that Jesus offers us a clue. Jesus had to suffer, and indeed to die. But through death, came resurrection. There is hope at the end of all tunnels of suffering, for those who trust in God's essential goodness. And for those who are open – like Lucy – to hearing God's voice in the midst of suffering.

So, may you come to know the power of God that is often revealed in suffering. May you come to know the power of denying self, and taking up the cross that is offered to you. May you come to know that God's power is so often revealed in and through weakness - our own weakness, as well as the weakness of those we encounter and serve.

And it's alright…you don't have to sign over the deeds of your house to Sister Shelley!

Amen.

St Gregory the Great

Preached on Thursday 3 September 2020 by Bishop John

Today the Church commemorates St Gregory the Great, described by St Bede (the first great historian of the Church of England) as "our apostle", because he was the Pope who sent St Augustine of Canterbury in 597 on his mission to establish a church for the English people. It's not without reason then that Gregory is sometimes described as "the apostle of England."

Gregory came from a noble and wealthy Roman family which had been distinguished in both politics and the Church. One of his great-grandfathers had himself been Pope, and his father had been a senator and senior official of the city. Gregory seemed destined for an important public role. As an expert lawyer, he also became Prefect of the city. His real longing however was to be a monk. Even that did not save him from public service as the Pope sent him as an ambassador to Constantinople, which was then the capital of the Roman Empire. Like many of the most able and devout leaders of the early Church, Gregory was thus torn between a prominent public position, with all the temptations that brings, and his desire for a hidden life devoted to the service of Christ.

This same ambivalence characterised the way he exercised his own ministry when he himself was chosen as Pope. He brought with him all the experience and habits he had acquired as a senior servant of the state. He was decisive and could be authoritarian. But he was also a sensitive and skilful pastor not just in his care for the Church as whole but also in his attentive care for the different needs of the people entrusted to his care. One of his loveliest writings was a book "On Pastoral Care" –while Archbishop Michael Ramsey said he used to reread every time he was preparing to ordain a new bishop.

So, that's a bit of the background and character of the saint we commemorate today.

His title, "the Great", should not mislead us. Whoever would be great, said Jesus, must make himself least and the servant of all. One of my favourite 20th century saints, Charles de Foucauld, said that Jesus has so taken the lowest place that no one can take it from him" – and all who follow him must follow him in this too. Gregory understood this, and one of his favourite descriptions of himself was "the servant of the servants of God."

Greatness, Christian greatness, is something very different from how the world understands greatness. Do you remember the little battle between Jesus and Peter we heard about in Sunday's gospel? Peter had protested when Jesus spoke about his coming suffering. This shall never happen to you, Lord. Peter clearly thought that Jesus should trounce all his enemies and meant to do everything in his power to help him do so. Peter wanted a triumphant Jesus, a glorious Jesus – in this he probably was not too far from those two brothers James and John who asked to have places of honour in God's kingdom.

Jesus' whole life and message was a protest against that way of thinking. In worldly terms Jesus was, to quote a modern phrase, a loser, the ultimate loser. Hence his sharp words to Peter: "the way you think is not God's way but man's." The world's way is to lord it over others or at least find ourselves higher in the pecking order and have other people at our beck and call. Christ's way is very different. After all, he came, as he himself said, not to be served but to serve and to give his life as a ransom for many.

May St Gregory pray for us individually and as the Church of England, that we may all learn how to share the lowest place with Jesus Christ and, following his example, wash the feet of our brothers and sisters.

In the *Name* of Jesus

Tom Kennar's Sermon on 6 September 2020

Text: Matthew 18.15-20 (compare with John 14.13-14)

What's in a name?

In the name of Jesus. In the *NAME* of Jesus. In some churches, you'll hear that phrase used over and over again – all through the prayers they say. It's a kind of magic phrase which some have come to believe will make real whatever the prayer is about. 'Father God we pray for wealth and health, in the NAME of Jesus. Abracadabra!'

But is this what Jesus meant for us to do when he taught, in John's Gospel, that whatever you ask in his name he will do. Or, as we heard in today's Gospel, 'whenever two or three gather IN MY NAME I am there with them.

What does it mean to pray, or gather, in the name of Jesus?

In western culture, names are thrown around without a great deal of thought. We tend to give names to children because we like the sound of them, or because they are the name of a much loved family member.

In older times, parents would choose names which they hoped would be worked out in the behaviour of the child as it grew. So, names like Grace, Chastity or Patience were especially popular in Victorian times. The stained glass windows in our choir stalls have three lovely ladies in them, called Faith, Hope and Charity.

A few years ago, I was accosted in the churchyard by a dear lady of somewhat dubious mental health. She harangued me for quite a while about the fact that we don't, in fact, call Jesus by his proper name. Actually, she was right. The name he was given was in fact 'Yeshua' – which is anglicised to Joshua. Over time, through translations from Aramaic into Greek then into English, the consonants and vowels got changed – leaving us with the modern rendering of his name: Jesus. Yeshua is what Jesus would have heard when his mother called him for his dinner. And it means 'God saves'.

Which makes Jesus an extraordinary name for a child to be given, because there was an expectation that he would live up to the name he was given and go on to genuinely save people from their sins.

There's no mention in the bible of Jesus having a surname, but that isn't hugely surprising. At the time Jesus lived, an individual would be known by their given name, and then perhaps the place they were from. Jesus of Nazareth would be good example. Perhaps their occupation - like Matthew the Tax Collector; or maybe who their father was, like James son of Zebedee. What is certain is that Jesus' surname wasn't 'Christ'. No-one approaching him in the street would have said 'Good morning, Mr Christ'. That wasn't his surname – but rather it is a Title…a word which means 'saviour'. So, if you like, you can call Jesus Christ 'Yeshua Saviour'. Certainly the old lady in the churchyard would be much happier if you did!

Giving people a title is another way of renaming them, to describe something about them. Ken Dodd, of blessed memory, sometimes referred to himself as the 'Chief Tickler of Britain'. And then there are the plan daft titles which are creeping into the world of work. Recently I heard of someone called the 'Chief Wizard of Light Bulb Moments'. Turns out he was a Marketing Director. And I rather like the title of 'Grand Master of Underlings'…which turns out to be a Deputy Manager!

There is one title, however, that we can all aspire to because of Yeshua Saviour – Jesus Christ. The whole point of Jesus living among us was to show us what God is like. Jesus wanted us to see God differently than how he has been viewed in the past. Jesus showed us that God wasn't a distant deity, perched on a mountain-top or a cloud, viewing the world from a distance. Instead, Jesus gave God a new title – the title of Father…or, actually, the title 'Abba' – which means 'Daddy'. Jesus, born as a child himself, invites us to view God as a parental figure…the Daddy, or the Mummy, who cares about their children. And so, we are offered a new title – the title of Child of God.

I've had many names and titles throughout my life – Tom, Dad, Grandad, Rector, Reverend, Canon. Idiot. But the one which matters most to me is the simplest of all, the one modelled by the baby in the manger…child of God.

I am Tom, child of God.
And Sandra is a child of God.
And Lucas is a child of God.
And everyone here…we are all children of God.

That title is one which every member of the human race can claim. We are all God's children. The only choice we have to make is whether we choose to be part of the family of God as well.

And if we do, if we choose to bind our self to the names of God, and especially to the name of Jesus Christ, then we will surely desire to live and to pray in the ways that he lived and prayed. To pray, or to gather, in the NAME of Jesus, means to align ourselves to Jesus' will for the world – revealed to us in the Scriptures.

What was his will? We see it worked out in his prayers, and in his teaching. We willed that we should Love God with all our heart, soul, mind and strength. He willed that we should love our neighbours as ourselves. He willed that all his followers should be one, and that the hungry would be fed, the prisoners cared for, the sick healed. He willed that the whole community of people who call themselves after Christ – the Christians – would bear his light to the world. By our actions, by our generosity, by our commitment to our community, by our prayers…all of us bent towards the transformation of the world in which we live.

Now that's a prayer for which we can pray, and for which we can gather, in the name of Jesus!

Love your enemies…really?

Preached on Thursday 10 September 2020 by Tom Kennar

Text: Luke 6.27-38

Love your enemies? It's one of the more apparently crazy statements that Jesus made, isn't it? I mean, surely we should batter our enemies? When an enemy comes at you with an army, or a suicide bomb, or a nuclear missile, loving him isn't going to be much of a defence is it?

It's just this kind of namby-pamby rhetoric from Jesus that gives religion a bad name, isn't it? Christians are so easily dismissed by a population who lived through the rise of Nazism, or who watched the Twin Towers fall. People say to themselves 'why on earth would I follow a religion which has such an impractical message at its core. Love your enemies? Preposterous!

But to dismiss Jesus' teaching so contemptuously would be unwise. History is full of examples in which conflict has ultimately been solved by Love. The history of Europe is just such an example.

After the First World War, the Allies imposed punitive sanctions on Germany. War reparations were demanded from the German people, and as a result, their economy went into freefall. The Allies effectively continued to 'hate' their enemy, even after the Armistice was signed. The result of this hate-filled demand for retribution led directly to the rise of Adolf Hitler. He was able to tap into the poverty of the German people, and their festering resentment against the Allies, to promise a rise to greatness. He promised to 'make his country great again' (where have we heard that phrase recently?).

After the Second World War, the victorious Allies realised that punishing Germany again – continuing the hate – would not achieve the aim of lasting peace. Instead, the Marshall Plan was devised – by which the United States donated the equivalent of 5% of its gross domestic product to the rebuilding of the shattered cities and lives of Europe – including what was then West Germany. Whilst other political issues were also at play – such as the pushing back of communism – essentially the Marshall Plan was a practical attempt to 'love enemies', and to 'do good to those that have hurt us'. The end result was the creation of NATO, and ultimately the European Union, which has preserved peace and fostered co-operation for over half a century.

Perhaps Jesus wasn't such a crackpot after all? And Jesus' advice works on an individual level too. How often do we hear stories of neighbour going to war with neighbour? It's usually over some trivial matter – at least at first. I know people who have fallen out over paint colours, or the mis-placing of a boundary marker. Hatred and enmity builds in these circumstances, as each side justifies their own bad behaviour towards the other. Whole families can get drawn into such disputes…and sometimes whole communities.

Into such arguments, the voice of Jesus cries out. 'Love your enemy!' he pleads. For he knows that the ONLY answer to the healing of such disputes is love.

But let no-one imagine that this is namby-pamby easy stuff to do. It's often much easier to roll with the hate…however much stress that induces. It's in our human nature to be compelled by conflict, motivated by it, energised by it. Anyone who has ever found themselves in the middle of a legal case will know exactly what I mean. Seeking the defeat of one's enemy is both stressful and exhilarating – all at the same time.

But it takes a truly courageous person to choose the path of love. The Loving path doesn't seek to win. In the words of St Paul from 1 Corinthians 13, the path of love is patient and kind. It doesn't keep a record of wrongs. It always hopes. It always perseveres. It always seeks the good of the other. And its hard work.

Which is why we should all pray, constantly, for the strength, the wisdom, the fortitude and the commitment to Love our enemies. Amen.

Forgiveness

Preached by Tom Kennar on 13 September 2020

Text: Genesis 50. 15-21 and Matthew 18. 21-35

You have to take your hat off to Joseph, don't you? He had been his Father's favourite son. He was given a coat of many colours (I know you can all hear the song in your head!). But then, he gets sold into slavery by his own brothers. He spends years in an Egyptian prison, but then with God's help, rises to the second most powerful position in the land. His brothers, now penniless and starving come to him for help. What a chance he had! What an opportunity to get revenge on those who had treated him so cruelly! But what does Joseph do? He forgives. He forgives his brothers, and promises to take care of them.

In so many ways, Joseph represents God in this story. He lives out the very heart and nature of a God who freely offers forgiveness to ALL his children.

As a priest, who has heard many a confession or life-story, I know that forgiveness is one of the hardest callings of the Christian faith. How can someone be expected to forgive another who has abused them, or stolen from them, or falsely accused them, or hurt them in a myriad of ways? Or how can we, as a society, forgive the bombers of 9-11, 19 years ago, or of Manchester?

And yet Jesus calls us to forgive those who trespass against us…as much as seventy times seven, he says metaphorically to Peter. As always, context is everything. Peter and Jesus are talking, on this occasion, in the context of a church fellowship. Note that Peter's original question is 'if a member of the church sins against me, how many times should I forgive him?'. The original word here is 'brother' (not 'member of the church' – but inclusive language is highly valued these days. But the discussion is focused on how a lack of forgiveness can completely wreck a church fellowship.

And I guess we've all at least known people who have been affected by an inability to forgive in churches, as well as other social institutions. The classic conflict often seems to arise between flower artists and vicars, resulting in the classic joke, often repeated in vicaring circles, 'what's the difference between a flower artist and a terrorist?' (Answer: you can negotiate with a terrorist!). I have to say that our brilliant flower artists are nothing like that!

But the reality is that sometimes, an inability to forgive some slight, or careless action by another member of the church can so often, sadly, lead to long-term pain and a continuing and deep sense of hurt. But Jesus suggests a radical alternative….

To forgive someone is, quite literally, to give up one's right to feel aggrieved or hurt by another. When we do that, we actually deny the person who has wronged us any power over our own emotions. We take away their ability to hurt us, or damage us in the longer term. Altogether.

In fact, true forgiveness means giving up the right to feel hurt before the hurt even has a chance to take root in one's soul. To forgive is to give up the hurt before it can take hold.

But does this mean that the person being forgiven gets away with whatever they have done wrong? Well, perhaps – especially for the little things…the annoying word, the careless insult. By forgiving someone for that, we recognise them for what they are…symptoms only of that most common of diseases…the disease of being a failing human being. Just like us.

But what about the really big things…the systematic abusers, the scammers, the murderers, the suicide bombers? Well, for such people, Jesus offers further advice. In Matthew chapter 10 he advises that we need to be 'as wise as serpents and as gentle as doves'. If I know that someone has the potential to cause great harm to another, I have a duty and a responsibility to do all I can to prevent that harm. So it is only right that I must, and should, involve the appropriate authorities in stopping them. But never out of revenge. The gentle dove releases the hatred. But the wise serpent makes sure – as sure as they can – that the wrongdoer is prevented from causing further harm to anyone else, and suitably punished for the wrongdoing they've already wrought.

This is why we have a justice system, after all. Having forgiven the wrong-doer, so that they no longer have the power to hurt us, we hand over the responsibility for punishment and correction to the society in which we live. There, appropriate punishment is meted out, without passion, without hatred. A just punishment is handed down, hopefully, but not by the person who was harmed. Not least so that the harmed person is not further damaged by committing some act of violence or retribution themselves.

So, may you find the strength to let go of the hurt that others have done to you. As Joseph did, and as Peter was encouraged to do, may you release your heart from the resentments it holds onto, so that your heart may fly free, and straight into the heart of the forgiving God of Love.

Father, forgive us our trespasses as we forgive those who trespass against us. Amen.

Amazing Grace

Preached on Thursday 17 September 2020 by Tom Kennar

Texts: 1 Corinthians 15.1–11 & Luke 7.36–end

This morning's readings are intended to inspire awe in us. Awe, because the focus of both readings is on the amazing grace of God.

In the first reason, while reminding his readers of the basic story of Jesus' sacrificial death and resurrection, Paul confesses that he was a dastardly sinner. He reminds his readers that he was a persecutor of Christians – which, in his day, means that he was no doubt responsible for death of many. From the book of Acts, we know that he stood by watching, with approval, the stoning of Stephen – the first Christian martyr. Paul had been a bad man – one whose religious zealotry was so certain, and so passionate, that he could approve of the public lynching of a man who spoke only of God's love.

But as we know from Paul's story, Jesus reached out to him, via a vision on the Damascus road. He calls Paul to follow a new path. He gracefully uses one of the fledgling Christianity's most ardent opponents, and he offers him new life and new purpose. Without a word of repentance being said by Paul, God reaches out through Jesus and saves him.

In the second story, a woman whose name we do not know, is described as 'a sinner'. Readers of the time would have understood that to mean that she was probably what we would call a sex worker. (It says a lot about the morality of the time that a sinner is someone so desperately poor that they are forced to sell their body and their dignity to a succession of sweaty men). This so-called 'sinful' woman falls before Jesus, and bathes his feet with her tears and then with ointment. Jesus, again, acts gracefully towards her. Without a word of repentance being said by the woman, Jesus offers her complete forgiveness of all her sins.

What might we notice about both these stories? For me, both stories talk to me about how God reaches out to us. That's what Amazing Grace is like. It's why John Newton, the hymn-writer, was inspired to coin the phrase. As you probably know, Newton had been a slave-ship captain. Like the sinful woman who washed Jesus' feet, and like Paul who tortured Christians, Newton couldn't get over the fact that God's grace was powerful enough, strong enough, loving enough to forgive even a 'wretch' like him.

Have you ever wondered what the difference is between 'grace' and 'mercy' – two of the most powerful descriptions of God? Well, 'mercy' is when God withholds punishment that we deserve. 'Grace' on the other hand, is when God gives us gifts that we don't deserve. (Try reading that again!).

In other words, mercy always precedes grace. By rights, because of the way we all sin, and all fail, God would be within his rights to punish us. But he doesn't. By his mercy, he withholds that punishment, and he instead pours out his grace.

What does this mean for us? How do these stories impact on us? For me, the message is clear. It doesn't matter who we are, or what kind of life we have led. Society may have labelled us a sinner. Our lives may have been driven by hatred, or zealotry, intolerance or extremism. We may have been selfish, or arrogant, or lazy or greedy. Whatever our sin, God offers mercy, and amazing grace. God invites each one of us, just as did for Paul, the chance to take a new road, and to co-operate with him. He frees us from our past, and offers us a new future as one of his beloved children, invited to take his hand and walk towards to the light.

And that's pretty amazing.

Amen.

Havant Commemoration of Our Lady of Walsingham

Preached on Thursday 24 September 2020 by Bishop John Hind

Today the Church commemorates Our Lady of Walsingham, so this is a special day for all members of our parish cell of Our Lady of Faith; but not only for them, because Walsingham and its message are for everyone.

Although the origins of the image and the shrine are lost in the mists of time and legend, Walsingham's title, "England's Nazareth", should set us thinking. There is only one Nazareth, of course, where Mary received the angel's message that she would be the mother of God's messiah and where Jesus grew up, receiving his early experiences and where he was formed for adult life.

That may be enough reason for us to have a special affection for that little Galilean village whose well, synagogue and carpenter's shop have left such a mark on human history. But it has never been enough for Christians to remember holy places from afar. We need to know what difference they make to us now. Indeed, we might think of Pope Gregory's advice to St Augustine of Canterbury at the very foundation of the Church of England, "Do not honour things because of the places they come from, but honour places because of the good things that come from them."

Nazareth matters because that's where Jesus came from, so it is a small step for Nazareth to be a kind of symbol of wherever Jesus is present. Many Christians all through the ages have found a pilgrimage to Nazareth a powerful way of joining their own sense of Jesus NOW with the story of Jesus THEN. But of course for most people travelling to Nazareth has always been an impossible dream. It is hardly surprising then that they have sought more local ways of celebrating what God did there and then in order to rekindle their faith here and now.

So that is the point of Walsingham. It's why the Shrine was established in the first place and it is why for so many centuries people have travelled there in faith, hope and love. It may be a long way from Havant, but we can get there even if the journey may require some effort. But now, especially this year, when the Shrine is closed and pilgrimage impossible, we are forced to ask what Nazareth means for us –not in Galilee or even in north Norfolk, but here, in Havant, in our homes and in our own lives.

Pilgrimage is not religious tourism; it is ultimately a journey inward, a journey to discover the presence of Jesus Christ. In a wonderful passage in his Confessions St Augustine of Hippo wrote, "You were within me, and I outside; and I looked for you outside and I rushed towards the lovely things you made. You were with me but I was not with you."

Just think about that for moment. God, the creator of heaven and earth, the infinite, the unbounded, than whom nothing greater can exist or even be imagined, is pleased to make his home in that tiny, very particular bit of creation that is my own heart. There is a wonderful traditional image of Mary showing her with Jesus in her breast: the title of the image is "She who contains the uncontainable." "Containing the uncontainable" is not only a privilege of Mary: it is something to which we are all called.

Nazareth and Walsingham, wonderful and evocative places as they are, exist to remind us of the supreme truth that in Jesus, born of Mary, we meet Emmanuel – God with us, not just in Nazareth and Walsingham but always and everywhere. God did indeed make himself at home in Mary's womb, but he makes himself at home in each one of us. Remember that every day. When you receive holy communion, and those of you participating in this Eucharist online in making an act of spiritual communion, know that you are the tabernacle of God himself, and consider what honour and reverence you owe to his presence.

Is the Lord among us, or not?

Bishop John Hind's Sermon from 27 September 2020—Trinity 16

"Is the Lord among us or not?". Those words from this morning's first reading come from the Bible's account of the Exodus, God's people's escape from slavery in Egypt. It is a question that is asked in every time of crisis. "Is the Lord among us or not?" In times of crisis we are always tempted to put God to the test. Where is God in all this? How can God allow this to happen?

Six months ago when lockdown began we were advised that the problem would soon pass. In words reminiscent of the early days of the First World War we were confidently told "It will all be over by Christmas", and even some of our religious leaders, who should have known better, assured us that the crisis would pass.

I can't comment on politicians who seem to think that stating the desirable somehow makes it happen, but I can say that as Christians we should regard any predictions of how things in this world will turn out with the utmost suspicion.

The reason I say this is because Jesus himself told his first disciples, and through them us as well, that "in the world you will have trouble" – although of course they and we hardly need Jesus to tell is that. What was new, distinctive, and the cause of endless hope, was what Jesus went on to say: "but be of good cheer; I have overcome the world." Jesus did not say that bad things won't happen, or that they are less bad than they seem – but rather that bad things do not have the last word.

Trouble and delight are both permanent features of life. Yes, trouble and delight. What a strange mixture of experiences we have, and how important it is to find a way of making sense of both joy and sadness in our picture of the world we inhabit. Do you remember the reaction of Job in the Old Testament when he was told about four tragedies that had befallen his sons and daughters "Naked I came from my mother's womb, and naked I will return. The Lord gave, and the Lord has taken away. Blessed be the name of the Lord…… Should we accept from God only good and not evil?"

The traditional English expression "the patience of Job" is not accurate if patience simply means being uncomplaining in the face of suffering. The Bible talks rather about his steadfastness. He raged against what had happened, but refused to curse God despite the encouragement of those around him to do so.

The whole of the Book of Job is a wonderful and agonizing exploration of the mystery of human suffering, but it leaves the mystery at that: it doesn't attempt to give any easy answers but invites us to trust God, come what may. And that's the point. There is no simple intellectual answer to the question "Why do bad things happen?" In any case, having an intellectual answer wouldn't give any comfort or help us deal with our wretchedness. The more pressing question is "What are we going to do about it?"

This brings us straight to our present crisis. Despite the brave words I mentioned at the beginning, we are now told that the Corona Virus is here to stay and that we need to learn to live with it. That does not mean there is nothing we can do about it. We have rather to recognise that some of the changes we have had to get used to about the way we live and interact with each other will have to be permanent. And because they will be permanent, we may need to be more subtle about how we apply them. To give just one example, we should alter our language: let's not talk about social distancing as if it means we should have less to do with each other – let's talk rather about physical distancing, maintaining a healthy space while at the same time doing all we can to be closer to each other in other ways.

Above all, however, let's stop complaining about why things are the way they are but commit ourselves to improving how things are, to living with what cannot be escaped, knowing that the answer to the question in my text from this morning's first reading "Is the Lord among us or not?" is a resounding YES.

To repeat Jesus' words: "In the world you will have trouble" of course, that's just the way things are, but remember how he went on to say, "be of good cheer, I have overcome the world."

The harvest is plentiful, but the labourers are few.

Preached on Thursday 1 October 2020 by Tom Kennar

Text: Luke 10.1-12 (Jesus sends out the 72).

In these days of the Covid Pandemic, a remarkable thing has happened. There are no firm statistics to support it yet, but all the anecdotal evidence is that the church is growing. The mass movement of churches into online services has meant that people all across the country, and across the world, are accessing opportunities for worship and study in new and exciting ways. In some cases, these are people who might otherwise have been stuck at home, through frailty or illness. But in many other cases, I've found, the 'new worshippers' have been people who only had a very loose affiliation with church.

Perhaps, for some, the very thought of entering a church has been scary, even though they have been interested in faith. That might seem strange to those of us who feel at home in a church. But perhaps we might reflect how we would feel entering, say, a mosque or a Hindu temple. Where should we sit? Are we allowed to sit? What words do we say? When is the right time to stand or sit? If I sit here, will I be sitting in someone's favourite place?

Offering our services online has enabled some people to engage with worship without any of those apprehensions. They can sit in their own chair, and watch when they want to watch. If something intrigues them, they can pause. If they want to visit the bathroom, they can pause! For many, therefore, worship online has enabled them to gain a window into the previously nerve-wracking world of 'coming to church'. And that's a good thing. It's why we plan to continue live-streaming our worship for as long as anyone is watching it from home!

Another group of people we've seen attending online church is the group of folks who walked away from church at some time in their lives…but who are now, slowly, gently, finding a way back through internet worship. If you are one of those – then you are welcome too!

The happy upshot of all these online engagements is that the number of workers for the harvest of human souls is somewhat larger than it was. The harvest is indeed plentiful…there are literally millions of people who have not yet heard – or perhaps understood yet - the good news that they are children of God, that God loves them, and wants them to find new, purposeful life and healing for their souls. 'Salvation'…if you prefer.

But how are we to encourage online worshippers to engage in that task of being workers in the harvest field? Well, here's a few suggestions, from today's Gospel reading...which really apply to us all, whether we worship in church, or at home.

First: Jesus calls us to engage with the world. He sent out the seventy disciples as his ambassadors. He wanted them to prepare the ground on which he was planning to walk – telling the people that the Kingdom of Heaven is at hand. We too are called to this work. Wherever we are – at home or at work, at school or out shopping – we are all the bearers of wonderful news. God loves us, and calls us to live fulfilling lives, and to find healing for our souls. We can invite our friends, our co-workers, our family to access the online resources which are now available – whether it's to watch a service like this, and to think about the sermon – or whether it's to join in with the Church's daily prayer initiatives, or an internet discussion group. Or whether it's by passing on the Corona Chronicle to a neighbour or family-member. By just chatting with others, about how helpful WE have found these resources, we can draw others into the light of faith.

Secondly: Jesus tells us we are not alone. He sent out the seventy disciples in pairs. He understood that we all need companions along the journey of faith – to correct us, to uplift us, to encourage us. Who is your companion on the journey of faith? Perhaps it's your life partner? Or perhaps it's a close friend with whom you share your thoughts and feelings? Perhaps just the very act of tuning-in regularly to online worship, or by actually coming into church, you feel that you have companionship along the journey of faith? Whatever works for you – whatever lifts you, comforts you, encourages you, challenges you – keep on doing that.

Thirdly: Jesus tells us to wipe the dust from our feet. Jesus knew that his good news of abundant life would not be welcomed by all. Sometimes, people are just too attached to their own ways of doing things. They are no longer teachable. They think they have nothing to learn. Jesus encourages us to not waste our time with such folks. Leave them to God's loving mercy.

That's a lesson I've had to learn – especially on the internet. It's very easy to get riled up about someone's frustrating, or ignorant comment. Part of me wants to turn into a 'keyboard warrior' – and to smash down the walls of their ignorance (or plain stupidity) with facts. But I've had to learn that doing so is just a waste of time. Someone who has allowed false news to dominate their thinking is only going to view me as deluded. Their ability to reason has already been taken from them. Wiping, sadly, the dust from my shoes, turning off the internet or leaving the conversation in the street are my only options.

So…engage with the world, do it with others, and don't waste your time on those who will not, or cannot hear the life-saving words of God. That's the nub of today's Gospel…and whether we labour in the streets and workplace, or from our screen and keyboard, the harvest is plentiful. Thankfully…the workers are not quite so few!

St Faith

Tom Kennar's homily our Dedication Festival,
commemorating St Faith of Aquittaine and Agen (our 'patron saint').
4 October 2020—Trinity 17

There are many so called holy places in the world. They are those places where, somehow, the veil between our mortal world and the spiritual world seems more fragile. Some people call then 'touching places', or 'thin places' – places, that is, where one seems to be able to reach out and almost touch the out-stretched hand of God.

Attributions of holiness have been given to many places over the millennia. Stonehenge was once considered holy by its builders – as far as we know. Great cathedrals and churches were considered holy, thin places, because they often contained the bones of great saints. For devotees of our patron Saint, Faith of Agen, the abbey-church of Conques, France is one such place. There are laid the bones of the young martyr – cruelly murdered under the rule of the Roman emperor Diocletian, because she refused to renounce her faith in Jesus Christ. Ask Bishop John and Janet Hind for their account of the place – for they visited it only a couple of years ago.

And yet there is a danger, isn't there, in investing all our energy into buildings. Anyone who has toured the ruins of great churches around the UK should know that faith is not kept alive by holy places alone. They, like all physical things, must pass. For as King Solomon prayed at the building of his great temple, '…will God indeed dwell on the earth? Even heaven and the highest heaven cannot contain you, much less this house that I have built!' Where is that great Temple of Solomon now? Gone. Just a few stones which comprise the so-called 'Wailing Wall' remain.

In fact, if we are honest, holy buildings can sometimes get in the way. In the Jerusalem temple, for example, human priests created a holy of holies – a place in which God was said to actually dwell. It was a place so holy, that the High Priest could only go into it on one day of the year, after elaborate rites of purification. The New Testament tells us that the curtain of that 'holy of holies' was torn down at the death of Jesus. It was not a helpful picture of God. It had to go.

Even our own beautiful building has some challenges – in terms of the story it tells about God. For example, the way that the whole focus of the church is fixed on the High Altar, could suggest that God is distant from us…. that he is far away, and only to be approached on bended knee, in front of a Sanctuary that ordinary people dare not enter. That is not, I think, the picture of God that Jesus offers us. He wanted us to understand God as our heavenly parent – the father who cares for his children and who walks alongside us. Jesus taught us to expect to find God's spirit along us, leading us into all truth, dwelling within us. These are not images of a distant God. A church which has its altar in the centre of the people might well be a much more accurate picture.

Some of our images of Jesus – in this beautiful building – are rather problematic. The blond, bearded man on the cross in our East Window looks nothing like the probably clean-shaven, dark-haired Jewish man who died for us. What picture of God does this building convey? It's a picture of God as an Englishman – a blond one at that! That kind of image undermines all that Jesus and his followers taught us about being one family of humankind, in which there is neither Jew nor Gentile, black nor white.

And yet, as those who steward and care-for this church throughout the week will testify, the building has immense value to all those who enter its doors throughout the week, seeking solace, peace, or a place to seek God. That is why, for all its theological confusion, I think that our continuing efforts to refurbish this place are worthwhile. Its very age and architectural idiosyncrasies are precisely what draw in those seekers of a thin place, a touching place.

But at the same time, we must not forget that this building is not 'the Church'. It is only a shell…at the end of the day, a shelter from the rain in which the actual church can gather. Fundamentally it is no different from the church of St Nicholas in the parish of Nswam, Ghana – which I visited in 2015. A few palm branches, spread over a frame. Just a shelter from the elements.

For, as St Peter says, we are "living stones…built into a spiritual house, to be a holy priesthood". We are the church – not these stones. We could – if the Diocese would let us! – tear this whole place down – leaving a pile of rubble in the middle of Havant. That would not mean that the church was gone. The people who make up the church would still be here (if a little damp, when it rains!).

We have perhaps learned the truth of this even more during the COVID pandemic. We have discovered that we are still the church, even when the building is locked and bolted against infection. Through the internet, through phone calls, through loving and caring for each other and our community, the church has continued, without its building at all.

Next week we will focus on our plans for the future, during our Annual Meeting – plans which will certainly include the ongoing care and development of this beautiful building. But also plans which will aim to build up the living stones of our congregation, as we seek, after the example of St Faith, to Live, Pray and Serve as followers of Jesus Christ.

Asking and getting

Preached on Thursday 8 October 2020 by Tom Kennar

Text: Luke 11.5-13

One of the great battles of medieval world, was over the correct interpretation of Scripture. For centuries, the established church had kept somewhat of a lock on the Bible. Only selected texts were read, and only authorised ministers were allowed to preach. Quite often even those sermons could only be sermons which had been written by higher authorities within the church. Pre-prepared texts, if you like. Scripture itself was often read in Latin, so that it was largely beyond the comprehension of most of the population.

The problem, as the church authorities saw it, was that if you put the words of Scripture into the hands of ordinary people, they would mis-understand it. They might, for example, pick up the book of Genesis, and actually believe that it was a factual, historical account of creation – rather than the allegorical story that it is.

But this wasn't good enough for the Reformers, like Martin Luther, John Calvin and, famously William Tyndale who was the first to mass-produce Bibles in English. They argued that everyone has a right to read Scripture for himself, and, guided by the church, to arrive at a correct interpretation. The advent of the printing press made this move almost inevitable, just as the arrival of the internet in our time means that it would be impossible for the church to keep the Bible under wraps now.

But this new found freedom to interpret Scripture for oneself does lead to difficulties. We have before us, this morning, one of the most frequently mis-understood texts of the Bible: "Ask, and it shall be given unto you".

Sadly, there are churches all over the world where this text (and others like it) are taken at face value, without any scholarly context or interpretation being applied. As a result, the worshippers in such churches find themselves believing that if they want to get rich, all they have to do it pray for it. They are taught by their poorly educated leaders that if they don't get rich, then that's because they don't have enough faith. So the worshippers try desperately to believe, believe, believe! Then, these false church leaders tell their congregations that in order to receive, you first have to give. Congregations are persuaded to give what little wealth they have to the church leaders…in the desperate hope that they will yet become rich.

It is a terrible, terrible con-trick…and it drives millions into abject poverty all across the world. And all because this one line of Scripture is taken, completely out of context, and used as a maxim for prayer and the religious life.

For this particular verse, what appears to be a straight promise from Jesus' lips – "Ask and you will receive" – turns out to be not so straight forward, after all. It needs to be read alongside other renderings of the same promise, in other gospels. (That's why we have more than one Gospel – so that we can form a balanced and healthy view of Jesus' life and teachings, from the variety of voices who told his story). Matthew's gospel has an account of this very same teaching of Jesus – in Matthew 7.

But actually, we don't even need to look at the other renderings of Jesus' promises on prayers. Luke provides all we need to know for a sound understanding of what Jesus was teaching. At the end of today's passage, we read these words:

"If you then, who are evil, know how to give good gifts to your children, how much more will the heavenly Father give the Holy Spirit to those who ask him!"

So, it turns out, prayer is not an open invitation to present God with a shopping list of things we'd like. Jesus is teaching us to ask for the gift of God's Holy Spirit! He encourages us to be persistent – like a man knocking up his sleeping neighbour and asking for bread. But the object of our desire is not for bread, or even gold. The object of our desire is the gift of the Holy Spirit.

Why? Because the Spirit is the comforter, and the teacher. He is the one who helps us in Augustine's words of today's Collect, 'to find our rest' in God. He is the one who Jesus promises will 'lead us into all truth', and who will empower us to live, move and have our being in God. How could we desire anything else?

I rather like the saying of St Theresa of Liseaux, who said "God always gives me what I want, because I only want what God wants to give." (Try reading that again, slowly!)

St John expands on his understanding of what Jesus was saying, when he says this: "If you remain in me and my words remain in you, ask for whatever you want and it will be done for you".

Do you see what I'm saying? For those whose wills are aligned to God's will, by the gift of the Holy Spirit, prayer can indeed become a powerful force in the world and in our own lives. If we ask for something which is not central to God's plan for saving the world, then the answer will be "no". But if our prayers are bent towards the will of God, seeking his face and his will for ourselves and for the world, then we should get ready for showers of positive answers to our prayers! Amen.

The Wedding Robe – Part II

Tom Kennar's Sermon on 11 October 2020—Trinity 18
Text: Matthew 22. 1-14

By a strange serendipity, the Lectionary has offered us a Gospel reading on which I preached only about two months ago, at a Thursday morning service. 'Oh good', said I to myself as I sat down to write today's sermon. 'I'll just preach that one again – no-one will notice, and the Thursday congregation is a largely different bunch of people'.

But then, I realised that our newly discovered skills at using the internet would probably shoot me in the foot. After all, the sermon I preached on the 20th of August has been widely shared. At the latest count, 293 people have watched the service of that day, and an additional 154 have been reached by the separate posting of the sermon, and another 14 have read it online. In addition, it was published in the Corona Chronicle, which currently goes out to around 250 people in the parish.

Preaching a sermon again is something we preachers often do, if we can get away with it. 'After all,' we reason, 'if it was true then, it's still true now. And all the hours of preparation can be put to other good uses'.

I'm reminded of the apocryphal story of the Vicar who preached the same sermon two weeks running, and then again on the third week. Thinking that his Vicar had finally gone mad, a churchwarden approached after the third occasion and said 'Father, did you know that you've preached the same sermon three times now?'. 'Yes,' replied the Vicar. 'And when I see evidence that the congregation has heard what I've said and acted on it, I'll preach another!'

Another aphorism of preaching is that most sermons, if we're not careful, can be boiled down to three basic messages: Please pray more, attend more, and give more! That's a temptation I try to avoid – but I'm not always successful!

Jesus had a similar problem. His message was essentially a very simple one – "the Kingdom of Heaven is at hand, and you are invited to be a part of it". But his task was to communicate that simple message to as wide an audience as possible.

He wanted people to know what the Kingdom of Heaven was like – so he gave them multiple images and stories to conjure with. The Kingdom of Heaven is like a mustard seed, or a wheat field, or a light shining on a hill. Its citizens are like salt, or light, or – in the case of today's Gospel reading, like guests at a wedding.

But Jesus doesn't only describe what the Kingdom of Heaven and its citizens are like. He also helps non-citizens – immigrants from the Kingdom of Men – to learn how they can become citizens of the Kingdom of Heaven. 'Repent', he tells them. 'Love God, and love your neighbour as yourself' – which he then illustrates with a variety of new images. Be a 'good Samaritan', sow 'good seed', don't hoard your wealth in barns, be constantly ready, like wedding guests waiting for the bridegroom. Be persistent like a woman knocking on a judge's door, or like a man seeking bread from his neighbour in the middle of the night.

Out of Jesus' stories came many a memorable phrase. 'Don't cast your pearls before swine'. 'Ask and it will be given to you'. 'Repent, for the Kingdom of heaven is at hand'.

We're going to be proposing a memorable phrase this morning – at our APCM. It also comes out of the story that we've been telling ourselves – the story of a congregation, here at St Faith's, who want to live out the mission that God calls us to live. It's a story of five years of real progress, under the leadership of your brilliant PCC. And it's a vision of the next five years. The phrase we've given this story – the title, if you like – is this: Live, Pray, Serve. As you'll hear, when our Churchwardens unfold the plan, we want to:

Live as followers of Jesus Christ – whose example we cherish

Pray alone and together by building on the historic practices of faith we have inherited, and…

Serve – young and old, rich and poor, black and white – loving our neighbours at least as much as we love ourselves.

The only question – for each one of us here today – is whether we will choose to put on the wedding robe that is being offered to us by the Master of the Feast. Will we choose to roll up our sleeves and get stuck into the task of advancing the Kingdom in Havant. Or will be like the wedding guests who are just too busy or too occupied, to accept the Master's invitation?

Kill the Prophets!

Preached on Thursday 15 October 2020 by Tom Kennar
Text: Luke 11.47-end

In our Gospel reading of today, Jesus, we might say, is clearly not a happy bunny, or a happy camper. He is effectively declaring open hostilities with the traditional teachers of the faith, the scribes and the Pharisees. The question is: why would he pick such a fight? Wouldn't it be easier to have kept his head down, and lived a peaceful life?

The answer of course is that Jesus, the living Word of Wisdom and Truth, could not stay silent. From the history of the Hebrews, set out in what we call the Old Testament, Jesus knew that time after time, the Leaders of the nations had killed the prophets, sent from God. They silenced them through murder. Jesus reminds the Leaders that from Abel (the first prophet) to Zechariah (the last prophet), their reaction had been to 'rid themselves of these troublesome priests' (to mis-quote King Henry II before the death of Thomas Becket).

This is a theme that Jesus picks up later in Luke's account, in the form of the parable of the wicked tenants (Luke 20. 9-19). Jesus tells the story of a wealthy landowner (meaning God), who rents out a vineyard (the Land of Israel) to some tenants (meaning the Hebrew nation). Then at harvest time, the Landowner sends out some servants to collect the rent – the servants, of course, standing for God's prophets. But the servants get murdered by the tenants. So the Landowner sends his own son. Surely the tenants won't harm him, for surely they love him? But no…the tenants murder the son, and thrown him out of the vineyard. In this simple parable, Jesus underlines again the way that people in power automatically resist anyone who challenges their power, or their status.

But this is precisely the role of prophets. Prophets are those who, despite being disregarded, ignored, or even murdered, are prepared to stand up for truth against the powerful people of the world. They are those who seek to transform the cultural norms of the society they serve – calling people to a transformed vision of the world.

There are prophets in every generation. God continually calls out people of Wisdom whose unlucky task is to try to shift the culture of the day to something more life-giving, more Godly. From our own time, there are many. For Christian prophets, we might look to the example of Martin Luther King, who dreamed a dream of racial equality. Or William Wilberforce, who led the campaign against state-sanctioned slavery. We might think of Mother Theresa, who by her life and example reminded us that every human being is God's child. We might hold up Archbishop Desmond Tutu, who brought Truth and Reconciliation to South Africa.

But Christians don't have a monopoly on the truth. There are secular prophets too – or at least people who don't use the language of religion to try to shift prevailing cultures. We might think of Ghandi, who shifted the colonial culture of India. We might think of David Attenborough and Gretta Thunberg, who are calling a largely deaf humanity to halt the destruction of Creation. We might hold up the example of Malala Yousafzai, the young woman from Afghanistan who passionately argues for the education of girls throughout the world.

Few of these prophets ever really succeed – at least in their lifetimes. Martin Luther King and Ghandi were murdered. Mother Theresa, David Attenborough and Gretta Thunberg are treated as figures of fun – to be joked about and lampooned. Malala Yousafzai faces the prospect of the Taliban regaining political authority in Afghanistan. And so the cycle of the way the prophets are treated – called out by Jesus – repeats and repeats.

It's a tragedy. As much as it was for Jesus, it is for today's prophets too. The fact is that the powerful people of our world lack the motivation to change their ways. They are comfortable and wealthy. They hold the levers of power – whether it's the media (which lampoons the prophets), or whether its henchmen who can carry out murders.

But our task – is to carry on being prophetic. We, who are followers of the Word of Truth and Wisdom Incarnate, we have a mighty task thrust upon our shoulders. Wherever we live, work, study or play, we are called to speak truth to power. We are called to stand up for what it right, and fair, and just in every situation. In the words of the prophet Joel, we are called to "Declare a holy fast; call a sacred assembly. Summon the elders and all who live in the land to the house of the LORD your God, and cry out to the LORD".

Render to Caesar…

Preached by Tom Kennar on Sunday 18 October 2020 - Trinity 19

Text: Matthew 22. 15-22

Politics, politics, politics. It's a slippery business, isn't it? It's a business that I know something about. Before I was ordained, I spent five years of my life working in Westminster. I worked in a building in Great Smith Street, just across the road from Church House – the offices of the Church of England. Often, I would look out from my ivory tower across the road at the administrative home of the Church I was about to serve…and I would wonder.

I would wonder at the link between the church and the state. The formal link between state and church that we have in the United Kingdom is, in fact, a pretty rare thing – compared to the rest of the world. The link between us – the church – and our nation is cemented in Law, and presided over, on both sides, by our Monarch.

So how are we to interpret Jesus' teaching to 'give to the emperor what belongs to the emperor, and to God what belongs to God'. Many have argued for centuries that Jesus wanted the link to be 'disestablished' – and that Jesus' words should be taken to mean that's time for the link to be dissolved. Those who oppose this view rejoice in owning the longest word in the English language: antidisestablishmentarianism!

So is Jesus's statement a great cry for the disestablishment of the church from the state? Is this a cry that religion and politics don't mix? I don't think so! Jesus stood in the tradition of all the ancient prophets and teachers, who legislated for the way that the whole State was to act, in all matters of human endeavour. Everything, from…

- the ways wars should be conducted,
- the way prisoners should be treated,
- the way foreigners should be welcomed,
- the way that the poor should be supported,
- the way that disputes should be settled,
- the way that the ownership of property should be regulated,
- even the way that banking and the charging of interest should be conducted.

There are laws in the Hebrew Bible for all of these things…and many more. And Jesus went even further. He came to fulfil these laws, by proclaiming a new kind of Kingdom. Kingdom is an inherently 'political' word. Repent! Turn around! Do things differently! Live according to God's rules and God's ways. Live in God's Kingdom.

The real problem, I want to suggest, is that our state, here in the UK, has already become effectively disconnected from its religion. Our society looks less and less like the religion we claim to respect. The poor are neglected and discarded. For example, the new universal credit system requires people with nothing – no money – to live for around six weeks without any support from the rest of society. For those with no savings, because any work they did have was very low paid, this is enough to bring about utter destitution.

Whereas the Scriptures teach, boldly and courageously "there shall be NO poor among you". (Deuteronomy 15:4). We ignore that teaching, and then we wonder why desperate people break into churches to steal what they can to live on.

Here's another example. Our economic models are driven by the charging of interest, which the Scriptures call usury, and illegal. (Exodus 22:24 –commands, "you shall not charge interest on loans to your brother"). And another. We take for granted the accumulation and passing on of capital through our families. Yet the Scriptures, on the other hand, advocate 'Jubilee' – the principle that fairly-shared land shall be returned to the original owners every 50th year. (Leviticus 25). I could go on – at some length. But you'll get cross with me if I do and start waving your watches at me. Let me finish with this suggestion.

Far from being a call to separate politics from religion, Jesus' call to render to Caesar and God that which is theirs should constantly remind us that both the state, and God, have a call on our lives. These two calls must be held in a state of constant dialogue. A state without a religion is a state out of control – prey to the whims of the mob who would drive it ever towards the human kind's baser instincts...blame of the other, the fracturing of community, individualism and consumerism, and the total disregard of the poor and the suffering.

Cont'd...

A religion without a state is just as much in danger. A religion practiced without the tempering reality of human life can also become a deeply damaging thing. Personal religion can so easily become an individualistic search only for personal peace and holy experiences. The songs of stateless religions are always the songs of the individual search for God…cries for God to 'touch me, heal me, fill me'. They are just as much a danger – and just as much worthy of correction.

The state needs religion. And religion needs the state. Each keeps the other in balance. Each invites the other to think outside of the narrow confines of the self.

Yes, we must render unto Caesar that which is Caesar's. We are the State – and we owe a debt to the community which sustains us, feeds us, houses us, and cares for us. But we must also render to God what is his…and never forget his cries for justice, for loving one another, for caring for the poor and the plain unlucky, and for placing God's priorities above all else. Amen.

Not peace…but division!

Preached by Tom Kennar on Thursday 22 October 2020

Text: Luke 12. 49-53

[Jesus said] 'I came to bring fire to the earth, and how I wish it were already kindled! I have a baptism with which to be baptized, and what stress I am under until it is completed! Do you think that I have come to bring peace to the earth? No, I tell you, but rather division! From now on, five in one households will be divided, three against two and two against three; they will be divided: father against son and son against father, mother against daughter and daughter against mother, mother-in-law against her daughter-in-law and daughter-in-law against mother-in-law.'

I'm sorry – but this morning's Gospel always makes me giggle. As does the corresponding passage in Matthew's Gospel. It's the reference to mothers-in-law. It always takes me back to my childhood, and to the humour of its time from such comedians as Les Dawson. He used to say things like "We always know when my mother-in-law is coming up the path. The mice start throwing themselves at the traps!".

We still find such humour amusing, don't we? Because we've all experienced – or at least observed – the sometimes-strained relationships of family-life. As the old saying goes, 'you can choose your friends…but you're stuck with your family!'. It's natural for parents and grandparents to have different ideas about how to bring up the grand-children, for example. Or different ideas about what job that a son-in-law or daughter-in-law ought to be doing. And sometimes, within families, we struggle to 'zip-it'!

But Jesus adds another layer to this natural tension. He warns his followers that just by choosing to follow him, division will almost inevitably flow. Jesus says that his followers may have to make some pretty tough decisions about where their allegiance lies. "Whosever does not take up his cross and follow me, is not worthy of me..." and so on.

The Christian faith, openly declared, is dangerous to the world. It is a way of life which stands in opposition to the way that many people chose to live. It is a way of peace, not war. It is a way of self-control, not pleasure-seeking. It is a way of poverty, simplicity and charity, not materialism and consumerism.

Now please don't get me wrong. I'm not saying that families are a bad thing. God loves families! God invented families. The best families give us companionship and love, a place to feel secure, a place to make mistakes, and still be accepted.

But Jesus says to us, through this reading, that we have an even higher loyalty...a loyalty that only a God could claim...a loyalty to Him.

And that, Jesus warns, will bring division even between members of the same family, and (through the lens of Matthew's account) even a kind of metaphorical sword. Because God has an even higher claim on our loyalty than our families.... even if our families don't acknowledge him.

That higher claim on our loyalties can have some difficult consequences. It can cause real tension between family members when some are trying to follow the Way of Christ, and others are following the way of the world. Big family decisions can be fraught with tension.

Perhaps, for example, there's a debate over where to go on holiday? One side of the family fancies maxing-out the credit card with an expensive trip to the other side of the world. But, perhaps the Christian in that decision wants to question whether a cheaper holiday, closer to home, would be a better use of the resources God has given.

Perhaps, for example, there's division about how the whole family should spend Sunday together. The follower of Jesus feels drawn to church, to express their love and worship of God with other believers. But the other family members want to head to the beach, nice and early, to get a good spot.

Perhaps, for example, there's an argument about how much money to give to charity, or to the work of God's church. The follower of Jesus Way knows that extravagant generosity and charity are fundamental to the

Christian life and the nature of God. But other family members want to hold on to as much money as possible, if only to hand it on to the next generation.

Perhaps the tension is over what TV programmes to watch – violent, sexist, racist fare? Or something life-giving and spiritually awakening.

And so on. Time and again, families which are not working together towards a common spiritual goal find that these kinds of tensions arise. They are nothing new. Even Jesus' own mother, brother and sisters tried to pull him aside from the path he knew he was called to follow.

There is little comfort to offer about these situations. Jesus was utterly truthful, and utterly honest when he warned that following his Way comes with a heavy price. For Jesus himself, that price included persecution, torture and death. He asks us to follow his Way – offering only that peace which passes all understanding that comes from a life lived with God, rather than against God.

May God give you the strength to stand up for Jesus, and for his radical call to a Way of truth, justice, simplicity and charity. May you carry your cross, even when your family or neighbours tempt you to another path - an easier path, a path of least resistance. Pray for your families. Be strong in the Lord. Carry your cross. And hold out for the reward of heaven. Amen.

The Word of the Lord?

Tom Kennar's Sermon from Sunday 25 October 2020 –
The Last Sunday After Trinity

According to one survey, the Bible has sold more than 6 billion copies in more than 2,000 languages and dialects. Whatever the precise figure, the Bible is by far the bestselling book of all time.

On the other hand, the Bible is also the least read book in the world! Very few Bibles ever get opened. They are often given as gifts. But, unfortunately, they often remain as pristine as the day they are given.

Why is this? There's a number of reasons. Sometimes the translations of the Bible are just too difficult, too archaic for modern minds to grasp. Other people find that they do try to start reading the Bible. But they soon get lost in a sea of numbers and laws.

Others, having skipped the laws, find themselves in the Psalms, or in the Prophets...and there they quickly find their attention wandering. For such writings come to us from a very different mind-set and culture. And so, frustrated (and perhaps feeling a little guilty) people lay aside their Bible, and reach for a Catherine Cookson or Jeffrey Archer instead! We find that we have a whole generation of Christians, in churches all over the world, who have been told time and again to read their bibles...but who find that they just can't do it.

In my experience, if that's YOU, you will undoubtedly be a good Christian. You will be someone who tries to follow Jesus every day. You will be someone who worships your Creator, loves their neighbour, and who gives generously to the work of God. And yet, you will be carrying around this weight of guilt that you never actually open your Bible.

So, how am I to respond to this fact? How would you expect me to react? Perhaps I should pull myself up to my full height and call you all 'Sinners!'?

Hmm...I'm not sure that would help very much, would it? Because, actually, if you are one of those who finds the Bible difficult to read...I agree with you! The Bible is not a novel. It's not a newspaper. Some people have described the Bible as 'the Maker's Instructions'. But for many, it's the kind of instructions which come from the Far East, translated by someone who learned their English in primary school...like this bit of helpful instruction from a computer hard-drive I recently purchased: "More simple under USB interface, it only can do until the 3rd step and deleted is present channel". And let's be honest – that's how some of us hear the Bible. I know – I watch those eyes glazing over!

But the Bible is not an instruction manual. Neither is it a well-planned novel from a single writer, who sets out to tell a story. Instead, it is a collection of writings; 66 letters and books, assembled over a period of about 1,600 years. (The word Bible itself means 'library'). It contains legal codes, songs and poetry, prophecy, myths, history, stories and some pretty complex theology. Sometimes these different genres are separate. Sometimes they are all woven into just one of the books! (The gospels are a good example of this.)

So does all this mean that we don't need to bother with the hard work of reading the Bible? No. It doesn't. One of the things that the Protestant Reformation gave us, was access to the precious pages of Scripture for ourselves. With that access comes the chance to grow daily in our understanding of God. But unlike a Catherine Cookson or a Jeffrey Archer, reading the Bible is the work of a lifetime. Its beauty, and its huge complexity, takes a lifetime of learning to even begin to master.

But, the church Fathers of old were right about one thing. They knew that, unless properly understood, the Bible can be so easily mis-used and manipulated. That's why the quote "you shall not suffer a witch to live" was used so mercilessly throughout the Middle Ages. It's why the letter to Philemon was used for so long as a justification for slavery, and why the letters of St Paul are still used to silence women's voices in church leadership circles.

The underlying problem is that in some very loud quarters of the church, the Library of books, stories, myths, laws, poems and theology we have inherited has gained a status which it does not claim for itself [1].

Some of the loudest voices declare that the 'Library' is 'the Word of God'…as if God had personally written down his thoughts for us, as fully-formed instructions for us to slavishly follow.

---

[1] * *Theological discussion-point: some may be tempted to quote 2 Tim 3.16-17 ("All Scripture is God-breathed…") to dispute my statement. My opinion is that this oft-quoted phrase refers to the way God has inspired writers (like a mountain-view inspires a painter). It does not suggest that God himself dictated the Scriptures. It is also worth noting that chronologically, this text was written (most probably) BEFORE much of the New Testament - so it refers only to the Old Testament (Hebrew Bible) Scriptures.*

Well…I might be about to shock you now. I am happy to declare my view – that the Bible is NOT the Word of God. Rather, it is a collection of writings which point us towards the actual Word of God – the Logos of God – which is Jesus Christ. That's why, in our services, after a reading from the Bible, we say 'For the Word of the Lord' – rather than 'This is the Word of the Lord' – as most churches still do.

That's a subtle distinction – and some of you may not have picked it up. But by saying 'For the Word of the Lord', we give thanks for those parts of the Scriptures which DO point us to the reality and the truth of God. But we also give ourselves permission to understand that some of the Scriptures we have inherited simply do not contain such truth. Rather, they are an echo and a reflection of a time when our spiritual ancestors were reaching out of their stone-age ignorance - towards the very idea of a Divine Being at the heart of all things.

Along the way, they made some terrible mistakes – which we can read about in the Scriptures. They murdered, raped and pillaged in the name of their God, led on by leaders who told them that such was God's will and instruction. They conquered the land of other tribes. They kept slaves and subjugated women. They allowed religious ideas to be SO sacrosanct that even children could be stoned at the city gates for blasphemy. They were contemptuous of foreigners, and miserly towards the poor. None of these things are the Word of the Lord – they are only a record of humanity's faltering quest for him – the actual Word of God.

For it is in Jesus Christ that the Scriptures find their target, and their fulfilment. In the life and teaching of that one perfect human-being, we find the inspiration and the focus of the whole Library we call The Bible. He is both the author and the perfector of our faith – the first and the last. He inspired the writers of the Bible to seek for him through its pages, like a mountainside inspires a painter. And through his teachings, his life, his death and his ongoing inspiration – he leads us ever onwards to the sun-lit uplands of our Faith. Amen.

A truth worth dying for?

Sermon of Bishop John Hind on Thursday 29th October—'Thursday after the Last Sunday after Trinity'

In the south transept of Southwark Cathedral there is a memorial to a man who lived from 1475 to 1556. Those were tumultuous years for England and its church. In 1535 the Bishop of Rochester, John Fisher and Thomas More, the Lord Chancellor, were beheaded. Twenty years later Hugh Latimer and Nicholas Ridley, former bishops of Worcester and London respectively, were burnt at the stake to be followed in 1556 by Thomas Cranmer, previously Archbishop of Canterbury

Perhaps before we feel too sorry for all these martyrs we might just remember that More and Latimer at least had themselves played prominent parts in the condemnation and execution of a number of those they considered heretics.

Many terrible things were done by the disciples of Jesus Christ to other disciples of Jesus Christ, and in both cases persecutors and victims alike thought they were doing God's will. There followed a bloody century in which there were more Christian martyrs in England than ever before or since.

Given this history, it is perhaps not surprising that so many people by and large reckon Christianity scarcely worth the candle if its adherents could do such things. The other side of this is that they simply can't believe that any faith could so grip people as to enable them to endure such things. But Fisher, More, Latimer, Ridley and Cranmer would have understood each other far better than any of them would have understood the exceptional irreligiosity of England today, Catholic or Protestant.

What drove those Reformation martyrs, what has driven all the martyrs throughout the ages, was the conviction that the truths of faith are truths, and that they are worth dying for. That is one of the reasons why we find the past so inaccessible and indeed not only the past, but also the greater part of the world today.

The question really is, is there anything that matters so much to us that we would be willing to die for it?

Now the point of my mentioning the memorial in Southwark Cathedral lies in the final words of the epitaph. Bear in mind those dates: 1475 – 1556. The text concludes, "He lived and died an honest man". We know little of the details of his life, or how he comported himself in the midst of the political and religious turmoil of those tyrannical times. We do not know whether he found a careful way of negotiating without sacrifice of principle or whether he just kept his head down. We do however get a sense of integrity and straightforwardness – and that he survived with those virtues intact! That's no mean tribute.

To maintain integrity and straightforwardness is always a challenge and very particularly in times of crisis like the present pandemic. Different difficulties from those of the sixteenth century, but the challenge no less.

I'm prompted to say this today because yesterday was the feast of two of the early martyrs of the Church, Simon and Jude. We don't know much about either of them, although Simon's nickname "the zealot" gives us a clue. This doesn't mean that he was enthusiastic but rather that he had belonged to a particular group of contemporary terrorists determined to overthrow the Roman occupation by force. His conversion transformed his zeal from violence into faithful discipleship. The very passion which had previously made him so angry became the source of the bravery that led him to martyrdom.

Like the figure in the Southwark memorial, Simon and Jude are honoured for their steadfastness, their honesty in the midst of turbulent times. Unlike him, they paid for their honesty with their lives.

Honesty and zealotry have their dangers, but indifferentism may in the long run be an even greater danger. No one should doubt the capacity of religion, gone wrong, to do great harm. But equally, no one should doubt its capacity to motivate to the greatest deeds of love and sacrifice, the most fearless intellectual enquiry and the most beautiful and uplifting art. The knack for human life lies in the constant struggle to distinguish the two. Amen.

All Saints

Tom Kennar's Sermon from 1 November 2020—All Saints Day

Those of you who have suffered my sermons for a few years will know that I always look forward to All Saint's Day. It gives me an opportunity to rehearse my list of funny and quirky saints – most of which I have culled from a book by the priest and broadcaster, Richard Coles, called 'Lives of the Improbable Saints'.

For example, have you ever heard of St Ronald of Buckingham? Apparently, he was born into the world like any normal baby, and immediately preached an amazing sermon.... before promptly dying. Then here's St Theophilus the Myrrh-Gusher. It's a great name isn't it? It refers to the belief that the bodies of certain martyred saints secrete a sweet smelling liquid from their wounds. Apparently, St Theophilus' body did just that, in copious amounts!

Then there's St Isodore, who in the 1980s was designated the patron saint of the Internet – because he was a scholar and compiler of information. I like to imagine the scene in Heaven when God told Isodore that the Church has just designated him as the patron of the internet? "I'm the Patron Saint of WHAT?!"

And then there's the number one weird saint of all time...the Patron Saint of finding a parking place – Saint Mother Cabrini. Apparently, in New York, car drivers circling a block can be heard muttering this prayer: "Mother Cabrini, Mother Cabrini – find me a space for my driving machiny."

All these Saints are jolly good fun, but there is more than grain of truth in many of them. Sometimes, saints become patron saints because of the terrible things they were made to suffer for their faith in Christ. So, for example, St Apollonia is the patron saint of Dentists, because she had all her teeth extracted as a punishment for believing in Jesus. And let's not forget our own St Faith... roasted alive on a griddle-iron, for refusing to give up her Lord. I could tell you a lot more horror stories...but it's a bit early in the morning for that!

So, All Saints is a good time to be reminded of extraordinary lives of the Saints who now 'from their labours rest' - as we shall sing at the end of our service today. But are there saints among us now?

The Bible refers to all true believers as 'saints'. So the answer to my question must be 'yes…there are saints among us today'. There are, and must be, those who in the words of John's first letter which we heard just now, are 'children of God'. They are those who yearn and hope for the final revelation of Christ, so that they can become more and more like him. They are those who constantly seek to purify themselves, because Christ is pure.

Or, if you prefer, from Jesus' lips in the Sermon on the Mount, the saints – the blessed ones - are those who hunger and thirst for righteousness. They are the poor in spirit, the meek, the merciful, the peacemakers, the pure in heart.

But is that me? Is that you?

Our brothers and sisters in the Orthodox church have an insight to offer. They teach that all Christians have the potential to become so like Christ that they can become kinds of gods themselves. Orthodox theology calls that process 'deification' – and it's a goal for which all of us are encouraged to strive.

But what does it look like, in practice? Much has been made recently of the sainthood of the medical profession, tirelessly exerting themselves on behalf of the COVID-suffering population. Other saints have been recognised by awards and honours – like Captain Sir Tom Moore, and Marcus Rashford MBE. And locally, our own wonderful Sandra Haggan, recently recognised by the Spring's awards programme. Hmm…St Sandra. I like that!

But are saints measured by what they do? Yes, of course…to an extent. The true nature of our heart is often demonstrated by our actions. But what about those who cannot do anything? Is it possible to be a saint who is tied by illness to the hospital bed, or trapped at home by being shielded from COVID? Well, I want to say 'yes' to them too. Being a living saint is not just about what we do. It's about who we are. To be a saint is to become more and more like God. But how?

Well, here's a way of thinking about an answer to that question. There's been a thought winging its way around social media recently. It's one of those 'feel good' sayings that we all encounter from time to time, which gets lots of people clicking 'Like'. This particular one goes something like…

"I don't care if you are black or white, gay or straight, rich or poor. If you are good to me, I'll be good to you". On the face of it, it's a nice thing to have said – essentially 'all that matters is how we treat each other'.

But it's not a particularly Christian thing to have said. Being nice is not an exclusively Christian virtue. Jesus calls his followers beyond human nice-ness. He calls us to extraordinary love, in the pursuit of holiness. If Jesus had written that 'meme', he might have added – "It doesn't even matter how you treat me. Even when you insult me, or beat me, or kill me...I will still love you".

Christian love is the kind that says 'Father forgive them', even when 'they' are nailing you to a cross. Christian love is unconditional – like the love of Jesus, who we strive to be like. It is a love which does not stop even when, like St Faith, we are being tied to a roasting griddle iron. Or as Christians in Nice encountered this week, being knifed by a religious extremist. It's a love which sees beyond the poor behaviour and poor choices of failing human beings, and which begins to see all humanity as God sees us – children – who often fall down, and constantly need picking up and hugging from time to time.

Now of course, I realise what a challenge it would be to continue to offer love to a knife-wielding madman, or an abuser of children, or a corrupt politician. Simple common sense says that, of course, society needs protecting from this kind of behaviour. But hate is never the right response. Hate only produces more hate. The ONLY possible remedy against hate, is love. It won't always work – but it's the only path worth even trying. And it's the path of Jesus. It's the path of holiness. It's the path of saint-hood.

Of course, that kind of holiness is beyond human norms. It's super-human, in fact. It's not something I would find easy to do, on my own. But, with God's help, and by God's grace, maybe I could love someone that much. Maybe I too could be considered a saint. Hmm...St Thomas of Havant....has a bit of ring to it….

And if we are open to it, we can all take up the challenge to become Holy ones, deified ones, Saints, ourselves.

Anxiety, Panic and Fretting

Sermon of Tom Kennar Kennar on Thursday 5th November

So…another Lockdown eh? I don't know about you, but I confess to a certain level of rising anxiety this week. I'm find myself anxious about a lot of things. There's the Lockdown, of course…I'm anxious about the number of rising infections. Will I fall victim to this virus? Will my family? Or any of my parishioners and friends? This week, I've been especially anxious about doing the right thing for our Remembrance Sunday commemorations. And I've been anxious about how we can continue to pay our parish bills, with all our ways of making money closing down again.

But I'm anxious about other things too. Like the state of world politics, especially in the United States right now (as we wait for the results of the presidential election). But our own British politics gives enough cause for anxiety, don't they? We are only weeks away from the end of the Brexit transition period. What's going to happen?

Today is, of course, November the 5th. So that adds a new layer of anxiety – especially for those of us who have pets or very small children. We want to protect them from the stupidity of letting off fireworks – usually by people who have no idea who Guy Fawkes was!

Anxiety is, of course, a normal human reaction to the changing circumstances of life. It's part of our natural protection mechanism. We cast around for threats to our security, or comfort. We are on our guard…and that makes us anxious. We become more alert…less likely to sleep…and therefore more anxious.

In our first reading, St Paul describes the kind of anxiety that he has lived with, all his adult life. There's an almost Trumpian level of boasting on display as he talks about all the ways that he tried to work himself up into being acceptable to God. He was 'circumcised on the eighth day, a member of the people of Israel, a Hebrew born of Hebrews a Pharisee, a persecutor of the church; righteous under the law and blameless. (You can just hear Donald Trump at this end of that list can't you? 'No-one has ever been more righteous-er than me!').

There's a lot of anxiety on display in today's Gospel reading, too. First, there's the anxiety of the Pharisees and scribes. They were anxious about this new charismatic preacher in their midst, who appeared to be leading people away from their way of doing religion. They were anxious about losing their authority – losing their power base.

And then, in Jesus' parables about the lost sheep and the lost coin, his main characters display anxiety too. The shepherd is anxious about his lost sheep – so much so that he leaves all his others, to go in search of the one who was lost. The woman who has lost a silver coin is anxious. How will she feed her family, or have dignity in her old age, when she has lost her coin?

Both the shepherd and the woman are offered to us as pictures of God. Now, we need to be careful about making God in our image – but there is a sense in which Jesus sees God as being anxious about the spiritual fate of his children. The Scriptures in general give us a picture of a God whose whole being is anxiously focussed on the salvation of humanity. He seems anxious to communicate his wisdom for living, sending prophet after prophet to teach us his ways. When that stratagem fails, he sends his son – his very self in human form – to teach us from his own mouth, and then to die in order to show us the way to life.

And ultimately, it's God's sheer passion – anxiety if you will – for his children which saves us. Paul ultimately discovers that all anxiety about faith, all his chasing after righteousness was 'rubbish' compared to the experience of finding out that God loves us, anyway. We have no need to try and earn God's favour – because he is already favourable towards us. He loves us…enough to have come to live among us, and die among us. For, what greater love is there than this…that a man should lay down his life for his friends? This is the kind of God who will search out the lost sheep, or the valuable lost coin. This is the kind of Father who stretches out his hands to his children and says 'Come unto me, all ye who travail and are heavy laden…even in a pandemic, even when the politics of the world are in chaos, even when the climate is catastrophically changing…and I will give you rest.

So, to my own present anxiety, and to yours, I say this: let us use the coming days to rest in the Lord. Let's stop chasing after the things of creation which we think will make us happy, and look to the source of all creation instead. Let's take time to rest in the loving gaze of our heavenly father, to contemplate his teachings, and receive the power of his love.

Remembrance

Tom Kennar's Sermon from 8 November 2020

It is our enormous privilege, here at St Faith's, to host Havant Borough Council's Civic Service of Remembrance each year. And that's because outside these walls we also have the privilege of hosting the Havant War Memorial – built by public subscription in 1922. This year, the pandemic has caused us to radically change our approach – but we look forward to gathering again, next year, with thousands of our neighbours, to commemorate the Fallen.

It would be inappropriate to say that I enjoy this service, each year. How can one enjoy the necessity of remembering all those who have given their lives for us? But I do confess to gaining a certain satisfaction from our annual gathering.

Why? Because this is one time in the year when we lay aside our politics, our arguments about the Havant Regeneration Plan, or Brexit, or the handling of the Pandemic, or any number of other contentious issues – and we come together, as a community, to say 'thank you' to the Fallen.

It is a strange irony that War, and its effects, has a way of bringing communities together. We stand united against a common foe. Or we stand united in grief and commemoration. There's something about war – its scale, its sheer horror – which causes us to lay aside our petty differences, our political, theological and philosophical struggles – and to come together. It is sometimes only during war that the very worst – and the very best – of humanity gets seen.

We all know about the very worst, of course. The awful machines of war – the tanks, and the machine guns which can mow down a whole platoon in seconds. But the best of humanity can also be seen. Human ingenuity. The coming together of communities like the East End of London during the Blitz. Great art, poetry and music. Leaps in medical and scientific knowledge. The common endeavour of capitalists and socialists, monarchists and republicans, black and white, Christian, Muslim, Hindu and Sikh (for all of them fought with the Allies in the Great War). And, perhaps above all, the best of humanity is shown by the willingness of human beings to lay down their lives for their families and communities.

When you think about it, that's an extraordinary thing to do. In what other circumstance would you, or me, be prepared to give up our life for another? Let's say, for example, that you learned today of a neighbour who was dying of a serious heart condition. But then you learn that this neighbour's life could be saved, if you (or me) were willing to give them our own heart – but only by dying first. Which of us would be willing? Who would raise their hand and say 'take my heart!'?

War, then, is the ultimate canvass on which to paint the very worst and very best of humanity. It is perhaps why war is so deeply embedded in the human condition, and reflected throughout all the great religious scriptures of the world. Our wars reflect the cosmic battle between good and evil. The battle between light and dark, fought out all around us in space. The battle between growth and decay – between the gravity that binds, and the entropy which destroys. The battle, if you will, between God and the Devil.

For Christians, this battle was supremely fought in the sacrificial death of Jesus Christ. He demonstrated that greatest trait of humanity – the willingness to lay one's life down for one's friends. Jesus volunteered for the suicide mission of the Cross. He knew what the result of going to Jerusalem would be. He warned his followers, in advance, that he would be taken down by the elite political powers of the day. And yet, he stepped forward. He allowed the very worst that human beings can do to each other to overwhelm him…and then, and then, the power of his sacrifice overcame all that death and suffering. By rising from the dead, he demonstrated that the very best instincts of humanity CAN overcome the very worst.

Jesus announced the coming of a new kind of world – or as he called it, a new kind of 'Kingdom'. It was a world in which the greatest traits of humanity would not just be shown in the crucible of War – but in everyday life. He called his followers to lives of sacrifice for others…not just on the battle-field any longer, but in everyday living. He called his followers to be prepared to pour out their lives for others, just as he had done.

And what was the result? The flowering of the best of humanity, flowing from the heart of God. The Christian church – like all the great religions, became the home of charity. Great universities of learning, advances in medical science, superlative art – music, poetry, drama. And the very principle of giving, sacrificially to others – all these flowed from the example of Jesus.

Of course, it was not always rosy. The cosmic battle between good and evil was fought, and continues to be fought, in the crucible of the church as much as in the rest of the world. Powerful men gained control of the levers of power, and corrupted the teachings of the Founder. Power was mis-used to dominate, to fight, to tear down – to even burn each other at the stake. Because that's what we human beings do. We relish the battle. War is found at our core. Religion became not the anti-dote to war, but sometimes the cause of it.

Does that mean that we should have nothing to do with religion, anymore? Of course not. We do not judge a religion by the stupidity of its followers. We judge it by the teachings of its Founder. And in the case of Christianity, the Founder said this:

"Love God, and love your neighbour as yourself"

And

"No-man has greater love than to lay down his life for his friends"

And

"The Kingdom of heaven is among you"

So, today we give thanks for the sacrifices of the past, sometimes compelled by conscription and fears but often offered willingly. And we find that we too are called to demonstrate the very best traits of humanity. We too are called to lives of sacrifice for others. We too are called to be prepared to lay down our preferences, our prejudices, our wealth, our abilities and, yes, even our lives in the service of all humanity.

For that is the example set for us by the Fallen, and the call of the God who sacrificed everything for us.

On the road to freedom for ALL God's children

Sermon of Tom Kennar on Thursday 12th November

It is a sobering fact that the Bible appears to support the idea of slavery. In the letter to Philemon, which we've just heard, Paul begs his brother (that is Philemon) to accept back into his service one Onesimus, a slave. Presumably, Onesimus had run away from Philemon, and then found himself serving Paul, during his imprisonment. Along the way, Onesimus had become a Christian – and Paul appeals to Philemon: 'Please take back Onesimus, not just as a slave, but as a Christian brother.'

This is rather shocking to us. Paul does not appear to condemn the idea of slavery itself. Instead he simply asserts that, because he is a Christian, Onesimus is more than a slave. The issue of his slavery is not at question. At all.

This passage was one of the key reasons why it took so many years for the British Empire to abolish slavery. After all, if slavery appears to be perfectly acceptable in the Bible, why should slave owners feel any guilt about it? (Or so the slave owners argued). It took years and years of patient exposition, mainly by the likes of William Wilberforce and the Clapham Sect, to persuade the British Parliament and people that there were higher biblical principles at play. They reminded them that slavery was simply considered 'normal' in Biblical times. No-one questioned it – even the slaves, mainly, accepted it. It was just the way things were. But Jesus brought about a transformation in the way that human beings began to think of themselves, especially in relation to one another. He invited us to see ourselves as sisters and brother of the same heavenly Father. And, later on, Paul himself would write that we are all equal before God. "There is neither Jew nor Greek, slave nor free, male nor female, for you are all one in Christ Jesus." (Gal.3.28)

The letter to Philemon then, arises at a time when such thinking was only beginning to percolate. The Good News of Jesus for all humankind was only just beginning to take root. The Holy Spirit was only just beginning to nudge humanity towards the Kingdom. And writings like the letter to Philemon are a snap-shot in that process.... they are like a still-frame photo of an opening flower. Half open, but not yet fully revealed.

And that's the danger of using any Scripture to justify any kind of hatred or antagonism towards others. Scripture only ever offers us a snapshot in time. It is a snapshot of what people OF that time thought about God. In the Hebrew Bible, that includes snapshots of a time when people thought that God wanted the Hebrews to forcibly possess the lands of other tribes. It's a time when they thought that God wanted parents to stone their own children for blasphemy at the city gates. It's a time when the people thought that the world was made in six days, and that God insisted that no-one should wear cloth made from two different types of fabric! (Bad news for anyone wearing a poly-cotton shirt today!). It's from a time when people thought that God could be contained in a Temple, or that he lived on top of a mountain.

The New Testament is also a product of its time. It's from a time when slavery was considered the normal way to structure a society. It's from a time when Paul could say that he would never permit a woman to speak in church…and get away with it! It's from a time when a woman was commanded to obey her husband, rather than form a partnership of equals. It's from a time when non-binary relationships were still considered a sin, and not an inevitable consequence of a gloriously diverse creation.

But since those days, as we move inexorably towards the end of all things, and the coming of the Son of Man, the Holy Spirit has continued His work among God's people. Slavery has been abolished – in every legal sense (although it still exists, illegally, tragically, underground). The status of women as priests and bishops, writers, artists and business people has been made legally equal to men – at least in most of the Reformed Churches and Western nations. And now, the last of the great taboos – the appalling treatment of Lesbian, Gay, Bi-sexual, Transgender and other non-binary people – is at last rising to the top of the heap.

Which is why I delight in the fact that this week, the Church of England has launched an exciting new initiative, to listen again – with even more attentiveness – to the experience of people who experience their bodies in ways that are different to the majority. The Bible teaches us – right throughout its pages that we are on a trajectory of change…leading towards a future, glorious day, when EVERY knee will bow at the throne of the God of Love. The Holy Spirit has led us, along the way, to work hard to rid ourselves of slavery, of racism, of sexism, and paternalism. My prayer is that in the coming months and years, we will also say goodbye to homophobia….and embrace the truer, deeper reality that we are ALL made in the image of God. Amen.

Talents and Abilities

Tom Kennar's Sermon from 15 November 2020

Text: Matthew 25.14-30.

I'm sure that most of us who have heard a sermon on this passage will immediately associate it with money – and especially with giving money to the church! But I already do quite enough begging for God's mission in Havant! So I'd like to broaden things out a bit.

As many of you will know, I teach that context is everything. We need to understand the context of the original speaker of any words, the context of the person who wrote them down, and our own context as hearers. Context, context, context – the three C's.

For the first of these (the context of the speaker) let see where this passage figures in Jesus' story. The Parable of the Talents is part of a long sermon from Jesus about the end of the world. From the beginning of chapter 24, Jesus does these things:

- he foretells the destruction of the Temple,
- he describes the signs that will be seen at the 'end of the age',
- he predicts the persecutions of the Christians,
- he foretells the coming of false messiahs and prophets
- he describes the 'coming of the Son of Man'

And then he tells a number of parables to illustrate and underline the kind of behaviour that he expects from his followers while we await the end of all things.

- He uses the illustration of a fig tree whose tender leaves foretell the coming of summer to encourage us to be watchful.
- Then Jesus talks about the kind of lives that he expects his followers to live, while awaiting the end of the age. They are to be those whom the Master finds 'at work' when he arrives - not eating and drinking with drunkards, but 'at work' about their Master's business.
- Then comes the story of the Ten Bridesmaids, that we heard last week - another encouragement to be prepared and watchful for the coming of the Lord.
- Then - at the end of all that! - comes today's story of the parable of the Talents, which we'll deal with in a moment.
- Finally, the whole section concludes with Jesus famous story of the end of time, when the sheep will be separated from the Goats – when those who fed the hungry, welcomed the stranger, and who

visited the sick will be separated for all eternity from those who did not.

Can you see the context in which the Parable of the Talents sits? The narrative force of the whole section is one of pointing us to the end of days, the end of the age, the Second Coming of the Messiah. And this is where the second context comes in – the context of the writer, or the recorder of a person's word. Matthew seems convinced that the end of the world was going to happen very soon. He even records Jesus saying that the end of the world will take place while some of his followers are still alive. (Which is an interesting theological conundrum that we'll leave for another day!).

According to Matthew's understanding – Matthew's context – Jesus is coming again! Let me say that one more time...Jesus is coming again! It's something we declare in the 'mystery of faith' during every Communion service...'Christ has died, Christ is risen, Christ will come again'. It is a central tenant of our faith that we believe the Kingdom of God to be both among us now, but also yet to come in all its fullness. That, of course, is a subject for a whole sermon of its own. So we won't dwell there for now.

The point is that while we wait for the Master, according to the parables, we are to be busy about our Father's business. And that, finally, is OUR context. Whatever skills and abilities we have, whatever wealth we have been given in financial terms or in terms of abilities, Jesus the Master expects us to use them in his service. We are not to bury them. We are to grab every opportunity to use the gifts we have been given for the work of the Master.

What does this mean in practical terms? Let me quote theologian, Fred Craddock. He says this…

"Most of us will not this week christen a ship, write a book, end a war, appoint a cabinet, dine with a queen, convert a nation, or be burned at the stake. More likely the week will present no more than a chance to give a cup of water, write a note, visit a nursing home...teach a Sunday School class, share a meal, tell a child a story, go to choir practice and feed the neighbour's cat. "Whoever is faithful in a very little is faithful also in much." (Fred B, Craddock, Luke, Interpretation (Louisville: Westminster/John Knox, 1990. 193))

So, I want to encourage each of you to spend some time this week thinking about that very question. Go into a quiet place, and let your mind wander free through God's mission field. Is there a homeless person who needs your care? Is there a friend or family member who would be SO uplifted to receive a call from you? Is there a function within the family of the church that you could carry out...but which you have ignored for a while? Is there some money you could give to alleviate the suffering of another human being, or expand God's mission in Havant?

And let me finally, ask you to ask that question with the kind of urgency that Matthew wants his readers to hear. What will the Master say to you when he comes? Will you be one of his 'wicked and lazy slaves'? Or will he call you his 'good and faithful servant' and cry 'well done! Enter into the joy of your Master!'?

St Hilda and the Battle for Unity

Sermon of Tom Kennar on Thursday 19th November

Hilda is a name we don't encounter very often these days. In fact, I only know one Hilda within my entire circle of friends and church members. Few of us who are older than 50 can hear the name without remembering the infamous Hilda Ogden, of Coronation Street – a strong, forceful character, with a piercing voice, who made the life of her poor husband Stanley rather complicated!

But, in fact, the name Hilde has a long and proud history in the British Isles. Originally it was a Viking name, and it meant 'battle'. Not a bad name for the fictional Hilda Ogden – who picked plenty of fights with Stan and her neighbours! But perhaps it's an even better name for the saint whose memory we honour today – St Hilda of Whitby.

Hilda was a relative of the King of Northumbria, who established a monastic community somewhere near Whitby. She was much loved by her community, and highly venerated in her life-time as a wise and compassionate leader. As such she battled against rural poverty and ignorance, and battled to establish her community of love and learning. She is known as a patron of the arts, because – in particular – she fostered the music of a sheep-herder called Caedmon.

But she is perhaps most famous for playing a large part in an important gathering of the early British Church, which took place in the year 664...known as the Synod of Whitby. At the time, the Church had already been well-established in the British Isles – since at least the first century after Christ. In fact, medieval scholars asserted that the first Bishop of Britain was a man called Aristobulus – who was believed to have been one of the 70 disciples, sent out two-by-two by Jesus himself. Since those early days, the church had flourished, all across the British Isles. The names of great Saints like David, Patrick, Aden, Alban and Cuthbert come down to us from those years. But, being somewhat distant from Rome, and especially after the fall of the Roman Empire, British Christianity had developed as a somewhat distinct version of Christianity, with many of its own local traditions.

But in the year 597, Pope Gregory sent Augustine, from Rome, with a brief to evangelise first the Anglo-Saxon tribes of Kent (who were said to be a pretty Godless lot, apparently). Then, once established at Canterbury, Augustine set off to bring the rest of British Christianity fully under the authority of the Roman church. Many British Christians were not too happy about this. We Brits don't take kindly to attempts to rule us from other European cities! Great debates ensued, about the supremacy of Rome as the seat of St Peter, on whom Jesus had said he would build his church. One particular focus for this debate was on how to calculate the date of Easter. Different parts of the British Isles celebrated Easter on different days – depending on what calculation they used. That meant that some Dioceses in Britain were cheerfully proclaiming Easter, while others were still in the solemnity of Lent. The Kingdom of Northumbria, and especially the Episcopal See of Lindisfarne, was one such place.

So, the Synod of Whitby was called, by the King of Northumbria – King Oswiu. After much debate, it was agreed that Northumbria would fall into line with the practices of the Roman Church. In reality, the Synod of Whitby was just one of many such gatherings at that time, and part of a process of harmonising the British Church with the historical Mother Church of Rome. But, some revisionist historians like to point to the Whitby Synod as a pivotal moment when a native, Celtic church came 'under the heel' of its more powerful Roman neighbour. The truth is rather more complicated – as the truth so often is. But those who fear the exercise of power over the British Isles from foreign capitals often point to the Synod of Whitby as a kind of 're-enslavement' to Europe, like the earlier enslavement under the Emperor Tiberius…an enslavement which was only undone by Henry the Eighth, nearly 900 years later.

St Hilda played an important part in the Synod. And it was perhaps her greatest battle. As a senior leader in the Northumbrian church, she spent much of the following years persuading and cajoling those around her to accept their place within a worldwide, or 'catholic', church. In that sense, Hilda's battle was for unity. She longed for the body of Christ to be one – clearly and powerfully speaking with one voice, and being prepared to give up some individualistic practices and traditions for the sake of the greater good. It was her defence of the Roman Church's right to rule, while still being proudly a British Christian, which means that she is venerated as much today in the Catholic church as she is in the churches of the Islands of Britain.

St Hilda then, stands as a focus of Unity – for the worldwide church, as well as for political unity (remembering that the church of her time was much more than a purely religious authority). That makes her a challenging saint for us Brits to contemplate (and indeed venerate) – especially while we anticipate Britain's present attempt to free itself, once again, from the perceived shackles of another European super-power.

On Sunday we will celebrate the Feast of Christ the King, when we will ponder what it might mean for the whole of creation to come under the Lordship of Christ. In the meantime, the battle for Unity of St Hilda of Whitby might offer us some food for thought.

Christ the King – and a bit of 'woolly' thinking!

Tom Kennar's Sermon from 22 November 2020

Text: Matthew 25: 31 - 46 - The Sheep and the Goats

As you know, today is the Feast of Christ the King – the Sunday before Advent. Its put here, on the last Sunday of the church's year, to remind us to keep our eyes fixed on the end of the story, even us as prepare to contemplate its beginning at Christmas. The humble babe of Bethlehem was destined to be the King of Kings, and the Lord of Lords…Christ the King. To help us picture that ultimate destiny, Matthew gives us today's story, of the separation of the sheep and the goats.

When I say the word "sheep" to you – I daresay that you have a vision in your mind of something round and fluffy, with a big thick woolly jumper. On the other hand, the word "goat" brings to mind something bigger, stronger, with a rough wiry coat, and big horns. It is quite possible that was not the image that Jesus had in mind.

Something I've learned through my trips to Africa in recent years is that primitive breeds of sheep and goats are remarkably similar. Woolly, English sheep, and strong wiry goats are the result of selective breeding over many centuries. But in hotter countries, where thick wool would be a distinct encumbrance, there is only one way to tell the difference between a sheep and goat in a hurry… namely that sheep's tails point downwards, and goat's tails points up.

The story of the Sheep and the Goats comes at the end of a long section of Matthew's gospel, when Jesus has been talking about the End of All Things. It all starts back in Matthew 24, when his disciples say to him "Tell us...what will be the sign of your coming and of the end of the age?"

So this parable, which is part of Jesus' response to their question, could easily start with the words "At the end of the age"...or, as we might say, "at the end of the day". At the end of the day, this parable teaches us, there are only two kinds of people. They are pretty similar, these people - it's hard to tell them apart, in fact. They all lead fairly normal lives, they marry, have children, go to work, watch Eastenders. But there is a difference. And the difference is found in the way that they relate to other people.

All the people of the world, the sheep and the goats, are surrounded by others in need. At the end of the day, the difference between the lost and the saved is indicated not by the way they look, but by the way they behave. The difference is seen in the way they respond to the hungry, homeless, thirsty, naked, sick and imprisoned. Jesus is saying "if you want to know who will be saved, look at the quality of a person's life...at the decisions they make about others in need".

That is the heart of the story of the sheep and the goats. At the "end of the age", at the "end of the day", how I have lived towards other people will show whether or not I have attained the salvation of my soul. Or to quote Jesus, earlier in Matthew's account, "By their fruit shall ye know them".

But of course, it's not as simple as that. How I have lived towards others is only an indicator. It is the outward sign of what's going on inside of me. Every human being is capable of being generous, from time to time. Adolf Hitler was famous among his friends for the gifts he gave them.

I wonder how many of us have supported Children in Need this year? Good for you, if you did. Nothing wrong with that, at all. But woe to you, if that is all you have done for others this year! I feel nothing but sorrow for those who can only respond to the plight of others when it is put in front of them in graphic detail on the television. My friends, such people are goats. They are the ones who look like sheep, but whose obedience to the radical call of the Gospel is only skin deep.

Becoming a sheep –a true believer, a true Christ-ian, takes a complete transformation of our inner being...or what the Bible calls being 'born again'. Crucially, it takes a daily commitment to the abandonment of 'self'. Earlier in Matthew's gospel, specifically Chapter 16, Jesus says this...listen to him:

"I anyone would come after me, he must deny himself and take up his cross and follow me. For whoever wants to save his life, will lose it, but whoever loses his life for me will find it. What good will it be for a man if he gains the whole world, yet forfeits his soul?"

Salvation, or being 'born again', is not achieved at a moment in time...just by saying a prayer. It is the work of a lifetime, to keep on carrying our cross. When Jesus died on the cross, he gave up his rights to everything, even the robe that he wore, and the life that he had. But even while he was hanging there, he found time to forgive his executioners, make provision for his mother, and give a comforting word to a thief.

When Jesus calls us to 'take up our cross', he means that for us to find salvation, we need to embrace that kind of radical giving. And then, when the moment of testing comes (as it did for Jesus) the way we find ourselves behaving will be the best indicator of the kind of person we are. And of whether our tail points up or down.

The Whore of Babylon

Sermon of Tom Kennar on Thursday 26th November
Texts: Revelation 18 and Luke 21.20–28

In case you didn't know, we are in the dying days of the Church's liturgical year. The new year begins for us on Sunday, with the first Sunday of Advent. In the midst of winter darkness, we seek shelter, warmth and light. With our ancestors of faith, we await the promise of a coming Messiah, who will save us and lead us beyond the darkness.

But in these dying days, the Lectionary does not let us rest in peaceful slumber. After the glorious vision of Christ the King which we shared on Sunday, we now find ourselves confronted with apocalyptic visions. In Revelation, today, we meet the 'Great Whore of Babylon', and witness the promise that her reign over the earth will one day end.

And then in the Gospel reading, we read Jesus' dire predictions of the destruction of Jerusalem – which actually did take place, about 40 years later. These visions are reminders to us that although Christ reigns today in heaven, 'on the right hand of the Father', his work of fully establishing God's kingdom on earth is not yet done. There is still much struggle ahead.

'Babylon' is a very particular biblical metaphor. Based on the idea of the city which carried off Jewish leaders into Exile, 500 years or so before Jesus, the Babylon of the book of Revelation is generally thought to represent the city (and the political and economic structures) of Rome. When John prophecies the overthrow of Babylon, he predicts the Fall of Rome. Later scholars have suggested that Babylon represents any economic or religious structure which runs counter to the principles of the Gospel. Throughout history, Babylon has been associated with Jerusalem itself, the Roman Catholic Church, and these days, even the cites of Washington DC, Brussels, Strasbourg and London!

Too many religious leaders – especially among the Christian churches – have tried to read the book of Revelation as if it were a coded message to the 20th or 21st centuries. "Look!" they will say, "the downfall of the whore of Babylon is a description of the American war against Iraq (which is modern-day Babylon)". Then, they will make a leap of prediction, and claim that this means Jesus is coming soon…any day now. Unfortunately, the messy history of church claims about the imminent return of Jesus suggest that they are probably wrong.

But as with all biblical prophecy, we must be cautious of trying to fit our context into the context of the biblical writers. We need to hear the hope, and the fear that they were expressing about their own time and their own world – and then consider what parallels there are for us today. For there are indeed many parallels between our world and the world of the Bible.

The kinds of signs which commonly accompany 'end times' prophecies are exactly the sort of things we see and hear around us today. Wars and rumours of wars. Famines and earthquakes. And plagues. No biblical writer ever heard of COVID-19...but after the 'hell on earth' of 2020, we know all about plagues!

War. Famine. Earthquakes and sickness. These are the Big Four – the things which have the most potential to disrupt our comfortable existences. These are the four major events that human beings feel most powerless about, on an individual level. But it is our very impotence in the face of such existential threats which offer the chance for God to break through. Confronted by the reality of war, many people will seek peace. Confronted by the reality of famine and earthquakes, many people will respond with charity. Confronted by a plague, even politicians may come together in common purpose, and find the resources to help scientists find a vaccine.

You see, this is what God does. He enters into the darkest corners of human existence, and by his presence he redeems us. His spirit whispers 'Make peace' to the Generals who could unleash hell. His spirit whispers 'share your wealth' to the rich nations, when famine or natural disaster strikes the poor. His spirit whispers 'come together, co-operate' when pandemic plagues threaten the world.

The most graphic example of Jesus turning darkness to light is perhaps the work of the Cross, transformed into Resurrection. But that's just the most graphic example. For this work – of turning darkness into light, despair into hope, sickness into healing, war into peace…this is the work of Jesus, every day. In this sense, Christ the King is truly on his throne – proclaiming through the Spirit of Truth the Laws of the Kingdom to all his subjects. "Seek peace, give love, co-operate together and bind up the broken".

So as we move towards the time of anticipation which Advent affords, let each of us ask ourselves whether we have truly heard and answered the call of the King of Kings. Let each of us commit ourselves anew – let us be 'stirred up' (in the words of this week's collect) to 'seek peace, give love, co-operate together and bind up the broken'. Amen.

Tired of waiting – (Advent 1)

Tom Kennar's Sermon from 29 November 2020

When, I wonder, did we forget how to wait for something. None of us like waiting, for anything. We want what we want, and we want it now! And, if we are one of the 1% of the world who have enough money to buy pretty much anything we want, we tend to get it…now.

A couple of years ago, Clare came back from visiting a friend's house, extolling the virtues of the new Amazon 'Echo' device. 'It's fantastic', she said. 'You can just ask it to play the radio, or for a summary of the news headlines, or what the weather will be! I really fancy one for Christmas.' Three days later, one arrived in our house!

The Season of Advent is the beginning of the Church's New Year, and it is designed specifically to be a time of waiting. For the rest of our society, the New Year starts with a bang and fireworks…with a sense that we've 'arrived' at something important. That's odd, when you think about it. Why should the simple turn of the Calendar be something to be celebrated with dancing in the street and all night parties? But the Church, deliberately, counter-culturally, starts its new year with two important words …'Coming' (which is what 'Advent' means) …and 'Wait'.

This year, with the challenges of COVID, none of us can wait for the whole messy business to be over. We don't want to wait. Even the Government has felt pressured to relax sensible rules of social distancing over Christmas, because, they felt, society in general is simply incapable of waiting. 'Don't ruin our Christmas!' they have cried – even though many of them will go nowhere near a church, nor even ponder for a moment the meaning of the coming of Christ. What would it matter if we delayed Christmas by a few months, until we've all been vaccinated? But no, we don't want to wait. We must have what we want, and we want it NOW!

In Advent, we can't help looking forward, because we see the way the world is now. We yearn for God to put things right. The writers of the Gospel's shared in that sense of urgency. Mark and Luke, for example, repeat a saying attributed to Jesus, which is (for me) one of the most intriguing lines of the New Testament: "Truly I tell you, this generation will not pass away until all these things have taken place". Jesus is reported to have promised that his second coming was SO imminent, that the current generation would not pass away before that great event happened.

Well, that didn't happen! This is one of those examples of where we need to understand the context of the writers of Scripture. Mark was writing at a time when Jesus had been gone for perhaps 30 years, and the early church was feeling the iron boot of Rome on its neck. Peter was probably in prison, along with Paul. Rome was becoming increasingly hostile towards both Jews and the new cult of the Christians.

It should not surprise us that Mark, in reporting Jesus' words from three decades before, has rather let his imagination run away with him. He didn't want to wait for God's plan to be unfolded in God's time. Despite reporting that Jesus said 'no-one will know the hour or the time of his coming', Mark let his inner-optimist get the better of him…I suggest.

Or perhaps – Jesus is, in fact, already come, stealthily, in clouds. That by his Holy Spirit, he is already among us. That he is even now, continually, gathering his elect – his followers – from the ends of the earth. Gathering us into churches, love-factories, for the spreading of his message of Love.

And, while we wait for the completion of the Reign of God, there is a very real sense in which God is already among us, already coming – in fact already here.

- Every time an army lays down its weapons and seeks peace – Jesus comes.

- Every time politicians and scientists combine their efforts in unprecedented action to produce a vaccine – Jesus comes.
- Every time a family is raised up of fear by the organisation Stop Domestic Abuse, Jesus comes.
- Every time a lonely person finds a friend in our morning church-opening, or forthcoming Christmas Market, Jesus comes.
- Every time one of our church members phones another church member just to chat – to make a connection – Jesus comes.
- Every time a hungry family is fed by the Beacon or PO9 Foodbanks, Jesus comes.
- Every time homeless people sleeping in our town are treated like the human beings they truly are, Jesus comes.
- Every time that an alcoholic, a gambler, a drug user turns up to one of our Pallant Centre support groups, and says 'NO!' to their addiction, Jesus comes.
- Every time an item of clothing is recycled through our shop, rather than added to the pile of human refuse, the planet is loved, and Jesus comes.
- Every time a young person develops their human potential through Dynamo Youth Theatre, or a person with learning difficulties grows in confidence through Creating Chaos, or a teenager with mental health challenges is helped by MIND – Jesus comes.
- Every time that SSAFA helps the poverty-stricken family of an armed services veteran, Jesus comes.

You see – signs of the kingdom are all around us. Our task, like an alert house-owner, is to keep awake. To see the signs of the kingdom with open eyes, and join in with the activity of God, wherever it is found. Amen.

The wise and foolish men

Sermon of Tom Kennar on Thursday 3 December
Text: Matthew 7.21, 24–27

Today's Gospel reading is one of those which always takes me back to Sunday School. Do you remember the song?

"The wise man built his house upon the rock (repeated three times)
And the rain came tumbling down.
The rain came down and the floods came up (repeated three times)
And the house on the rock stood firm."

Then the whole thing got repeated for the foolish man who built his house upon the sand, till 'the house on the sand fell FLAT' (at which point we would clap and laugh hysterically!)

The surface meaning of this parable is, of course, completely obvious. Those who build their lives on the teachings of Jesus will have strong and stable lives. But those who build on other foundations are doomed to live on shifting sands.

This principle has always been true for Christians. Millions upon millions of us can attest that a life built on the teachings of Jesus is a life filled with purpose and meaning. It's a life of hope and love. A life of service and fulfilment. But what are the alternatives?

Doubtless, there have been many sermons over the centuries which have offered alternatives to the teachings of Jesus. Perhaps the teachings other religious leaders have been held up as shifting sands – especially at times when the apparent advance of competing ideas was seen as a threat. Perhaps lives of drunkenness and debauchery have been suggested, at times when abstinence was seen as a top priority for the Band of Truth or the Salvation Army. Or perhaps it was lives lived in pursuit of wealth, the empty promise of gold or over-stuffed barns (as Jesus suggested)?

But I think that recent events in our World have offered us a whole new desert of shifting sand to contemplate. As a society, we have built our entire house on some very perilous shifting sands. In the last hundred years, this foundation of sand has become so ubiquitous, that we hardly give it a second thought. It is so ingrained in our society, so much a normal part of our lives, that we almost never stop to examine it or question it. What am I referring to?

I'm talking about the sand of consumerism. And I think the consequences of that sandy foundation are now becoming all too plain to see. Our house is sinking fast. The floods are rising.... quite literally in the case of climate change caused by rampant consumerism. It is consumerism which fed the mass transit systems of our lives, which in turn led to the rapid advance of a little local virus into a world-wide pandemic. It is consumerism which pumps smoke into the air, and plastics into the water. It is consumerism which causes armies to fight over literal deserts, in the hope of possessing the lakes of oil underneath them. It is consumerism which feeds individualism, which in turn leads to Nationalism, and paranoid fears about outsiders. And it is consumerism which provokes the backlash of angry extremism, and the ideologies which seek to return us to the stone age. And it is the collapse of consumerism, under the weight of the pandemic it caused, which is putting so many people out of work right now.

Have you ever noticed that every world economy is measured not on levels of happiness, or by the way it takes care of its most fragile members, or the benefit it offers to the climate, or the benefit it offers to the intellectual and spiritual health of humankind? Instead, the single most important factor in determining the health of an economy is said to be growth. Which is frankly, nuts. If the economy of every country grew by just 2.5% per year on average, then in 10 years' time, the world would need to produce 25% more stuff than it does now. 25% more smoke in the air. 25% more plastic in the sea. In 20 years' time – the world would have to give up 50% more than it already does to feed and please the consumerist armies of humans swarming across its face. It's nuts. It's crazy. It's the self-defeating, civilisation-ending strategy of the mythical lemming. Something has to change. Something has to shift. Or we're quite simply not going to make it. The house on the sand will fall FLAT!

Against this terrifying vision, Jesus offers us a solid, rocky, alternative. His teachings are granite-hard foundations on which we could choose to build. Jesus wasn't an economist. But the principles he espoused can be converted into economic theory, without very much effort at all. Principles like – prioritising care for the poor and the sick. Principles like sharing, giving, and spreading, instead of hoarding, taking and keeping. Principles like 'rendering unto Caesar' could transform an economy in which the wealthiest people currently pay the very least tax for the common good. Principles like teaching the priority of community, over individualism. Principles like valuing rest and retreat, instead of 24-hour shopping and frantic holidays. Imagine how different things would be right now, if we valued healthcare, education, medicine, scientific enquiry, spiritual growth and community service as much as we value restaurants, pubs, cappuccinos and department-store shopping.

CONsumerism – the clue is in the name. It's a CON. It's a con, perpetrated on the whole of our society by the con-men who currently pull the levers of power. How can we change this? How can any of us hope to turn around the Titanic of consumerism which is about to crash into the ice-berg of destiny, taking us all to the bottom with it?

The answer of course, lies with Jesus. We do it one person at a time, just as he did. One soul at a time. We spread his word, person by person and we live his life. And we encourage others to do the same. Perhaps, if you agree with my hypothesis, you could share the video of this sermon, on Facebook? Or pass on your copy of this Corona Chronicle to a neighbour? Or share this link to my sermon blog with a friend: www.tomkennarsermons.blogspot.com

Consumerism only took root in our society because one by one, we allowed it to. The opposite is also true, and also a possibility. Frankly, it's the only hope we have.

So, if you agree with my hypothesis…what will YOU do about it. What changes will you make today, to fashion some life-boats for the Titanic. Will you, once more, fall prey to the marketing gurus who will have you buy billions of plastic toys for children this year? Will you fall prey to the titans of industry who want you to decorate your home with their laser lights, and their plastic tree? Will you succumb to the message that comfort and joy can only be found through an over-stocked larder, a Christmas edition of 'Strictly…' and a mountain of chocolate? Will you build on sand again, this year?

Or will you stand up for Jesus – and for his way of life? The way of charity, simplicity, and love? Will you take time to draw apart from the madness, find some simplicity and some peace?

Will you prioritise charity over chewing, giving over getting, and loving over living-it-up?

Just not getting it....

Tom Kennar's Sermon from 6 December 2020—

Texts: Isaiah 40.1-11 and Mark 1.1-8

Today – and indeed next week too, the Lectionary invites us to consider the place and role of John the Baptiser. We call him that, these days, because the word 'Baptist' has become linked to a particular theological viewpoint. Today's 'Baptists' believe that adult baptism is the only legitimate baptism and that just about every other mainstream church is wrong in baptising children who can't confess their own faith. That is a fascinating argument…of course. But there isn't time to go into it now.

So let's focus down on John the Baptiser – the man. Mark launches straight into his story by reminding us of Isaiah's prophecy (which we've also heard, this morning). It's a prophecy of a messenger who will be sent ahead of the Messiah. Mark is absolutely convinced that John is that messenger – so he goes on: "John the Baptiser appeared in the wilderness, proclaiming a baptism of repentance for the forgiveness of sins".

John is the last of the Old Testament prophets. He follows the tradition of living apart from civilisation, and of calling people to repent of their evil ways. Picture the scene: Imagine a rather dirty fellow, with mad scruffy hair, dressed in camel-skins, and covered in bee-stings (from raiding wild bee hives). He's probably got blobs of honey stuck to his shirt, and he's munching on a locust...and declaring at the top of his voice "Repent! For the kingdom of heaven has come near".

I wonder what our reaction would be if we met someone like that in the streets of Havant – or even here inside the church. I think we'd try to get him some serious mental health support!

But there was something about John that attracted people to him. There was something about his message which, according to both Mark and Matthew's Gospels, attracted people out into the desert from "Jerusalem, all of Judea, and all of the region along the River Jordan" (Mt 3:5)

According to Matthew's rather expanded account of Mark's passage, John was not a man to mince his words either. He taunted the religious leaders of the day with phrases like "You viper's brood" (Mt 3:7). He warned them against the complacency of their religion: saying, "Just because you are Abraham's children, don't go thinking that gives you an automatic right to heaven." (Mt 7:8 - paraphrased)

There are, in fact, a number of puzzling questions about John. First there is the fact that he didn't join up with Jesus. Why didn't he set aside his baptising, and become a follower of the Lord? And then there's the fact that when he was in prison he sent word to Jesus to ask him if he really was the Messiah.

I think that John had a different vision of what the Messiah would be like. John's Messiah would be full of swift judgment against the evil people of the day. See what he says about Jesus in Matthew's gospel, chapter 3: "...he will gather his wheat into the granary; but the chaff he will burn with unquenchable fire". (Mt 3: 12)

John's expectations of the Messiah are rooted in the language and concepts of the Old Testament. But, uncomfortably, Jesus simply doesn't match up to John's expectations of what the Messiah would be like... should be like. And he was Jesus' cousin!

I wonder how many of us sometimes do that? How often do we simply assume that God will be as we expect him to be…rather than how God actually is? How often do we assume that God must surely agree with our beliefs? How many Conservative-voters assume God is a Tory? How many socialists are just certain that God would surely have voted for Jeremy Corbyn? How many racists or homophobes automatically assume that God agrees with them? How many religious extremists – on every side, assume that God condones their violent actions? We all have a tendency to make God in our own image – rather than seeking the truth of God in whose image we are made.

John's language is the language of criticism and warning. "You'd better do what I say, or God Almighty is going to smite you!" John's kind of repentance is a rather mechanistic, transactional thing. "Repent, and be baptised, and you will be forgiven of your sins – you'll be saved from the wrath that is to come". John is offering a rather simple passport to heaven – rather like the indulgences that Martin Luther rightly condemned 1500 years later.

Jesus' language, on the other hand, is of forgiveness, acceptance, and love. He speaks of journeys and the Way of faith. John is the apocalyptic doomsayer. Jesus offers life, hope and an exciting journey.

Mind you, Jesus is not immune from the apocalyptic tradition. Certainly he gives plenty of warnings, and he even appropriates John's use of the phrase 'viper's brood' – to describe the religious leaders of the day. (Mt 12.34). But on balance, Jesus' tone is rather different to John's. Instead of calling us to a desert of repentance, he invites us to commune with each other and with him around a meal. He even includes

Samaritans, Zealots, tax collectors and even his future betrayer into that community. He even includes women – which in his time was an incredible thing to do.

Jesus speaks the language of radical inclusion, whereas John speaks of unquenchable fire and winnowing forks. Jesus invites all of us on a journey of faith, self-discovery, community-life and growth. He calls it the Way, and the Kingdom.

Jesus call us to turn away from making up our own ideas about how things should be. He calls us instead to tune-in to God's loving, merciful, ultimately positive view of the universe. The baptism of Jesus marks the very start of an entire journey of faith.

That's why, incidentally, I do believe in infant baptism. For I think that it is never too early, in God's inclusive Kingdom, to invite another person to journey with God. Amen.

John the baptiser – prophet and sceptic

Sermon of Tom Kennar on Thursday 10 December

This is certainly the week for thinking about John the baptiser – he's the focus of readings all through this week. Today, I'd like to home in on one particular facet of John's character – a facet which speaks directly to us today…and it's this: John was a sceptic. After being thrown into prison, by King Herod, John sent a message to Jesus asking, 'Are you the Messiah? Or are we to expect another?' This is the same John who didn't become one of Jesus' own disciples. He carried on ploughing his own furrow…doing things his own way: angrily calling people to repentance with dire warnings, while Jesus tried the tack of Love. So, John was sceptical about Jesus.

Scepticism is all around us, isn't it? We are – perhaps justifiably - sceptical about the Government's promises that Britain will boom after Brexit. Many have become extremely sceptical about politics at all, not least since politicians seem to be willing to deal with 'alternative truth' (as Donald Trump's press secretary once memorably suggested). We are sceptical even about the great national organs of balance and truth that we've trusted for generations, like the BBC or the great newspapers of our nation.

It's perhaps even more disconcerting that, in our time, we've become sceptical of the claims of science. 'Anti-vaxxers' have been a growing voice in national discourse for a while – ever since some rather spurious claims (in my view) were made, linking the MMR vaccine to cases of childhood autism.

Scepticism doesn't just pervade our national life though. It also pervades our thinking about God. Just like John the baptiser, we wonder whether Jesus' claims to be God's Son, indeed God himself, can really be true. And, if we are not careful, our scepticism can drive us to throw aside everything we believe, and on which we have based our lives.

But scepticism is not, in itself, a bad thing. Scepticism is part of a process of growth. It's part of 'putting away childish things' (as St Paul so memorably said – see 1 Cor.13). For a sceptical mind is ultimately a questioning mind. It's the kind of mind which asks 'where does this information come from? Is it trustworthy?' Philosophers and theologians have a long name for this kind of enquiring thought – they call it 'epistemology' – which essentially asks the question 'how do we know what we think we know?'.

Sceptical thought should lead us to deeper thought, and to greater understanding. When John asked, via messengers, whether Jesus was the Messiah, Jesus said this to the messengers: "Go your way, and tell John what things ye have seen and heard; how that the blind see, the lame walk, the lepers are cleansed, the deaf hear, the dead are raised, to the poor the gospel is preached". (Lk 7.22).

Notice how Jesus doesn't get angry at John for his sceptical, doubting question. Instead, he answers the question with a powerful illustration. And invites John to arrive at a new understanding.

Sadly, we don't know what the results of Jesus' answer to John's question were...not least because the poor fellow literally lost his head a short time later. But we can see that expressions of doubt, and scepticism, were not rejected by Jesus. Instead, he confronted the sceptic head-on, and gave him new facts to consider. And this is how the healthy work of scepticism should work for all religious people. We should never be afraid of doubt, because doubt is part of the process of digging for truth. Scepticism, used wisely, is the shovel we use to unearth the gold nuggets of real truth.

Of course, like any human characteristic, it's possible to take scepticism too far. At the far end of religious scepticism, for example, we find the ultra-atheists, like every preacher's 'boogie-man', Richard Dawkins. I genuinely feel sorry for Dawkins. He is someone who has become SO sceptical of religions, and of religious thought, that he is no longer able to be objective in his sceptical enquiry. For him, scepticism is no longer a shovel with which to dig for truth, but a bulldozer to cover over any view which is not his own.

When I was a child, I thought like a child. But now I am a man, I have put away childish things. But even now, I still can only see through a glass darkly…and therefore I need to embrace the grown-up, adult-brained task of being sceptical about my faith, and about my own political and world views. That's the adult thing to do.

As the Christmas story unfolds around us again, perhaps you might find yourself sceptical about any number of things. Does it matter whether Jesus was born of a virgin? What is an angel, anyway? Why on earth would the civil authorities tell people to go back to the town of their birth to be counted in a census? These (and many more) are all good questions to ask.

And if you honestly seek answers to honest sceptical questions, I promise you that those answers will lead you into a much more profound, much more meaningful understanding of the truth. You too can unearth – with your sceptical shovel – new understandings of the depth of the story about when God came to town. A little town. Called Bethlehem. Amen.

Divine vengeance

Tom Kennar's Sermon from 13 December 2020—
Texts: Isaiah 61.1–4,8–11 and John 1.6–8,19–28

John the baptiser has had quite a bit of attention over the last week. In last Sunday's sermon, I explored how he had a subtly different understanding of who the Messiah was meant to be, and how he should act. Then on Thursday, I explored the sceptical side of his nature, and I suggested that scepticism is a generally healthy thing for all thinking people – and especially religious thinking people. Just now, we lit our third Advent candle, and reminded ourselves of John's pivotal role as a witness to the truth – as a burning and shining light for Christ.

Despite all this focus on John, we must never forget that his primary role was to be the announcer of Christ. As he himself said (in John 3.30) "I must decrease, so that he may increase". John recognised in today's Gospel that he himself was not even worthy to untie the sandals of the Messiah. As John the Gospel-writer stressed, John the Baptiser was not, himself, the Light…but rather, he came to testify to the Light.

It was Jesus – the Light of the World - that John pointed us to. And it was Jesus who, a short while after his baptism by John, who would claim for himself the opening lines of Isaiah 61, when he stood up to read in the synagogue of his hometown of Nazareth (see Luke 4:16-30). Here, again, are the words he both quoted, and then made his own:

"The spirit of the Lord God is upon me, because the Lord has anointed me; he has sent me to bring good news to the oppressed, to bind up the broken-hearted, to proclaim liberty to the captives, and release to the prisoners; to proclaim the year of the Lord's favour…"

Having read those words, according to Luke's account, Jesus put down the scroll and said to the congregation 'Today, these words have been fulfilled in your midst'. Jesus deliberately, and purposefully, declared his mission to be one of bringing good news, binding up, healing, and proclaiming liberty. He proclaimed that this was the year of the Lord's favour.

Which is all very beautiful. But I'm interested in what Jesus doesn't say. I find it fascinating that Jesus stopped quoting Isaiah at just that point. He didn't read the next line, which says '…and the day of vengeance of the Lord'. Jesus stops at the news that this is the year of God's favour.

There is a stream of consciousness which flows through the Bible, and especially through the Old Testament. It's a theme of judgement and divine vengeance, constantly invoked by prophets and seers throughout the ages, no doubt in an attempt to scare humanity into behaving itself. The very oldest stories of the Bible sometimes paint a picture of a kind of Divine 'bogey-man' who needs to enact some kind of punishment on humanity…

For the sins of Adam and Eve, they are cast out of the Garden. For the sins of all humanity, God apparently sends a flood to wipe out the earth. Pharaoh and his riders are cast into the sea for having stood in the way of the Divine will. Sodom and Gomorrah are destroyed, because the people failed to offer hospitality to God's angels. Time and time again, the Bible's writers reach for stories of divine vengeance.

But Jesus refuses to align himself with that kind of thinking, and with those kinds of stories. He doesn't, for a moment, deny the power of human sin, or its ability to destroy. But neither does he retreat into metaphors of divine vengeance as the solution. Instead, Jesus talks of God's love for the world. Just two chapters later than this morning's Gospel, Jesus says those words which we repeat at every Thursday Eucharist: "God so loved the world, that he sent his only son, so that everyone who believes in him should not perish, but have everlasting life". The God whom Jesus unfolds for us is that God who does not seek the destruction of his children. This is not the angry, vengeful God of former understanding. This is the God of love, of healing, of binding up, and of setting free. This is God the parent…God the loving Father.

And that, ultimately, is the good news that we are called to announce, this coming Christmas and then every day of the year. When we announce 'peace on Earth, and God's goodwill to all people on whom his favour rests', we speak of a transforming, overwhelming Love, a love which proclaims good news to the poor, which binds up the broken, and releases the captives.

I'm frankly tired of the religious voices who claim that every disaster which befalls us is some kind of divine punishment. AIDS was never a punishment from God, and nor is COVID 19. They were both self-inflicted wounds by an unwise humanity (who released otherwise harmless animal viruses into the human population). The devastation of earthquakes and even tsunamis are not divine vengeance – but the self-inflicted wounds of an unwise humanity, who build cheap houses and beach resorts in known earthquake zones. God does not wage war, and he never requires suicide bombers. God does not desire vengeance or retribution…these things are not the will of God.

God, rather, offers wisdom and love. Through Jesus, he offers us life – abundant life, filled with wisdom, healing, sharing, and liberty. It's Life which goes on for ever. All we have to do is look to the Light, and live in the Light, of the wisdom and truth of Jesus Christ. Just as John the Baptiser discovered that he must also do. Amen.

Taking the Bible seriously - not literally

Sermon of Tom Kennar on Thursday 17 December 2020

Texts: Genesis 49.2, 8–10 and Matthew 1.1–17

It has long been a practice of mine to preach, consistently, from the lectionary. Other ministers, quite justifiably, tend to choose readings which they believe are most relevant to the needs of the congregation they serve, at that moment in time. But sometimes, just sometimes, the result can be a fairly limited diet of Scripture.

The lectionary, on the other hand, is deliberately created to give us a broad overview of the principle Scriptures – making sure that we've heard, over two and three-year cycles (weekdays or Sundays), all the main stories, and the main theological principles.

But I have to confess that when I first opened the lectionary to today's reading, my heart sank! What on earth can one say about a long list of names of the ancestors of Jesus. And how on earth can I read them out, without tripping over my tongue?! But, as you've just heard, I decided to stay true to my self-discipline of just preaching from the lectionary!

If you have a really good memory, and if you've been listening to my daily readings from Luke's Gospel, then you may have noticed something quite intriguing about the genealogy I've just read from Matthew. It's this – Matthew and Luke's genealogies are quite, quite different. Right from the question of the name of Joseph's father. It was either Jacob (according to Matthew), or Heli, according to Luke. And from there, traced back through time, both genealogies are remarkably dis-similar.

This is a conundrum which has puzzled many bible scholars over the centuries – especially those who start from the premise of believing that the bible is the 'inerrant' or 'infallible' word of God'. It's a bit of a problem for those who claim that the Bible is a reliable historical (and indeed scientific) document. Various theories have been advanced over the years, including the idea that Luke's genealogy is actually Mary's (despite the fact that it plainly starts with Joseph and his father). Another idea is that Matthew's gives us a list of royal ancestors (to prove Jesus' descent from King David), whereas Luke gives us an actual list of biological ancestors. But none of these explanations really cut the mustard – and there is no reliable evidence for any of these theories.

So for me, these lists of names, right there near the beginning of two of the Gospels point me to a bigger truth. And it's this: never make the mistake of thinking of the Bible as infallible, or inerrant. It simply isn't – there are far too many internal inconsistencies, contradictory statements, and varying accounts of the same events. If this were a Bible Study, instead of a sermon, we could have great fun now going through the Bible and examining some of those inconsistencies for ourselves. Have you ever noticed, for example, that the second chapter of Genesis lists the order in which God created things…and that it's a completely different order to the first chapter of Genesis? But, tempted as I am to prove my point...this is not the place, and we don't have the time.

Instead, let me quote from one of my favourite theological thinkers, John Dominic Crossan, who said this: "My point….is not that those ancient people told literal stories and we are now smart enough to take them symbolically, but that they told them symbolically and we are now dumb enough to take them literally". Crossan is referring to ancient texts as symbolic. He understands, and teaches us, that ancient people were far less concerned than modern people with actual history. They told stories – sometimes based on real events, and sometimes just pure fiction - in order to inspire, to teach, to warn and to encourage. Another modern theologian, Rob Bell, teaches that it is not important whether something happened. What's important is that it HAPPENS – today, to us, to me. The stories of Scripture help us to examine and understand OUR lives. These stories transform US.

So, if you are one of the many people who struggle with the question of whether the Bible is true in any meaningful, historical respect, let me encourage you. If you are someone who wonders whether the Virgin Birth really matters, or what the precise meaning of Jesus' death on the cross really was, or whether Jesus really is 'coming again' despite 2000 years of apparent unwillingness…let me stand with you. Let me invite you to move, with me, BEYOND the questions of historical accuracy, and into the much deeper questions of what these stories have to teach us, about how to live today in the light of the Gospel. Let me encourage you to take the bible seriously not literally.

As we move inexorably towards Christmas, once more, ask yourself what your life would look life if truly lived in the light of the Gospel stories. What might a life look like if it was framed entirely in notions of living simply, generously, outwardly, selflessly? What kind of difference in the world could such a life make? What would life be like if the whole of our society recognised the poverty of the stable, the desperation of the flight into Egypt, the abuse of power of Herod, the generosity of strangers, and the proclamation of peace by the Angels. I actually don't care very much which aspects of this story are literally true. I only care that these stories, if we will let them sink deep into our hearts, have the power to reshape a dying world. Amen.

The subversive Christmas tree

Tom Kennar's sermon on Sunday 20 December 2020

First...a story...

Have you ever wondered where the tradition of Christmas trees started? Legends and folk-tales, my friends. The greatest legend of them all tells of a man called 'Beautiful Face', or Boniface, to his friends. A son of Devon, Boniface was a Christian missionary, a Bishop who travelled to the forests of Bavaria - spreading the good news of Jesus, the Light of all the world.

In the darkness of the Forest, he came across a massive oak tree. From its branches were hanging terrible things...bones, and skulls, including even the skulls of infants. Boniface searched nearby, and came across a tribe of pagans, the People of the Tree. They believed that something so mighty, the biggest thing in their entire world, must contain a great and mighty power. They sacrificed themselves, and even their children to this tree-god, in the desperate hope of pleasing it...lest it should destroy them all. Fear and superstition drove them to madness.

Boniface begged the tribe to understand that the True God, would never ask of them such a thing. In fact, he explained, the True God sent his own child to die for us! He would never ask us to harm one of our children for him. But the People of the Tree were not convinced. Their fear was too great.

So, that night, while the Tribe was asleep, Boniface took a mighty axe, and felled the great oak to the ground. In the morning, the Tribe gathered around, terrified, waiting for the god of the tree to smite Boniface for his act. But nothing happened...and gradually, the light of truth dawned in the minds of the Tribe. They saw the truth of Boniface's words, and began to worship Jesus Christ.

But these were people of the Tree. Without a tree towards which to focus their worship, they felt lost and bereft. So, in a flash of insight, Boniface bade them to focus their worship on the ever-green trees of the forest. They had no church, no building in which to gather - but instead, they could use ever-green trees as a symbol of the ever-green, never-ending love of God. Lights in the branches would remind them of Christ, the Light of the World. And so the legend of the Christmas Tree was born: a tree to remind us all, that God's love for all humanity is new every morning, and never, ever ends.

What we have just heard is but one re-telling of the legend of the Christmas tree. It comes from the 8th century (though I confess that most of the details were made up by me!). Nevertheless, it is one of the earliest mentions of the idea of trees and Christmas.

Some scholars have suggested that there is a connection between Christmas trees and pagan religions. The Old Norse festival of Yule is especially referenced – although any written evidence for the Yule-tree among old Viking records is pretty scant.

The Christmas Tree has a long history, therefore – and mainly a Christian one. In the story we heard just now, I suggested that lights in the branches of the tree were reminders of Christ the Light of the world. But there are many other Christian references to be explored…

For example - baubles are references to the fruit of the garden of Eden – the 'apple' which Eve ate, and by which disobedience towards God came into the world. But these 'apples' are balanced by many other symbols of light and hope. The star on the top of the tree points to the Star of Bethlehem. Or if you put a 'fairy' on your tree – you are actually referencing the angels who announced the birth of Christ. Presents, tied to the tree, are reminders of God's great gift to the world – in the form of his son. The very shape of the tree is a symbol…viewed in two dimensions, the tree forms a triangle, and is a reminder of the Trinity. The fact that

Christmas trees are ever-green is a reminder of the never-ending love of God (as good old St Boniface suggested in my story). The fact that the tree is a tree at all is a reminder that Jesus Christ was hung on a cross of wood, or a 'tree' as it is sometimes described.

In many ways, therefore, the Christmas tree is a subversive thing. It encompasses the whole story of God's rescue of humanity. From the Fall, in the garden of Eden, to the gift of Christ and his death on the tree, to the hope that the teachings of Jesus will be light to a dying world, each tree represents God's story. And many people don't know it! In most homes, and in most public squares around the world, trees are brought in. A blessing from God is carried into our lives, without us even being aware that God is at work.

And isn't that just like God? As the carol says, 'How silently, how silently, the wondrous gift is given'. It is precisely in quietness and peace, in silent but never-ending love, that God comes to us.

We find him, surprisingly, in a stable in Bethlehem. But we also find him, surprisingly in the gift of a home to a homeless family, or in the gift of welcome and sustenance to a refugee. We find him in the quiet march of scientific discovery, and in the gift of caring medicine which we've seen so much this year. We find him in the phone-call to the lonely person, isolated by COVID or their own frailty. We find him in the work of thousands of charities and volunteers who place the needs of others above their own. We find him in the gift of time and learning which teachers give to their students.

Just as the Christmas tree has crept into our homes, we find that God too has crept into our lives. And "where meek souls will receive him still, the dear Christ enters in". Amen.

Christmas....Just stop it!

Tom Kennar's sermon for Christmas Eve 2020

Gospel Reading: Luke 1.67–79

There are many for whom Christmas is a completely joyful time, filled with excitement, the tingle of anticipation, dreams of mangers and shepherds, parties and people. There are, I'm told, SOME people for whom the writing of Christmas cards is a joy, and for whom the wrapping of presents is an exciting activity. There are SOME people, apparently, who take pleasure from battling through the supermarket with an overloaded trolley, heady with anticipation of munching their way through its contents. There are those for whom the annual ritual of setting up a tree and decorating their home with shiny plastic baubles is joy-giving, and like-enhancing.

But, I suspect that for many people Christmas into actually fails to deliver the 'peace on earth' that the angels proclaimed. For many, the pressure to conform to society's idea of Christmas actually drives them into acute states of anxiety.

A little meme was doing the rounds on Facebook yesterday, which a lot of people shared. It went like this:

"My bedroom closet is full of Amazon boxes. Zero presents are wrapped. Laundry is everywhere. Kids are screaming and fighting. The house looks like a crime scene, and the only food in the pantry requires a recipe that I'm not sure I can pull off.

"Also, I'm 90% positive I'm forgetting something...or someone.

"This is fine. I'm fine."

Did you know that there is actually a diagnosable mental condition, called 'Christmas Anxiety Disorder'? And that applies to normal Christmases. This Christmas has anxiety piled on top of anxiety, like snow falling snow on snow. Many people will be jobless, or coping with only 80% of their wages on furlough. Many are reliant on foodbanks, or the kindness of strangers. Quite literally thousands of lorry drivers are waiting anxiously at Dover, for the chance to get home to their families for Christmas. Others will be grieving the loss of loved ones, some just a day before Christmas, from COVID. Medical staff, funeral homes, shop workers, teachers and council staff are on their knees.

Into this level of anxiety...how does a preacher preach? What possible comfort and joy can I offer, to a world so anxious? What can I say which would not feel like a little happy-face dinosaur plaster over a gaping wound?

The Father of John the Baptist, Zechariah, prophesied that the coming Messiah would lead us out of darkness and into light. He would create the circumstances in which we could serve him without fear – without anxiety – in holiness and righteousness all the days of our life. God's tender mercy would break over us like the dawn, and he would guide our feet into the way of peace.

So what happened? Where is this peace? Where is the holiness and righteousness we were promised? Where is the tender mercy of God?

Here is the problem: human beings consistently, and persistently, have rejected God's way to peace, holiness, righteousness and mercy. God has done his part. He sent his son to both live for us, and die for us, teaching us with his own mouth and body what God is like. God has done what Zechariah prophesied.

He has opened the way to life which goes on for ever. It's a way of selflessness. A way of charity. A way of generosity and sharing. A way of prayer, and of study. It's a call to worship God with everything we have, and everything we are. It's a way of caring for creation, and for one another. It's a way of putting God first, in all things.

But human beings, as a species, have chosen another way. We've chosen the path of pleasure-seeking, the path of self-realisation and individualism, the path of wealth-accumulation, the path of consumerism, the path of excess in all things. Rather than a simple, prayerful service of thanksgiving for the birth of our saviour, the Christ Mass has been turned into a hedonistic, resource-gobbling, greedy, pleasure-seeking excess of unrecyclable plastics and metals, rotten over-ordered food, frantic travel arrangements, and impossible expectations. It's no wonder that Christmas makes us anxious!

So what can I say as a preacher? I can say only what I believe God to be saying…and it's this: Enough! A silent night, in a sparsely-equipped stable, in the quiet arms of one's closest family was enough for the Lord of Heaven. Why isn't it enough for you too? What are you looking for? What do you think you're going to find among the glitter and the mountains of presents and the billions of cards? Stop it! It's enough!

Search for the kind of wealth that does not rust, and which thieves cannot break in and steal. Search for the light which shines in the darkness of all human life, not the plastic light of a Christmas decoration. Search for the Narrow Way of living a life in community with others, in forgiveness and love. Search for God, in a stable.

For where meek souls will receive him still, Zechariah's prophesy still has power. The dear Christ will enter in. Amen.

Christ LIVED for you!

Tom Kennar's sermon for Christmas Day 2020

The Corona virus has presented us with many challenges this year, hasn't it? This is by no means the first major Christian Festival which has had to be celebrated only through a camera lens. It seems a long time ago, but I well remember having to celebrate Easter from my front room – at a time when even I wasn't even permitted to be in the church building!

And now…Christmas. Easter and Christmas – the two greatest Christian festivals which stand like bookends, or perhaps bastions, at different ends of the church's year. Both of them speak about the life of Christ. His coming in human flesh in Bethlehem is the focus of Christmas. Easter turns our eyes towards his risen and eternal life.

And yet, despite these great festivals of life, the church seems (to me at least) to be sometimes just a bit too focused on the death of Christ. Our greatest and most ubiquitous symbol for Christ is not a manger, nor is it an empty tomb. Instead, the Cross has become the primary Christian symbol. The cry of so many evangelists, throughout history, has been 'Christ died for you!'.

This of course is utterly true – and I don't want to undervalue the rich layers of meaning which the death of Christ contains. We explored many of them together on Good Friday – as we shall no doubt do again in 2021. But, at this Christmas time, just as at Easter, I want to proclaim a different emphasis…a refreshed understanding of the Jesus story. Not so much that 'Christ died for you', but rather, that startling truth that Christ lived for you!

Jesus' death has much to teach us – it teaches us about the value of sacrifice, it warns us of the power of human governments to push God to the margins, and it provides theological, legal framework for the problem of sin (for those who find that helpful). It teaches us something about the love of a God who would send his own Son to give up his life for us. But the life of Jesus has so much more to teach us.

It is by his birth at Bethlehem, in humble and lowly circumstances, that we catch a glimpse of God's passion for the poor and the outcast of society. It is through Jesus' life among us, his teachings, his actions, his warnings, his encouragements, that we have the chance to really get under the skin of who Jesus was.

Some of you have been following me as I've read a chapter of Luke's Gospel each day during December (and well done if you've made it through all 24 days!). I really hope that experience has helped you to get a broader, deeper and more profound understanding of the God who lived, and who continues to live in each of us. And I hope you've noticed that the death of Jesus takes up just about half of one of those 24 chapters!

It is by Jesus' life and teachings that we too may find life. Jesus saves us by the Cross, yes, but also by the example of his life. A life lived as Christ lived his life will be a life full of joy, of fellowship, of community, of giving and sharing, of healing, simplicity and of love. These are not products of Jesus death – but of his life of earth. And by his resurrection, we are promised that that life can go on for ever and ever.

So, this Christmas, let us hear again the news the Angels bring…good news for all humanity…the news, the real and present hope, that it is possible to live differently, to live lightly, to live generously, to live gloriously in the light of the example of Christ. Christ has lived for us…alleluia! Amen.

A glimpse of the face of God

Tom Kennar's sermon for the first Sunday of Christmas.

I had a strange experience a couple of years ago. I was standing in my garden, in the early dawn, when suddenly I saw the face of Jesus looking back at me, from the grass. Just his head...as though someone had buried Jesus up to his neck on my lawn. It was quite a shock; I can tell you – until I realised that what I was actually looking at was a football which our dog had chewed to pieces. In the right light, it looked just like the face of a bearded man, looking right at me.

My first thought was 'E-bay'! I could make a fortune. The face of Jesus on a Vicar's football...that would be worth something! But then, it set me wondering. For a start, no-one actually knows what Jesus looked like. There are no portraits of him by anyone who knew him. We have a picture of him in our minds – white skin, long blond hair, beard, and so on. Just like the Jesus in our stained glass window behind me. But actually, the chances are that he would have had short hair, no beard (in the Roman fashion of the time) and a middle eastern face. So on reflection, I decided that pedalling dubious images of Jesus wouldn't be very appropriate. So I booted the ball back up the garden!

I wonder whether you have ever tried to imagine the face of God? It's impossible of course. But I think it is possible to imagine God's expression, at least. I imagine God looking, frankly, disappointed. I imagine him looking at the mess our world is in, and being rather perplexed, to say the least.

He must be perplexed at watching the uber-wealthy businessmen getting richer, while the homeless, the poor, and the COVID-related jobless struggle. I wonder how disappointed God's face appears when he ponders the inequality between nations – when he sees that some nations, like ours, will all be vaccinated by the summer; but some nations will never be able to afford the vaccine. I wonder what God's face looks like when he sees the rise of popularism and fundamentalism across the planet.

I especially wonder what God's face looks like when he contemplates the sheer waste involved in the celebration of Jesus' birthday. According the waste-disposal company, PHS, something like 4.2 million Christmas dinners are wasted in the UK each year. That equates to approximately 263,000 turkeys, 7.5 million mince pies, 740,000 slices of Christmas pudding, 17.2 million Brussels sprouts, 11.9 million carrots and 11.3 million roast potatoes!

Each year, the UK spends a combined total of around £700 million on unwanted presents! 227,000 miles of wrapping paper is thrown away each year. 1 billion Christmas cards are also put in the bin.

As well as imagining God's expression, I wonder if we could try putting ourselves in God's shoes for a moment. What would you do about all these problems? If you were God?

Perhaps you would be tempted to jolly-well sort it all out. Perhaps you would appear on a thunder cloud, and lay down the law with an iron fist, coupled with the threat of thunder bolts and lighting (very very frighteningly! Galileo, Galileo...). Perhaps you would use your almighty, omnipotent power to force people to be kind to one another.

But, if you did that...you might find that you have a new problem. Instead of a human race which chooses of its own free will to love you and worship you, you would have created a race of puppets. You would have reduced the beautiful thing that a human being can be into something not much better than a toy. Adam and Eve - reduced to Ken and Barbie. And any love or worship they offered you or one another would be a poor thing indeed. A mere shadow, a fabrication.

So, what do you do? How do you persuade human-kind that there is another way? How do you speak a Word to them that they will hear, and to which they can respond with all their hearts? Here's what you do...

You send them your Son - a human being who is so filled with God that he can say with integrity "I and the Father are one". You send them a Word clothed in flesh. You show them what a human life can be like if it overflows with God. You send them a Word which reveals the full glory of God by living the kind of life that God calls all his creation to live.

You send them...a baby. You send humanity the most fragile form of humanity that you can conceive. You do it so that humankind sees that the glory of God is not shown in acquiring wealth, or looking after number one, or living in hate - but the glory of God is shown in the weakest kind of human being possible...a baby, in a stable; the son of a peasant woman in a backwater of the mighty Roman empire.

If you could stand in God's shoes today, perhaps you too would send humankind a Divine Word clothed in flesh. For at Christmas, God comes to us as a human, to show us what it really means for us to be human. By a life of selfless giving, total sacrifice, total love and compassion, Jesus shows us the heart, and the face, of God. That's what the shepherds saw, and it's why they went away glorifying and praising God.

Perhaps we might do the same? Amen.

The sacrifice of light

Tom Kennar's sermon for the Last Day of 2020

Text: John 1. 1-14

Everyone loves a story – which is precisely why Jesus used parables, and why we all love movies and books. The Christmas Story is one of the greatest stories ever told. Its many characters help us to see ourselves reflected back – in the trust of the Shepherds, the wisdom of the Wise Men, the generosity of the Innkeeper, the faithfulness of Mary and Joseph, the abuse of power of Herod – and even in the evangelism of the angels who share good news.

The Gospel writers give us different perspectives on the same story. Luke is fired by the way Jesus reached out to the poor and the oppressed. So he gives us the story of shepherds, outsiders who are invited to be front and centre at the coming of the Messiah. Matthew, on the other hand, is fired by Jesus' message that God's love is meant for all humanity – so he focuses on the coming of Wise Men from Eastern Lands. These are non-Jews, outsiders, who are brought into the fold of God's love.

The oldest of the Gospel writers, Mark, actually says nothing about the birth of Jesus. And John, the most recent Gospel writer, is not interested in shepherds and wise men. Scholars tell us that John wrote his Gospel in his old age – after a lifetime of spreading – and reflecting on - the message of Jesus. John wants us to grasp the enormity of the Christmas event, the coming of Jesus, what scholars call the 'Incarnation' – that moment when God, who is Spirit, takes on human flesh.

There are two words which John especially plays with, in his poetic Gospel introduction. The first is 'Word', and the second is 'Light'. Let's break them down a little…

'Word' is the English translation of 'Logos' – a Greek word from where we get the word 'logic'. John is saying that the incomprehensible being we call God is many things – spirit, love, a creative force that binds the universe together. But he is also mind. He has thoughts. He has desires and intentions for the world that he has created. God's thoughts, God's logic, God's wisdom – these are his 'Logos' – his 'Word'. "In the beginning was the Word" – the Logos – "and the Word was with God and the Word was God". It's one of those great big thoughts that we human beings struggle to get our tiny brains around – that God can be thought of as having different aspects, but each of them is also fully God'. And that's ok. We are limited, created beings. We cannot ever really grasp the reality of God.

So John paints a different picture. He uses a metaphor. He has stated the truth as clearly as he can grasp it, by talking about the 'Word' dwelling among us. But now he chooses a different tack, and begins to talk about 'Light'.

Ah! That's better. 'Light' we can understand. We know about Light. We see its effects. We know that even a tiny spark of light cannot be extinguished by the darkness. We know that if this church was completely darkened, save for one candle, all our attention would be focused on that single solitary light.

"In Jesus", says John, "was life, and that life was the light of the world. The light shines in the darkness, and the darkness did not overcome it". And that, ultimately, is the message of Christmas. Darkness is all around us. The darkness of war, and famine, and poverty, and homelessness and selfishness and consumerism and loneliness, racism, homophobia, and fear of the stranger and all hatred and rebellion against the reason and logic of God. "But the light shines in the darkness".

In Jesus, through his teaching, his life, and yes even by his death, life is offered to the world. That's why we are going to mark Jesus' death in a few minutes, even in the midst of the 12 days of Christmas! Jesus' whole life is offered to us, by John and the other Gospel writers, as The Way to life. His way of living – generously, lovingly, wisely is offered to us as an example of what God's logic and reason look like. Jesus' way of dying – sacrificially, trustingly are still more examples of the Logos – the wisdom - of God. These are signposts for us. Lights in the darkness. Clues to how we too should live, if we truly want to find life.

The star of Bethlehem is of course another great symbol which the Christmas story offers us. It too is a light in the darkness, which leads others to the true light of Christ. And let's not forget that the light of a star is ultimately a sacrificial light. A star gives out light by burning itself up. All that the star is gets consumed, given out completely in the task of burning bright.

And that ultimately, is the task that we are given, as a response to the sacrificial self-giving of Christ. In a world only temporarily distracted by COVID, a world which will soon return to its selfish, greedy, destructive ways, we are called to be stars of Christ – sacrificially shining out into the darkness of the world.

So, here's my invitation, at the turning of the year. Let tonight be a turning point for you. Let the light of Christ illuminate and inspire you.

Draw from the spiritual energy he offers around his table, even taken in virtual form via this livestream. Follow and pursue the light of life every single day from this point on. It's what wise men did, 2,000 years ago. And it's what the wisest men and women today still do. Amen.

Autobiographies

Glimpses,
of our lives past and present

The Bellringers Apprentice

By Colin Browne – 30 April 2020

It was tea break on Thursday evening at our weekly 'a capella' choir practice when I asked a fellow Bass section participant what else he did with his leisure time. "Bell ringing," he said. "Where?" I replied. It would seem 'everywhere' as he reeled off a list of local churches that had active bell towers.

Now, as an ex Council house kid from Orpington in Kent. I said I had never been up a bell tower. The parish church on our estate back in the 1950's, and 200 yards down the road, was a more modern one and didn't have bells and the other one that we used to walk absolute miles and hours to on the monthly Cubs Sunday Church parade, did have them but as an 8-year-old, why would I care?

"Why don't you come along to Tuesday practice-night and have a look. We welcome everybody."

Well sure enough, off I toddle, and turn up at St Faith's at 19.30 on Tuesday evening. And so started an interesting struggle with trying to manipulate a 3/4 tonne piece of cast metal, tunefully.

The first thing to realise is that, despite what everybody tells you, it ain't as easy as it looks. Second is that the art has its own vocabulary. Thirdly, it would seem, the younger you are the easier it is to get the hang of. Yeah, right!! Fourthly, they are to be respected, as one appreciates pretty quick, they can and do bite you back if you don't. That means if you get shouted at it is for your own safety rather than for having done something wrong. Finally, belonging to this club means you are welcome at any tower, countrywide, as they are a very social, welcoming bunch of people.

As the 1½ hours of practise on Tuesday evening are for the whole band (group of bell ringers) then beginners are accommodated for half an hour before the main practice. It's a bit daunting as you have to be shadowed so you have an accomplished bell ringer supporting you as you pull the bell off on the hand stroke and they look after the back stroke. It's a bit like learning to drive a car when the instructor says 'this week we will teach you the accelerator and next week the brakes.' And so begins the first lesson. Tally Ho….

It's been an interesting journey. I started on the sixth bell which normally acts as the tenor if we are ringing the 6 bells. Never really got the hang of it, as despite all the encouragement, my bell control was non-existent. Then I switched to the fourth bell. That is a bit lighter and, as I found, easier to handle. And that is where I have been ever since. Time flies when you are having fun.

I said to somebody "in the five years I have been doing this I don't see any improvement." It wasn't till I looked at my emails that I realised I only started back in March 2017 when I took the Kings Shilling and got hijacked, so it's just over 3 years.

I have given it up countless times, as I have, in my opinion, never got any better. I found that if I went on holiday and came back to it, it seemed to improve no end. And then it didn't. Back to square one. And I would reiterate this is not for the lack of encouragement as the band are very supportive.

One thing that has, again in my opinion, been an absolute boon is the fact that bell ringers are needed to ring for the Sunday Service and that there always seems to be a space for me. So that means, good bad or indifferent, they have to put up with my, not always, inconsistent ringing. And practise, it would seem, does make perfect (whatever that means. I told you they have a different word for everything).

On a final note I would like to point out that a big plus for this as a hobby is that it doesn't take a big chunk of time out of your life. One evening a week for 1½ hours and 20-25 minutes on a Sunday and the occasional wedding, coffee morning and quarter peal. It's also great exercise.

Here endeth the Umpteenth Lesson.

Remembering HMS Coventry

by Bill Skilleter (Captain of the Tower)
21 May 2020

I was a crew member of HMS Broadsword during the Falklands Conflict maintaining The After Sea Wolf Missile system. On 25 May 1982, HMS Coventry and Broadsword were ordered to take up position to the north-west of Falkland Sound. There Coventry and Broadsword would act as a decoy to draw Argentinian aircraft away from other ships at San Carlos Bay. In this position, close to land and with not enough open sea between her and the coast, Coventry's Sea Dart missiles would be less effective.

Broadsword was armed with the Sea Wolf missile, which is for short range anti-aircraft and anti-missile system.

The two ships then came under attack by two waves of two Argentine Douglas A-4 Skyhawks. The first wave carried one 1,000 lb free-fall bomb each while the aircraft of the second carried 3 x 250 kg bombs. The four Skyhawks flew so low that Coventry's targeting radar could not distinguish between them and the land and failed to lock on. Broadsword attempted to target the first pair of attackers with her Sea Wolf missile system, but her own tracking system locked down during the attack and could not be reset before the aircraft released their bombs. One of the bombs bounced off the sea and struck the side of Broadsword coming out through flight deck which wrecked the ship's Westland Lynx helicopter then going over in to the sea without exploding.

The second pair of Skyhawks headed for Coventry 90 seconds later. On Broadsword the Sea Wolf system had been reset and successfully acquired the attacking aircraft, but was unable to fire as Coventry's turn took her directly into the line of fire. Coventry was struck by three bombs just above the water line on the port side. Within 20 minutes Coventry had been abandoned and had completely capsized. Coventry sank shortly after. Twenty of her crew were killed and a further 29 injured. Broadsword subsequently rescued 170 of Coventry's crew.

When I left the Broadsword after the Conflict my wife suggested that it might help me to start learning to ring bells, as she had already restarted this hobby whilst I was away. She learnt to ring when she was quite young but dropped it when we married. One of the things I vowed to do was to ring a quarter peal in memory of the Coventry, their crew especially those who lost their lives. Owing to the situation this year we are unable to ring but we will correct that once we are back to normal. On the 25th I will fall silent for 2 minutes to REMEMBER Them.

50 years of ordained ministry
by Fr Frank Hillebrand – 28 May 2020

A kind invitation has been extended to me to Preside at the 1030 Thursday Eucharist at Faith's (well – virtually!) on June 11th – the Feast of Corpus Christi (or as the C of E entitles it: "Thanksgiving for Holy Communion"). The reason for this is that the previous Sunday, Trinity Sunday, is the 50th anniversary of my ordination to the priesthood – and it was on Corpus Christi that I first presided at the Eucharist. Where did all those years go? Tom Kennar has asked me to share a little of my story, and for that I really need to "start at the very beginning…"

I was born in London in August 1946, my Dad having returned home in 1945 after 4 years abroad with the army in India, North Africa and Italy. He and my Mother had married in 1941 and he was posted just a few weeks later. For four years their only communication was by erratic letters whilst uncertainty not only surrounded Dad, but Mum who was actually living INSIDE the prime bombing target of the King George V Docks and working for the Port of London Authority. (And we are moaning about not seeing our families for a few months…?!)

Soon after de-mob Dad secured a position as Organist (and general organizer of the chapel) at the Royal Cancer Hospital (now the Royal Marsden) in South Kensington – and I was baptized there. Every Sunday I attended the 8am Holy Communion with my parents at our parish of St Anne's, Brondesbury (nr Queens Park) – after which Dad would dash off to the tube. I vividly recall kneeling with them week by week – and Mum explaining that when the sanctus bells tinkled and the priest raised the bread and wine on high – that this was Jesus coming to be with us in a special way. Wow! When I was about 8 years old I became a part of the 12-strong choir of boys that Dad recruited from the Kensington streets. With Dad, dressed in our Royal Scarlet cassocks, he and I went bed to bed around the wards before the service, asking the patients if they would like to come to chapel or would they like to listen to the service on their earphones? My Dad did this work for 30 years.

So from the very beginning, I now understand, a pattern was being imprinted in me – that in the Eucharist Christ comes in bread and wine to feed us, strengthen and inspire us, and in his strength we are granted whatever we need to go forth to serve.

In due time my voice broke. I was confirmed and became a server at St Anne's. I was just 17 and starting my final year at school when at the Youth Club Fr. Gubbins (lovely name – much-loved man) drifted over –

hands in cassock pockets as ever – for a chat. "What are you doing when you leave school?' he asked. I told him Dad had arranged for me to be Articled to a West-end firm of Quantity Surveyors. Fr G came back: "Does that fire you up? – Had you ever considered ordination?" What a crazy idea that seemed – and my friends thought it hilarious!! But somehow, soon, the surveying didn't appeal any more – and I tentatively entered into some conversations with Fr G – then with the Archdeacon and then Bishop Graham Leonard. Before I knew where I was, still just 17 years of age, I was off to a 3-day Selection Conference! Terrifying – everyone else was finishing university at least and I took my panic into Evensong that first afternoon! "Well Lord" – I remember praying in the manner of Laurel and Hardy – "what have you got me into now?!"

Short of ignominious flight there seemed no way out – so I resigned myself to just "being me" – on the basis that there was no hiding-place in this sort of selection conference and if I was really supposed to be doing this thing – or not – that might become clear. I was gob-smacked a week later to receive a letter unconditionally recommending me for training and ordination! I then took a year out, being so young, and worked as a shop-assistant and general factotum for Schott's Music Publishers in Soho. And bought an MGY!

Then it was off to Kings College London to study (as my Facebook profile states) Theology, Beer and Rowing! Marriage to Sue (whom I had met at her sister's wedding on my 17th Birthday) followed and we went off to St Boniface College, Warminster – King's own Fourth Year course to prepare for the practicalities of the ordained life – "How not to drop a baby whilst Baptising it" sort of thing!

Then there was a snag – ordination loomed but I was still under-age! Bishop Graham felt it would be silly for me sit around for three months until my birthday, so he obtained a Special Dispensation from the Archbishop of Canterbury. I was duly made a Deacon at St Pancras Parish Church in 1969 and Ordained Priest at St Paul's Cathedral in 1970. And so it began….

Two curacies of three years, as was then customary, completed 10 years of training. These were at St Michael's Wood Green and All Saint's Evesham (also Deputy Chaplain at Long Lartin prison). Amongst other things I trained as a Scout Leader which gave me youth-work skills which proved invaluable when the Bishop entrusted to me….

Holy Trinity and St Matthew's, on the "lively" Ronkswood estate, Worcester. I was there for seven hectic years – during which I was heavily engaged not only in the parish but also in founding St Paul's Hostel for the

Homeless in Worcester (check their website – it has developed into an amazing project which is immensely pleasing.) Our third child was born during this time too!

In 1980 I went to see my Bishop, Robin Woods, and asked if he might refer me to a Diocese in East Anglia (rationale: Sue came from a village near Frinton and my Dad needed to retire for health reasons = get parents together). He sent me to become Vicar of St John the Baptist KIDDERMINSTER! It was a fledgling Team Ministry: 2 parishes working in informal partnership with 2 Incumbents, a curate or two, a Parish Worker, an Industrial Chaplain – and close links to the newly-formed Hospital Chaplaincy and the Methodists.

It was an exciting time: we worked and played hard – Banks's was our local brew!! It was an awful decade for the West Midlands with traditional industries collapsing – many suicides, family breakup, broken town-centre. Led by the Industrial Chaplains the Church engaged with the unemployment crisis – the aisles of my church were converted with partitions for training rooms, from a caravan in the churchyard we ran a Gardening Training Scheme and from empty factories many such schemes were successfully run for all ages. Thatcher cut the funding eventually – furious at both the Faith in the City Report and Archbishop Runcie's insistence that he would pray for the Argentinian dead at the Falklands Memorial Service.... I became the first Team Rector of the West Kidderminster Team Ministry, and then it was time to move again!

1991 (Sue now a qualified Probation Officer) we moved to All Saints, the Parish Church of High Wycombe. This huge mediaeval building (seating 700 - up to 1000 at Christmas with extra seats!) was a mess – a Restoration and Re-ordering Project had stalled to the extent of communications passing via solicitors. The Bishop of Buckingham charged me: "This church is where our ordinations happen – many military services for NATO etc. - it should be the show-piece of our Episcopal Area – SORT IT!" The Church was consecrated in about 1087 by St Wulstan, Bishop of Worcester – where I was coming from – an omen?! Anyhow we seemed to pull it off and three years later we invited the then Bishop of Worcester back to re-dedicate it! (All Saints has an excellent and interesting website with lots of photos – well worth a look and even a short detour off the M40!).

In 1995 I was appointed Team Rector. It was the largest Team Ministry in England - with 6 Team Vicars, plus Curates, Non-Stipendiaries and Readers. In 1998 the Bishop noted that many new and worthwhile connections with the town were being formed and that this might be encouraged by changing my job to Team Rector and Town Chaplain - facilitated by another Team Vicar being added to take care of All Saints. It was an exciting plan which enabled Chaplaincies to the Police, the fledgling University, the business community etc. etc., but it turned out that not all of the Team (of disparate churchmanship and therefore understanding different visions of church) were prepared to back it wholeheartedly. The Bishop moved on – his successor did not understand Chaplaincy – so in 2000, in not a little disappointment at unmet opportunities, I decided I would shake the dust from my feet and made a final move - and I found myself "home"!

I saw an ad for an Anglican Chaplain at Portsmouth NHS Trust and, after interview and a basic training course at NHS Leeds, began an extremely busy, sometimes stressful but most rewarding seven years. The Ecumenical Chaplaincy Team then consisted of a Team Leader (who happened to be Methodist), 2.5 Anglicans, a Free Church minister, and a .5 RC priest. In due course we developed specialisms, and I found myself able to pursue an interest begun in High Wycombe in the area of baby-loss.

I also became part of the Women and Children's Divisional Management Team. We delivered a large teaching programme amongst staff at every level across the hospital, and our 24/7 care for patients was backed by 40+ trained volunteers. Sadly, the number of Chaplains is much diminished as a result of the recent decade of austerity and NHS cuts.

I retired in 2007 as Acting Head of Chaplaincy – a few years early as Sue had become very anxious to retire on her 60th Birthday. She was by then a Senior Probation Officer in charge of the Grange at Purbrook- a secure hostel for the more serious ex-offenders coming out of prison. In retrospect I think the beginnings of Alzheimer's Disease were already there for her – so it was good that I took retirement as we spent the next three years sailing our beloved 32' Fair Westering around the coast of Brittany. Gradually over the past 10 years I have become a "Carer" – since July 2017 sharing that responsibility with the wonderful team at Ferndale Care Home in Southbourne. We mostly worship at Westbourne – but have found a ready welcome at St Faith's Havant on occasions when there is non-Eucharistic worship at Westbourne.

Looking back on all that has happened as I approach the Golden Jubilee of my Priesthood I marvel at the (mostly!) wonderful experiences and privileges that have come my way – and am so grateful for my dear parents Joy and Stephen and what they taught and showed me of the Eucharistic life, and for Sue who also has held these things dear and still does even in her increasing confusion. On Sunday 15th March Ferndale "locked-down" to all visitors – but I was able to take the Reserved Sacrament to share with her. It was a very special moment.

So I look forward to Corpus Christi: Praise to you, Lord Jesus Christ, for the gift to your church of yourself in bread and wine – inspiration and food for our journey wherever that may lead.

A bit like Downton Abbey

by Margaret Tait – 4 June 2020

I worked for many years as a Credit Controller for a large local company, which sometimes involved flying around the U.K. to collect fat cheques. But it was stressful and, as my husband was made redundant from IBM at that time, we decided to take a different approach to our working lives.

I bought a copy of The Lady and, some weeks later, we were working in a 16th century country house set in around 400 acres of Surrey countryside. We were employed on a live-in basis to take care of a sweet, elderly lady and were given rooms in the annexe. My jobs were mainly to cook dinner for Mrs A., feed the cat and take her for a spree in her Mercedes. She would descend the stairs in her chair lift each morning and often spoke of her varied life: sheep farming in Australia and dining with royalty; her late husband had been a diplomat. She was kind and generous: on our days off we were allowed to use the swimming pool, tennis court and pavilion and to invite our family.

One New Year's Eve we gave a small dinner party for close friends and Mrs A. joined us for sherry. As she grew more frail and needed professional nursing care, we started to look again in The Lady.

Our next position was as live-in nanny and butler in a large mansion in West Sussex. The lady of the house was Mrs B, and as the daughter of the nobility she was extremely particular. Our accommodation had large rooms and sweeping views across the park. Think Downton Abbey on a slightly smaller scale.

There were four very unruly children so it was crowd control rather than nannying. At formal dinners I was required to wear a black dress with a white apron, but no cap fortunately. I didn't enjoy those occasions having to wait up until the last guest had departed and then finish hand washing the silver cutlery and ensure the oak dining table was clear of marks. There were four guest suites, each with a four poster bed to be supplied with clean linen, towels and toiletries before guests arrived. Mr and Mrs B also entertained royalty and attended royal weddings so it was interesting to peek in the visitors' book (when there was no danger of being seen)! My abiding memory is of constant exhaustion! There were three staircases, twenty-three chimneys, two dining rooms, plus the silver room, flower room, boot room and gun room......

But all good things as they say .... I was offered a completely different job - that of Escort for the local coach company, Lucketts Travel. I saw many places I would not otherwise have seen and met hundreds of people from all walks of life, serving them teas and coffees on the coach while hurtling along motorways. From The Channel Islands to The Orkneys, from Amsterdam to Galway, from Torquay to a Castle in Austria, where we battled swarms of hornets in the stifling heat, my memories are varied and pleasant; no other work could have provided such variety.

However, after nine years of this wandering life I decided to give my spare time to voluntary work. I could have covered several pages with memories of my time working for Mrs A. and Mrs B. not forgetting being an Escort! I hope the above abridged version has been enjoyable to read.

Why I chose to go to St Faith's

by Kim Sharpe – 4 June 2020

I have always attended church since a young age. I joined the choir at the age of 13. I was a Sunday school teacher too. When I moved to the UK, I tried a few churches but none that I felt happy in.

Then one day I was having a really bad time in my life and I was having a coffee in town with my best friend when I heard St Faith's bells ringing for a wedding. I had been informed of St Faith's before, but never knew exactly where it was.

So on the Sunday I got up early and sat in the congregation. I was made really welcome by Bill Jones and he looked after me that day. (That's one of Bill's great gifts! Ed.) It was such an amazing service and felt so warm and welcoming. After the service I spoke to Bill again and asked about joining the choir. Since then I have never looked back and have been so welcomed into the St Faith's family by everyone

Coronation Memories

by Colin Carter – 4 June 2020

The 2 June 2020, being the 67th anniversary of HM The Queen's Coronation, brought back memories to me. I had been in HMS DIAMOND, a Daring Class destroyer, for 9 months having joined her after 15 months training as a Boy Telegraphist at HMS GANGES, Shotley, near Ipswich. In those days the Communications Branch was the crème de la crème being the first to know what was happening – remember every signal at sea was sent in Morse code and encrypted – there were no satellites then.

The ship was alongside in Chatham, her home port, and it was exciting to do something different for 6 weeks after many days at sea exercising and visits to European ports. After rehearsing for the big day the majority of the ship's company were bussed to London the day before the event staying in Clapham.

It was an early start on the 2nd when we were taken to Northumberland Avenue to provide street lining. We were in position for many hours, with spectators behind us wanting to make conversation, before the procession came past on the way to Westminster Abbey. Whilst waiting there were some heavy showers that left us soaked! After the procession had passed we were fallen out, handed in our rifle and webbing and allowed to mingle with the crowds and watched the return from Westminster Abbey as the route after the Coronation did not pass along Northumberland Avenue. In the evening we went to Trafalgar Square and joined in the singing and dancing celebrations.

HMS DIAMOND sailed from Chatham to the Solent for the Coronation Review of the Fleet at Spithead held on 15 June (there were some 200 Royal Navy ships and 30 Commonwealth and Foreign ships making quite a spectacle).

After the review the ship then followed Queen Elizabeth II and the Duke of Edinburgh on their Coronation Tours to Scotland, Northern Ireland and Wales and the ship's company provided street lining in Glasgow (25 June), Belfast (2 July) and Cardiff (9 July).

We had the privilege of seeing The Queen and the Duke of Edinburgh on six separate occasions – albeit briefly as they swiftly passed by. Little did I know then that many years later (1988) I would have the honour of shaking Her Majesty's hand when she awarded me the MBE at Buckingham Palace!

Beattie's Sweet Factory

by Beatrice Mockford – published 11 June 2020

(from an old parish magazine)

As one of our oldest members, Beatrice (Beattie) Mockford has given a lifetime of service both to St Faith's and to the local community. Here is an article she wrote for the old parish magazine, a few years ago, which gives a fascinating (and very tempting) insight into some of her working life (kindly submitted by Hilary Deadman).

"Mr Hostler started making and selling toffee apples from his front room. By the time I started to work for him he had graduated to two factories in the Portsmouth area. The one I worked in, between 1945 and 1955, overlooked Pitt Street.

Whilst the war was still on and during the time of sugar rationing, Mr Hostler kept us busy as cleaners and decorators in the factory rather than laying any of us off.

I started as a labeller and moved on to pulling the mixture for the humbug machine, feeding it in and breaking the shaped humbugs into individual sweets.

After the war the factory had sugar and glucose and expanded its range of sweets. We started to make Southsea rock and rock for all the seaside resorts along the south coast. To make sticks of rock you start with a giant stick of rock about a foot in diameter with the letters running all the way through; it was hand rolled and pulled out to make it into thinner and thinner sticks until it reached the required diameter. The rock had to be rolled constantly even after it had reached the right thickness to stop it sinking into a flat lump, and we could only stop when it had cooled enough to become solid.

There was another machine for stamping out pear drops and eventually one for wrapping individual sweets. The toffee was made on huge oiled slabs, with someone constantly moving the boiling mixture until it had cooled and reached the right consistency to be cut and shaped.

In the winter the factory was a cosy warm place to work, but in the summer it was baking hot; we were given a ten-minute tea-break in the morning and again in the afternoon and an hour for lunch. Mr Hostler was a good man to work for and I only left when I started my family (as you did in those days).

Reflections of 1955

by Beryl Carter – 18 June 2020

65 years ago, on 4th March 2020, I arrived with my father in Southampton from Cape Town in the RMMV "Carnarvon Castle" after an exciting 14 days' passage – that's how long it took in those days as travelling by sea was the main mode of transport.

From Southampton we went by train to London where my mother, younger sister and two brothers, who had arrived six months earlier to set up home with the help of the Methodist Church, met us. That morning, I had never felt so cold in all my life having left Cape Town in the middle of summer and with the lovely hot weather during the voyage, especially when we crossed the equator, it was quite a shock.

People had said that it would be difficult for me being a teenager to move to another country, but not so at all. I very soon settled down and within two weeks of arriving found myself employment as a typist in the offices of George Payne (Tea Merchants) Co. Ltd at Tower Bridge. I was fascinated by all the London historic buildings, especially Tower Bridge, which I could see being raised and lowered from the office window. Also, the underground which I used daily, the hustle and bustle of London, the sense of humour of the office girls, and the different way of life from that of living in South Africa. However, I shall always have memories of beautiful Table Mountain, which I had seen every day.

Before the end of March, I was bridesmaid to a cousin's wedding in Surrey, on a bitterly cold day – just image how cold I felt in a short sleeved dress of taffeta and net!

So my memories of my first month in the UK were of excitement and also of feeling very cold – even the bed felt cold and damp – remember there was no central heating then. But when you are young you take this all in your stride.

The decision my parents made those 65 years ago in coming to the UK was one of the best things that happened in my life, which I have never regretted. By the end of that year, 1955, I had met a handsome sailor who became the love of my life – but that's another story! (Next month in July Colin and I will be celebrating our 62nd wedding anniversary).

Thanksgiving

by Alan Hakim – 18 June 2020

Memories of Bombay – or is that Mumbai?

My first job was with Thomas Cook in London, but in 1964 they suddenly sent me to be Travel Manager in their Bombay office. This was the second-in-command position. My boss Frank Lofthouse, who had been working in India since the 1930s, was the General Manager for the East and Far East. He had wide-ranging responsibilities so I was in charge of the whole travel department of some 50 Indians. We worked in a Victorian building in the style of a Venetian palace, and my department was approached up a magnificent marble staircase. It was open-plan, while Frank had a private office next to it.

For my first few months, he was very involved in negotiations with the Union about pay scales, and there were frequent low-level strikes. All the staff would leave their desks and form an impassable crowd outside his office doors, so that he was effectively locked in. Meanwhile, it fell to me to take all the phone calls. After an hour, everyone went back to work, and I went round delivering phone messages.

In August, at the end of the Monsoon, when it has stopped raining but the weather hasn't heated up again yet, I was approached with an invitation to attend the annual service of thanksgiving. "Thanks for what?" I asked. "For our good jobs," I was told. This was a surprise after all the strikes.

Still, I agreed to attend on Sunday morning at a Roman Catholic church in the inner suburbs, and all the Christians of my staff were there. We had a short informal service, and then retired to the Parish Hall for refreshments and dancing. This, at 10 o'clock on a Sunday morning. Of course, as the Manager it was my duty to dance with every one of the secretaries, and show no favouritism. And I wasn't even a good dancer. But the morning went off well.

The next August I had been in Bombay the better part of two years, and I decided to have some home leave. One of the perks of working for Cooks was very cheap airfares. And I thought I would be away for the annual service. But when I got back, they said they had postponed it for me, so it was next Sunday.

This time, there was no dancing. We all went off to the beach for a picnic and party games. It was all very jolly, but a bit hot in the open sunshine. It was possible to sit where there was a sea breeze, but unfortunately our beach was downwind of a Bombay Duck supplier.

Bombay Duck is a small fish which is salted and then hung in large numbers on frames to dry in the sun. Drying fish gives off a powerful smell, so it was better to swelter out of the breeze.

I had the opportunity to go back to Bombay a few years ago, and went to visit my old office. The exterior is still a Venetian palace, but sadly the interior was now an ordinary ground floor travel agent's office.

And if you are wondering about Bombay now being Mumbai, there is a simple explanation. Mumbai had always been the local name, but some 500 years ago, the Portuguese had changed it to Bombay, 'beautiful bay'. The trains carried both names on their destination boards, but Bombay was universally used until the Hindu Nationalists chose Mumbai for political reasons. Huge numbers of residents still use 'Bombay', and as I explained to my tour group, the plane might have been flying to Mumbai, but I was going to Bombay.

The Miracle

by Chris Elmes – 25 June 2020

The following story was submitted by Chris Elmes, who is married to Peter. She says that miracles might not always happen as a 'zap' from God. Sometimes, just being in the right place at the right time can be miraculous too...

"Happy Birthday Dad, and may there be many more" said David, lifting his wine glass towards his father. The twelve other people sitting around the table lifted their glasses and a chorus of Happy Birthday rang out. It was a family tradition for the whole family to gather together to celebrate Donald's birthday, and this was often the only time during the year that everyone was able to get together.

Donald responded by lifting his glass and looking in the direction of his older sister said "To Sandra, without whom I would not be here."

"May I ask why, Donald? What did Sandra do?" asked the latest addition to the family, his most recent daughter-in-law, fascinated by such an odd toast. Although most of the others already knew what had happened so many years ago, Donald took a deep breath and began to tell his story.

"It was all a very long time ago now, but I've never forgotten the debt I owe my sister. When I was a young child there was no National Health Service and if you needed medical help you had to pay for it or pay into a medical club that would pay the bill for you. Straight after the war, money was very short and my father had had no luck in finding a proper job so his payments to the medical club had lapsed. It was just after my sixth birthday when I became ill" he went on, staring into space as if he could see his childhood home in front of him.

After a brief pause he continued with his story. No-one had known what was wrong with him, and old Doctor Field had visited every day for a whole week with very little chance of ever getting paid. He had been unable to stop the constant headache, vomiting, dizziness and loss of vision. In desperation Donald's sister Sandra, who was two years older, went to her secret box hidden under the broken floor board in the scullery and counted out all the money she had been able to squirrel away. She had been collecting and returning empty bottles and used glass jars for some months, as well as collecting any old rags she could find and selling them to the rag and bone man. She had also run errands for neighbours and the local shopkeepers, who would sometimes reward her by giving her a penny. By dint of her own hard work she had so far been able to save the grand total of three shillings and four pence.

After carefully counting the money, and recounting it to be absolutely sure how much she had, Sandra had wrapped it all in her handkerchief, which she held tightly in her hand. Taking the money, she had slipped out of the house and hurried directly to the Doctor's house. She had seen that the front door with its huge brass knocker was open and she had marched inside without allowing herself to be frightened.

The Doctor had stared at her in absolute astonishment. "What on earth do you mean by walking in here? Get out."

"I can't go yet; I need a miracle."

"Frankly, I don't care what you need. I'm very busy indeed and am talking to a colleague and I want you to leave now. Do you understand me?"

"I'm sorry Doctor Field, but I just can't go until you listen to me. I need a miracle and I don't know how much they cost. I've brought all my money that I've been saving for ages, and I need to know if it's enough."

The stranger who had been talking to Doctor Field smiled at Sandra, bent down and spoke to her. "Why do you need a miracle, my dear?"

"Well, my little brother is very sick with something wrong inside his head. Doctor came and saw him today and he told my Dad we would need a miracle to make Donald better. I've got my money and I want to get him a miracle, because my Mum is crying all the time and I want things to be right again" she explained in a rush.

"How much money have you got?"

"Three shillings and four pence."

Taking the money from her hand he had replied "How very lucky. That is exactly how much a miracle costs. I'll come with you and talk to your Mummy and we'll see if we can't make your brother feel better."

Doctor Field's mouth had dropped open. "You can't rush off and interfere in one of my cases, Tim. It's madness. They just haven't got the money to pay for my basic care let alone for surgery, and I'm not even sure what's wrong with the lad, although I suspect a brain tumour."

"I can interfere and I will Richard. This little girl is prepared to give me all she has to save her brother. It's just lucky that I should be here when she arrived and that, as a surgeon, I can probably help. She has faith, and so should you."

True to his word, the strange Doctor had gone home with Sandra. After explaining his presence to her very flustered mother, he examined Donald and by pulling a few strings was able to arrange to get him in to hospital where he operated the following day. In less than a week, it was obvious to everyone that Donald was getting better and he was soon ready to go home.

Many weeks later, when Donald was well on the way to being his old self, his mother was talking to a neighbour about everything that had happened. "It was really strange, that posh doctor just turning up out of the blue with our Sandra. I dread to think what it would have cost us if we'd had to pay for a miracle like that."

Sandra smiled to herself. She knew exactly what a miracle cost. It was three shillings and four pence.

Typhoon Wanda – Hong Kong 1962

by Rex Plowman – 25 June 2020

I had been serving in the RAF since late 1959 and was part way through my Far East tour at RAF Seletar, Singapore followed by my detachment to RAF Kai Tak in Hong Kong. So, it was by August of 1962 that I was enjoying a normal, carefree and happy life, reflected in the Forces' popular recruitment slogan, "Plenty of opportunity for sport and travel"

However, because of its geography, there were very few places to travel on leave from Hong Kong. Japan, like Singapore, was some 1500m miles away. It was therefore decided by the Far East Air Force HQ that it would be a good idea to establish a small Recreation Site on one of the hundreds of islands surrounding the Colony. A small Island was chosen within Silvermine Bay, located to the North East of Kowloon which was an extremely popular recreational area for many of the people who lived in the Colony.

I was delegated to recruit eight volunteer Airmen for this new initiative. My C.O. was to organise not only the setup, but the date for the first week's visit. By late August we had transported all the necessary camping equipment to establish the site on the Island by the way of several trips in the RAF Air Sea Rescue Launch. To encourage the lads, I was first to put my name forward and indeed seven others signed up to join me.

It had been decided that the expedition would depart on the morning of Thursday 30st. August. Way out in the Pacific Ocean on Tuesday August 28th, a tropical cyclone had been forming some 700 miles to the north east of the Philippines. It was designated Tropical Depression No.59. Not too much notice was taken as tropical storms are normally quite erratic in their directional course. However, No. 59 was already heading in a North Westerly direction and it was the Typhoon season.

That evening, on Wednesday 29th at RAF Kai Tak, I was scheduled to play in a Combined Services hockey team against Hong Kong before their departure for the Asian Games in Djakarta. As luck may have it, or indeed not, within ten minutes or so of the game having started I turned an ankle, tearing ligaments which put me in hospital. I was returned to the Station later that evening with my right leg in plaster. I was particularly saddened by my injury, because now I could not accompany my pal Jimmy Campbell to the Island, with whom I played both rugby and golf.

The following morning, Thursday 30th, was the day of departure for the boys to their Island resort but, sadly, without me. By chance I had found an Airman who worked in the Photographic Section and had just arrived in Hong Kong, having taken no embarkation leave prior to flying out from UK. He was delighted to take my place.

So, although the Cyclone, now named Typhoon Wanda, was still heading in a Northerly direction, the decision was taken by the C.O. that they could sail to their Island on the original date. They arrived safely on the powerful RAF Air Sea rescue launch at their newly tented area late that afternoon to enjoy the beginning of their week's R&R (rest and recuperation).

Initially the winds were very weak as the tropical cyclone continued to follow a Northerly track, slowly growing in intensity but now heading towards Taiwan. On Friday 31st August whilst approaching South Eastern China, winds were recorded at 110mph. However, now veering to a North Westerly direction, Typhoon Wanda weakened a little before making landfall some 12 hours later on Hong Kong at 8.00am on Saturday September 1st. As the storm intensified some 10.5 inches of rain fell and the highest wind speed recorded at 161mph. The Typhoon moved inshore during the daily high tide resulting in an exceptional storm surge of 17 feet.

At about 10.00am, the eye of the storm passed directly overhead. To look up into the clear sky amid such mayhem was quite extraordinary. There now followed a ten-minute eerie lull of no wind and a raging sea. Rain hid most of the harbour where ships were blowing horns as they tried to go about prior to the winds lashing back in the opposite direction after a 10-minute lull. The rain fell horizontally. Cars were being blown away like the scattering of confetti. Trees were uprooted, plucked like weeds from a garden. At the quayside, a lighter[2] had broken its moorings and spilled out dozens of empty 50-gallon drums which with the help of the gale force winds raced down the runway at about 60mph before crashing into the Airfield's perimeter fence. Strong winds destroyed many vessels including a 10,000-ton freighter which had its bows settled upon a railway embankment nearly blocking the line.

By late that Saturday afternoon the RAF Mountain Rescue Team were on board the Air Sea rescue launch powering out in heavy seas towards the Island. The prospect for the safety of those Airmen on the Island was bleak. And so it proved to be, because they were eventually found dead, all huddled together sheltering in a derelict old building which had collapsed when it was hit by the huge tidal surge. The tented camp was nowhere to be seen.

---

[2] a flat-bottomed barge

Personally, it was an early experience of losing friends tinged with a guilt which will forever live with me. Especially for the young Airman who took my place. We were all in our 20's.

Records show that 434 souls were lost on that unforgettable day together with 72,000 poor people who became homeless in Hong Kong. Since that traumatic experience I have often been reminded of the Chinese proverb, "Keep facing the sun and let the shadows fall behind". A poignant reminder of our fate in life over which we have no control.

The Pingat Jasa Malaysia

by Colin Carter – 2 July 2020

In 2005 the Malaysian Government approached the Foreign and Commonwealth Office (FCO) to seek approval to present their new medal, known as the Pingat Jasa Malaysia (PJM), to British veterans and others who served in operations in Malaya/Malaysia between August 1957 and August 1966. The British Government believed it to be important to recognise, the generous gesture by the King and Government of Malaysia, and their wish to acknowledge the service given by veterans and others in the years immediately after Malaysian independence in 1963.

During the qualifying period I had served in the theatre of operations on two separate occasions.

Firstly, in 1957 & 1958 whilst serving in the destroyer HMS Cossack in charge of the wireless communications – it was Morse code in those days, not mobile phone technology of today - when the ship had provided naval gunfire support at various times for the army in areas held by the communists.

Secondly, in 1966 as the Communications Officer on the staff of the Commander Naval Forces in Borneo (there were only three naval officers – the Captain, Operations Officer and me – amongst many army and RAF officers), based in Labuan, an island north-east of Brunei. Indonesia had attempted to overthrow the Sultan of Brunei in 1962 to get its hands on the oil fields and had then started infiltrating into Sarawak and Sabah when it opposed the countries joining the Malaysian Federation in 1963.

It was a very interesting job which required flying from one end of Borneo to the other – Kuching and Sibu to the west in Sarawak and to Tawau in the east in Sabah – visiting Brunei, liaising with army and RAF personnel, visiting the naval radio operators and the naval helicopter squadrons based in the dense jungle sites. Visiting the naval helicopter squadrons was particularly interesting as it meant flying, in a small single engine Beaver aircraft piloted by an army sergeant, over the jungle tree tops and landing on small fields or dirt tracks in a jungle clearing – real flying!

The border between Sarawak and Sabah with Kalimantan (Indonesia) is 999 miles in length, so it was a large area for the military to stop infiltration with most of the terrain dense jungle – but it did – with the Gurkha's being particularly good at this.

What 'Lockdown' has meant for me

by Clive Barnett – 9 July 2020

A (very) personal reflection on what lockdown has meant for Clive Barnett, one of our Church Wardens

As I write this in early July, some fourteen weeks since the start of lockdown in the UK, I'm struck by how long ago that day in late March when it all began seems now. It was a very different world back then; we had so many freedoms which we took for granted and which have been since denied us. Yet, this weekend, we have the prospect of pubs opening again and, yes, places of worship for private prayer – with the strict proviso that this must be done safely and in a way that will not permit the virus to spread. So, this seems to be as good a time as any to take stock and assess the impact that the lockdown has had.

On one level for me at least, it has had little impact. I had never been a great clothes shopper, preferring to make my purchases online. I did shop for food but found it surprisingly easy to adapt to 'click and collect'. I enjoyed the occasional visit to the pub and eating out but not to the extent of wanting to do it every day. I did enjoy going to the theatre and to Lord's for the cricket – and have been a Chichester Theatre Friend and MCC member for nearly 40 years – so the realisation that this year's festival and county cricket programme would be scrapped was perhaps the worst imposition at the time. Otherwise, frankly, I welcomed the extra time to myself that lockdown would give; no more long car journeys to Salisbury for trustees' meetings or to Guildford to act as a governor, and a break from the carousel of lunches with friends which, delightful as they were, could so easily get out of hand.

I resolved to devote my time to those projects around the house and garden which I had never quite got round to in the five years since we moved back to the south coast. So, since late March, the garden has been transformed: the pond dredged and the reeds removed to allow the water lilies to see the light of day; the grass has been fed, watered and mowed far more regularly than before; flowerbeds have been weeded; vexatious ivy removed; roses pruned; raised beds re-planted; the summerhouse repainted inside and out. I've actually enjoyed the process of 'discovering' my garden. It had never been my forte: I had been a willing grass mower and hewer of wood but fancy stuff like planting had always passed me by. That's now no longer the case: I've started to take a real delight in watching the fruits of my labours take root and blossom.

The same applies to inside the house: painting has been completed; books, clothes and utensils have been sorted and earmarked for the charity shop or the local dump; filing has been reorganised and relocated; cleaning and hoovering have been prodigious – I have 'boldly gone where no man has gone before' with my vacuum cleaner. At the end of it all, I feel an undeniable sense of achievement; looking at my tidy shelves and clothes racks brings a great sense of satisfaction because without lockdown little if any of it would have been accomplished.

However, that is all pretty superficial. If I dig beneath the surface, what can I say I have achieved? Well – and I'm by no means the only one to say this – there has certainly been a reconnection with the natural world. The absence of road noise for much of the last fourteen weeks and of airplanes has made it possible to hear the birdsong which is normally drowned out by the busy-ness of everyday life. Many have observed how quickly the natural world has responded to the lockdown to the point of repossessing areas formerly relinquished to humans, and I was particularly taken by the news report, early in the lockdown, of the sighting of fish in the Grand Canal of Venice – something not seen for a century – as a result of the absence of gondolas and other waterborne traffic. To undertake my daily walk, along the path opposite my house which leads to the shoreline between Emsworth and the road bridge at Langstone, has been blissful especially in the beautiful weather of this year's spring and early summer. Whether working in the garden or standing on the shingle looking towards Hayling Island, I've been put back in touch with the rhythms of the natural world. More than anything, I hope that I don't lose that sense of heightened awareness when the lockdown ends.

I have also had the time to take stock of where I am on my spiritual journey and this has led me to some pretty uncomfortable truths. In particular, I had not been allowing myself to pray – really pray – for long enough each day. I'm trying to do better now and kneeling whilst doing the weeding or washing the car seems to be the ideal time when I can allow myself to reflect. I've been doing lots of kneeling in lockdown, and my sincerest hope is that this will continue into the 'new normal'.

So, what do I hope that the 'new normal' will look like? For myself, I earnestly hope that I do not return to the merry-go-round of meetings which occupied my weeks with remorseless regularity. Maybe I should relinquish some of the trusteeships and play a lesser role as a governor; perhaps it is the right time to allow other, younger folk to pick up the baton. After all, there is more than enough to occupy myself as a churchwarden at St Faith's, especially trying to keep Reverend Tom in check! As for those meetings which I will still have to attend, I hope that at least some can continue to be virtual thus obviating the need to spend quite so much of my time in a car. And I hope that this will be the case more widely in the world too, especially as so many have now realised that working from home carries with it many benefits. Perhaps it will not be necessary for so many to spend so much of their time commuting to and from the office. Maybe the shuttle flight to clinch the deal in New York will not be as necessary as it once was.

Lockdown has given all of us a God-given opportunity to rein back on our wasteful lifestyles. The climate has been given a chance to recuperate; the earth has been given the opportunity to regenerate; those who save lives and keep us all going in our everyday lives have at last been recognised for the heroes that they are. In view of this, I pray that we do not let go this moment in pursuit of all the old ways.

I really do not want to go back to the way things were.

More tales from Bombay

by Alan Hakim – 16 July 2020

Thomas Cooks attached great importance to getting payment for services provided, and taking care in granting credit. There was even a file circulated by Head Office of dreaded "Customers to be served on a cash basis only."

When I was transferred from London to Bombay, I found that things were not always so straightforward. Our business accounts were all reliable payers except one: a well-known British company who were always behind in their payments. I wouldn't have wished to do business with them.

But there were more unusual cases. One I remember was a Burmese gentleman who produced his British Passport and asked for some expensive travel on credit. He even uttered the words, "We British must stick together," always a signal to start counting the spoons. He claimed close acquaintance with Commander Smyrk, now a senior manager at Berkeley Street Head Office, who had served in India during the war. I consulted my boss, Frank Lofthouse, who had been in India for years. "Commander Smyrk?" he expostulated. "All he did in the war was sail a desk in Delhi." We agreed to write to him, and a week later the reply came back: "Cash basis only." And I saw no more of the Burmese.

Even more memorable was an elderly Sikh who turned up one day saying he was Finance Officer for a film in production, and they needed to book train tickets for the company to go up to a hill station for location filming. I said our Railway department would be delighted to arrange it, but he said, "No, you don't understand. We need credit for this." I demurred, not knowing him at all, and he explained that the film world was full of gossip, and if it became known he had had to pay in advance, it would have ruined his film's reputation.

I don't know how that argument would have gone down at Head Office, but in Bombay this was clearly true, and the only way we could get his business. So we came to a strict arrangement that he would come in with payment on the thirtieth day, and I sent him off happy to the booking clerks.

About a month later, there was a grisly murder of a well-known Indian film star, which was extensively reported in the papers. Not knowing much about the film world, I was not greatly interested. Then on the 30th day, the Sikh reappeared. He was full of apologies, but he couldn't pay me today. The dead star was a close friend of the man in his company who issued the cheques – and he was so upset by his friend's murder that his hands were shaking too much to sign with his proper signature. This story again had the ring of truth, so we parted, leaving me slightly worried about his large bill, and sure enough, two days later the Sikh came back with the cheque.

And I forgot it all, until several months later he turned up again. My heart sank at the thought of another negotiation, but no: the film was now on release, and doing good business in the principal Bombay cinema. He produced a wad of free tickets for me and the Railway department – and that was the first Bollywood epic I ever saw.

Early days in France

by Carol Acworth – 30 July 2020

It sometimes seems to me that being always foreign, and not being able to speak the language, (and being very lazy about learning it) is quite a high price to pay for living in the sun.

But sometimes the mistakes and misunderstanding are so funny that it makes it all worth it! Like the day I nearly crashed the car in astonishment on seeing a large Labrador dog driving the oncoming car, only to remember that actually the driver was sitting on the other side.

Like the day I walked into Schmidt Kitchens, thinking this is a likely place for a tap, only to be told with a certain politeness that they did not stock them. It gradually dawned on me that in Schmidt Kitchens, one bought a whole up-market kitchen, or one bought nothing at all!

Or the day I went into Mr Bricolage late in the morning and was browsing the shelves as I often do, and along came an assistant. "Can I help you?" he said in English. I was astonished. No one talks to me in Mr Bricolage, certainly not amongst the plumbing shelves, it's a man's place. Someone cares about me? I thought, highly flattered. "well" I said, embarking into an explanation of what I wanted, so relieved to speak

English. His response was unexpected. "Could you come back later?" he asked. "You see" looking at his watch, "we are trying to close the shop". The moral of this tale is that if you live in the south of France, get used to everything shutting for two hours at lunch time.

Or high moments at the art class. As the only foreigner there I felt rather that I did not quite belong. The teacher was very kind, spoke very slowly to me, corrected me, that what I called a brosse was actually a pinceau, and trying to fill me in with patient slow French as to what everyone was talking about. I frequently got the wrong end of the stick, and got teased for my overlong pronunciation of the word bouilloire, an item that interested me greatly, as I was always longing for the tea break.

One day a member of the class began tossing off all her clothes, accompanied by some strong French expletives, her face going an ever deeper shade of red, and creating a disturbance that turned every head in the room. The teacher sidled up to me. She felt I needed an explanation for this extraordinary display. She nudged me to get my attention, It was clearly going to be a new word for my vocabulary: "Tu sais Carol," she whispered, and then by way of explanation, dishing out each syllable with slowly emphasis: "c'est la 'Men . . ooooh . . . Pause!' She nodded sagely and wandered off, tossing over her shoulder as she went, "tu comprends Carol?"

Or the time I got a speeding fine, which, cursing as I did so, I paid up on the dot. Six months later I received a frighteningly official looking letter from the Ministry of the Interior. Opening it with trembling hands and reading it as best I could, it appeared to me that due to a speeding "infraction" six months previously I now had 12 points on my driving licence. I saw myself dusting off the bike and putting the car in the garage for a year. It turned out that they had put back the one point they seized when I drove too fast, and now, wasn't I lucky, I had all 12 points of my entitlement back again. That just seems the wrong way round to me!

John Burch's Life Story – in several parts!

by John Burch – from 23 July 2020 and several weeks following…

I was born in a war-torn London in 1938 at St. Giles Hospital, Camberwell. I am the third child of four, three boys and one girl. When I was 1 year old we moved to Devon where my mother gave birth to her fourth child. She was subsequently found wandering the streets in a confused state and so my Father, who was a military man, had her sectioned. I think today she would probably have been diagnosed with severe post-natal depression. She died three months later in hospital. I was taken back to London aged one but my brothers and sister went to relatives.

From London I was sent to Rhyl and placed with the C. of E. Children's Society in a village near Audley End called Ashdon. I started my first infant school. One of the helpers in the home was a dear lady called Mrs. Woodley. The Master and Matron were Mr. and Mrs. Maple, who unbeknown to me at the time, would prove to be a big influence in my life. We were surrounded by green fields full of vegetable crops and these were tended by German POW's. I used to converse with the ones who could speak English.

All 25 boys had specific jobs to do in the home. I must have spent five years in Ashdon before I was moved to "Pinehurst" in Camberley, Surrey. I was delighted to find that Mr. and Mrs. Maple had also been transferred there which made the transition easier. Pinehurst had beautiful grounds, once again I was one of 25 boys but, I soon settled in. However, it was not to be for too long!

I was nearly eight and very happy with my surroundings but I was soon to be off again. This time I was moved to yet another part of the country, Bexley in Kent which turned out to be The London Choir School famous for pupils such as Michael Crawford, Tony Hatch and Roy Chubby Brown, all of who were day pupils. It was a fee-paying School run by a man who said he was an ordained Priest but, as you will read a little later, he was an imposter. He was constantly walking around the grounds in his clerical shirt and collar.

I was a boarder and it was not until a few years later I was told that I had been sponsored by an anonymous benefactor. I never discovered who it was. Whilst at this school I was chosen to sing at many well-known London Churches: Holy Trinity, Brompton, St. Paul's Cathedral, where we performed the Passion of the Messiah, Eaton Square, The King's Chapel of Savoy which was attended by King George VI and Queen Mary and St. Martin-in-the Fields. I also sang in two films made at the Elstree and

Denham Studios. The "Guinea Pig" with Richard Attenborough and "No Room At the Inn" starring Glenda Jackson.

Around 1948-49 there was an investigation at the School regarding some serious misdemeanours involving the Principal. The News made the front page of The Sunday Pictorial and it transpired that he was not an ordained Priest at all and he was sentenced to 10 years for his offences.

I was taken out of the School by the C. of E. Children's Society and placed in
another Home in Wellingborough/Northants called Hatton Hall. I attended the local school settling in fairly quickly and enjoying my school work considering, I had had so many interruptions. But alas, it was not too long before it was deemed necessary to move me yet again, this time to Balham in South London which was classified as an Assessment Home looking where to place boys next.

I was quickly moved to Burgess Hill and this is where I was able to put my vocal talent into operation. Directly opposite the home was St. John's C. of E. Church and I joined their choir. The Home had spacious grounds with many apple trees which encouraged the boys to become quite good at scrumping...at which I excelled!

Part Two (30 July 2020)

After arriving in Burgess Hill the Master and Matron saw my potential as a leader and made me Senior Boy which, in some cases, did not go down too well with the more established older boys but after a little while they accepted me.

Our local school was the London Road County Secondary School with mixed classes. Yet again I had to adapt to my new surroundings. My teacher was Miss Philips who was a 'right old battle axe' but for some reason she took to me and I have to admit school suddenly became bearable. I was coming up to thirteen and was not always easy to control. I was always keen on sport and was selected for the school cricket and soccer teams and was Captain of the Shinty team, a game not unlike Hockey which was played a lot in Ireland.

As I progressed through the last two years of my school life I began to have thoughts as to what I would do when the time came for me to leave and step into the big wide world. I had one or two ideas and first and foremost I wanted to travel. Through no fault of my own, throughout my life, I have been a bit of a wanderer but, considering my circumstances is it any wonder. I was learning how to grow up and stand on my own two feet after years of being told what to do most of the time. At school we were known as the 'Lukey Boys' and often we were called upon to settle discrepancies that occurred in the playground. There were about 12 of us and we were situated in different classes according to our academic ability.

At times it was not a good place to be living as the Master and Matron were, on many occasions, cruel to many of the boys. On at least four occasions, I actually witnessed the Master kicking boys up and down the stairs. Thankfully, in todays' world this would not happen, but we as pupils had no one to turn to. Life could have been extremely uncomfortable as he was not a man to underestimate. A type of Jekyll and Hyde. Strangely enough I was also given the task of being their personal steward. My duties involved keeping the sitting room clean and tidy. A task I really enjoyed.

One day I collected the newspapers to put in their sitting room. I happened to see the front page in the Sunday Pictorial. It just said one word "IMPOSTER" with a large photo of my old Principal. I could not believe that not too long ago I had attended the very same school as a border. The following days paper had one big headline "UNFROCK THIS IMPOSTER". I have never forgotten those headlines.

Time was not standing still as it was approaching my fifteenth birthday: deadline day! Then you are released, and that is what it felt like, into the outside world with more or less no support. Fortunately, I had somewhere to go. A local family who had two children. Not having been used to a normal household, how was I going to manage was the big question. Fred and Flo were a lovely couple and made me feel so at home. I was finding it completely different to what I had been used to. Once more it was a case of adjusting to a new way of life. I found a job locally in a Grocers, were my duties were varied. Preparing cheeses, weighing out demerara sugar into little blue bags and keeping the shop clean and tidy…just up my street!

Part Three (7 August 2020)

I took the job at the Grocers shop but had other alternatives in mind for when I became sixteen. It had always been my ambition to see the world and go to sea but, having made enquiries in London, I had to wait. In the meantime, I had to work to pay Fred and Flo for my board and keep. Nearer my sixteenth birthday I paid a visit to the local recruiting office in Brighton to join the Royal Navy. I took the aptitude test and the medical which I passed, only to be rejected because I was one inch too short!

Needless to say I was very disappointed, but it made me all the more determined to go to sea, even if it meant not doing conscription as you were then classed as exempt if you were in the Merchant Navy. I applied to join in early November 1954. I was accepted and asked to attend the National Sea Training School T.S. Vindicatrix in Sharpness, Gloucester for a six-week training period to train in catering. I took my lifeboat exam which one had to pass to proceed with the course.

My training period concluded late in December. Very quickly I received notification to report to the Shipping Federation in London, King George V Docks, with a view to sailing immediately. After saying my goodbyes, I made tracks wondering what was in store for me. Arriving at the shipping federation I joined the National Union of Seaman was given the name of the vessel and the berth I was to proceed to. The Houlder Brothers ship "Ovingdean Grange". As I walked along the quayside, I passed many ships then suddenly out of the blue I looked up at this very unkempt ship from the look of her hull. This was to be my new home but for how long?, I was not told. I walked up the gangway, presented myself to the ships' cook who said "Ah you must be the new galley boy. This will be your domain for the forthcoming voyage." I asked where we were heading for and was told Rotterdam to pick up some cargo then on to Leningrad. Oh, my goodness I had hardly any clothes with me and Russia, at that time of year, would be very cold. What would I do?

On the 29th December we set sail for Rotterdam. Our cargo was to be timber which we would take to Leningrad. The ship I was on was a mere seven and a half thousand tons and we encountered very rough weather and were tossed around like a cork. Each movement of the vessel made me think, are we going to come back up or are we going to turn turtle. All this time we were shadowed by Russian naval ships and submarines. Very scary. We were only doing eleven knots, so the voyage was taking sometime.

We discharged most of our cargo in Leningrad, now St. Petersburg, and received new orders to sail to Murmansk and then on to Archangel both extremely cold places not far from the salt mines. I was very apprehensive and wondered if I would ever see 'Blighty' again. My first trip was very frightening and had not made much of an impression on me and I could not wait to get out of those Arctic waters.

We were reloaded once more with timber and grain bound once again from Amsterdam and Rotterdam. We encountered very heavy swells especially in the Barrents Sea and the North Sea. Once unloaded we were off again, hopefully back to London but, no, it was not to be and after bunkering and taking on water and stores we were off once again this time to Buenos Aires in Argentina then Montevideo in Uruguay. Up to Recife taking on canned corned beef and back to Bueno Aires to load more cargo for the long trip home. By the time I was twenty- one I had circum-navigated the world on many occasions on various deep sea vessels.

I left the Merchant Navy aged twenty-seven and have had many positions mainly in catering on cruise ships, Pullman trains, aeroplanes and in numerous hotels. I have also been a postman and a shop keeper.

I have lived in Havant for forty odd years and been a member of St. Faiths for over five years having previously been a chorister at St. Marks in North End.

Part Four (14 August 2020)

In 1964 I left the Merchant Navy and became a 'landlubber' again, I returned to Burgess Hill to decide what to do next, It wasn't long before I was on my way once more, this time to Jersey in the Channel Isles. I had made tentative enquiries at one of the many hotels and I knew that with the knowledge I had acquired whilst at sea, I could do quite well in the industry. My first post was at the Bay View Hotel en route to St. Aubins Bay. I was the 'Maitre D' in charge of the smooth running of the restaurant. It was not a live-in position but I found accommodation nearby.

Whilst working at the Bay View, I met a young lady and eventually moved into her mother's house in St. Aubins. We got to know one another better, Norah was her name and she was seventeen. One day she told me that she was 'with child'. I was shocked but, as you did in those days, we married in the local registry office, no frills and we started our married life.

I left the Bay View to take up a position as a 'Chef de Rang' at the Bonne Nuet Bay Hotel famous on the Island for its many lobster dishes for which people came from all over the Island to enjoy. My job was to greet and seat customers then revert to my Sommelier tasks. This involved me helping customers choose their wine.

As you came up the entrance stairs there were two very large water tanks filled with live lobsters. Customers chose which one they wanted for their meal. I only stayed there for about three months because this restaurant was situated at the far end of the Island making it difficult to get to especially when returning home after a long shift.

It wasn't long before I managed to acquire a position at one of the largest hotels on Jersey, The Hotel De France which was usually frequented by celebrities. Whilst I was there Shirley Bassey and her two children had a suite of rooms at the hotel. Most of the staff were Portuguese and their English was limited so I was given the job of looking after Miss Bassey who was a very pleasant guest.

Eventually it was time for us to return to the mainland as the season was coming to an end. Jersey in the winter is quite desolate with many places shutting down. Where were we heading. Only God above knew the answer to that question.

We headed for Brighton as I was familiar with the area. We found a flat in Norfolk Square and I secured a position in one of Wheelers fish restaurants. Wheelers were famous for owning the Ivy restaurant in the West End of London and both restaurants were the place for the stars and celebrities to be seen dining

We settled into our new surroundings but soon after the landlord put the flat up for sale and we were on the move again. I also put our name on the local council list and as Norah was now heavily pregnant so I kept pestering the council and eventually a two bedroomed house became vacant on the outskirts of Brighton near the racecourse in Woodingdean. We were both quite excited.

I also changed my place of work from Wheelers to another very well-known restaurant, The Three Little Rooms which was owned by Michael Wilding, Elizabeth Taylor's ex-husband. This restaurant had a reputation of specialising in various culinary ways of serving fish. It was situated in the Lanes, a fashionable part of Brighton then which still is to this day.

Norah gave birth to a healthy boy, Darren and a year after that she gave birth to another boy, Jason. Life was obviously very hectic but, we managed with a few hitches along the way but, although we tried very hard we were really not compatible and separated after five years.

During this time, I started a part time job at a brand new Hotel, the Bedford and was soon offered the job of Cocktail Bartender on an increased salary with a chance for further advancement. Although I didn't know it at the time, a certain young lady named Olive came into my life and, who was eventually to become my second wife and the mother of my third son Mark.

And so, our life took us on many more adventures, all over the county a few of which I will entertain you with in my final part next week!

Part Five (21 August 2020)

I saw a position advertised for an experienced cocktail bartender at the Mermaid Inn in Rye, West Sussex. I applied for the position and was successful. It was a live in position to include food. The weekly wage, which I received every Friday in a little brown envelope, was excellent. My colleague was, like me, a member of the U.K.B.G. "United Kingdom Bartenders Guild". We both regularly attended competitions all over the south of England and in the London area and were very successful. I was joined in Rye by Olive but this made things awkward regarding accommodation so I needed to get things sorted out.

For no apparent reason I suggested that we up sticks and go to Devon. I have no idea why, but I had been looking at a catering magazine and saw a vacancy in Ottery St. Mary. The vacancy was for a hard working couple and I applied and we got the job which included a flat. I became the Maitre D' at the Bowd Inn Sidford and Olive was in the restaurant. Soon, we found a completely fully furnished house in the main street called Cherry Trees. We settled in and it wasn't long before Olive fell for our son Mark. One day when he was a baby she went to the local butchers for some marrow bones and when she came home I said "Where's the baby?" She had left him outside the butcher's shop! She rushed back and the butcher had him in the shop with him and Mark was fast asleep. How different things were then. Olive said that it was strange to be pushing a pram after so many years having had two sons by her first marriage who were now in their late teens.

I was always looking for new adventures. I saw an opportunity in Lincoln and after discussing it with Olive, we upped sticks and we moved there. I was working in the Bailgate Hotel. However, the position was not exactly as advertised and unbeknown to me Olive approached the Manager and they had words and the next thing I knew I was called to the Manager's office and was told that we had to part company as he had had an altercation with my wife! He thanked me for my hard work and dedication and wished me luck. I have never been sacked before and was not at all happy with Olive.

This happened on a Friday and by Monday, after several phone calls, I was at Lincoln's main Post Office where I took an aptitude test which I passed and the following Monday I was a Postman. After an initial three-month training period learning about inward and outward sorting and doing a post round, I was made a permanent postman. We were living in Bardney but moved to Birchwood as it was nearer the depot. As I drove I soon became a rural delivery postman, serving many surrounding areas of Lincoln. In those days postmen and women had a distinctive uniform, had a badge number, a peaked hat and grey jacket and trousers. Unlike today's postman who are so casually dressed. On one occasion whilst delivering on a pushbike I decided to put on a French beret and wear a string of onions around my neck. I was reported to the Inspector by a disgruntled customer and I received a reprimand and a warning as to my future conduct as a G.P.O. employee. I spent five years as a postman and whilst we were at Birchwood Olive saw an advertisement for a couple to run a tobacconist and News Agents shop in West Leigh in Havant, wherever that was.

Olive made the long journey to Brighton to the Evening Argus offices for her interview and subject to seeing me was accepted. I went the following week and we were told to be ready the following week to be moved to Havant. Goodness what a rush it was. One day we said we will settle down and wondered if this was to be our final destination?

We took over a run-down corner shop taking around one K a week and when we left ten years later it was up to four and a half K. We started with four paper rounds and increased our circulation to eight rounds with ten paper boys using two boys as spares to cover absentees.

Although I had proposed to Olive on several occasions with no joy, out of the blue one morning she told me to go upstairs and make myself presentable as we had an appointment with the solicitor in Fareham. Off we went in our converted ambulance motorhome arriving in the car park opposite the Registry Office. Suddenly the penny dropped. I had to go over to a parked car which had three people inside it and ask if they would be our witnesses to which they agreed and so we got married. Finally, Olive was officially Mrs. Burch.

And so, for forty years we lived happily in Havant as I still do now, albeit on my own. I have many happy memories of holidays in our motor home and visits to the theatre and feel that I have been rather blessed even though I had an unusual start to my life.

Attending a Lockdown wedding

by Pauline West (Parish Secretary) – 30 July 2020

Well, the day of our son's wedding was upon us! Not quite as we had imagined but the happy couple were determined to go ahead and tie the knot despite the restrictions.

The day dawned, bright and sunny as we prepared ourselves for the event. What does one wear for a lockdown wedding? Should it be finery all round or smart-casual? The groom had assured us he was wearing smart trousers with a shirt and no tie or jacket. The Bride was wearing a blush coloured dress she had picked out to attend an upcoming family wedding. We opted for Kevin (my husband) to wear a smart white grandad shirt and suit trousers and I would opt for a flowery dress I had recently modified. Our daughter Steph, who lives with us looked lovely in a navy dress.

The traffic was light and we arrived at the venue on the outskirts of Uxbridge in plenty of time, having picked up my sister and her husband (our bubble family) along the way, so decided to stroll around a nearby lake. We enjoyed watching the swans and cygnets gliding gracefully through the water.

Eventually we made our way back to the venue and waited in the empty car park for others to arrive. Our niece and nephew, who was the best man, arrived with their partners making a total audience of 9. I received a text to say the happy couple were delayed in traffic as they had set off without the rings!! They had to return and collect them. Would I give the registrar a message to say they were on their way?

The registrar arrived and made her way inside. With 10 minutes to go, the bride and groom arrived with their maid of honour. They went in to have a pre-wedding chat to the registrar and then we were invited to enter the venue. We were all instructed to sanitise our hands prior to entry and to seat ourselves away from the aisle and with a clear row between each family set. The room was spacious for the 9 of us so we had plenty of choice of where to sit.

My husband Kevin was tasked with walking the bride down the aisle as her family lived in Bulgaria and could not attend due to the travel restrictions. I had been asked to film the ceremony on my phone so that the bride's family could view it and I was a little worried that I would muck it up. The music started and Kevin proudly walked beside the beautiful bride to present her to our son. The ceremony was very sweet with a light-hearted banter and much love and laughter. Before the signing of the register, the bride and groom had to sanitise their hands and also the witnesses, while the registrar and the administrator stood well back.

We took a few photos outside in the sun and were invited to attend a socially distanced barbeque at the newly married couple's garden in Shepherd's Bush.

The celebration was casual and fun with a happy family atmosphere. Veggie burgers are not my idea of a wedding feast, but needs must! It was lovely to sit outside and enjoy the company of our son and our new daughter-in-law and our family. We left at 5pm for our journey home. An emotional day.

The good news is that next year we will do it all again but this time the bride will wear her wedding gown and the groom a suit and we will celebrate with a proper crowd and with music and dancing and all the usual accoutrements of a wedding. Something to look forward to... all being well.

In the meantime, congratulations to Callum and Valentina, the new Mr & Mrs West!

Sandra bears (or is that bares?) all!

by Sandra Haggan – 30 July 2020

A tale…A few weeks into lockdown when I was walking everywhere I thought perhaps I should get my bicycle out of the shed and give it a try and thereby hangs a tale…

My bicycle had laid in the shed for about thirty years untouched so when I heaved it out it looked so very sad and obviously needed rather a lot of attention which was given by John my brother in law, then it was back to me. I got myself a helmet and a wicker basket to go on the front and then I was ready for a little test ride.

My daughter Tanya tells me that I have the full granny look now, riding a bicycle wearing a skirt and a helmet and a wicker basket on the front. The first time or two I just rode round the block early in the morning when hopefully there wouldn't be anybody about, then a trip delivering the Corona Chronicle to those who live close to me. I now thought I was ready for a longer journey.

My daughter and family live just a few minutes away by car, it takes me about fifteen minutes to cycle. I was invited to a socially distanced lunch in their garden so I thought it the ideal trial. Perhaps I should explain for those who don't know me I don't wear trousers, skirts and dresses are more me. So, I set off wearing my navy-blue pleated skirt realising quite soon that it was not a good choice. I tried pushing a bit of the skirt under my bottom but that didn't seem to work too well, so I gathered a handful of skirt in one hand and then put my hand back on the handlebars. I am not that confident so require two hands on the handlebars at all times.

I arrived at my daughters and enjoyed a lovely lunch with them, it was now time for the return journey. I had a plan, one which am sure other ladies will remember. When at school and doing handstands and cartwheels (neither of which I was any good at!) we used to hitch our skirts into our knickers so I did a bit of that and off I set on my way home – I hadn't gone far when the skirt came adrift and I had to re-think. So I gathered a handful of skirt in each hand, hands back on the handlebars, leaving a loop of the skirt in front of me and set off. It seemed to act a bit like a sail, anyway I thought best idea was to keep my head down and peddle as fast as I could. I didn't look at anyone and I do hope that no one looked or recognised me!

The lesson I learnt was to be careful which skirt I choose to wear but now thanks to the kindness of Kevin West the problem is solved. Following a chat with Pauline about cycling and the wearing of skirts, she thought that Kevin might be able to help and indeed he has. I needed a skirt guard and those available online didn't seem to be very good. Kevin drilled lots of holes in the mudguard and then threaded something like fishing line through it to make a skirt guard for me. It must have taken him ages but now I can wear any skirt I like!

A few things that I have learnt while cycling is that going up any kind of slope or hill is very hard work and coming down is a bit fast for me. The edge of the road that cyclists use seems to be the worst maintained, with humps, bumps and drain covers, it is all very hard on the bottom!

Having said all this I do rather enjoy the experience but most definitely I will be a fair weather cyclist!

Mave learns to ring…
by Mavis Floyd – 30 July 2020

Mavis Floyd is one of our longest-standing members and it's wonderful to hear of her early days in the parish, as 1940s teenager!

Following a recent conversation, I was having with Sandra (in awe of her daily flag raising task – albeit a labour of love) a chance remark led me back down memory lane which she said might also be of interest to others and suggested I put 'pen to paper' so here goes!

As a teenager in the 1940's we had a thriving young communicants group and together we would meet for chats, long walks, cycle rides etc. which gave us a real sense of companionship and belonging to our beloved St. Faiths.

During one of our meetings a newcomer who had arrived in Havant with her mother (who had taken on the task of church caretaker etc. with accommodation in church owned property nearby) asked us what night was bell ringing practice and which of us did it. Well of course we said it was only for men and she quickly surprised us by saying we could 'all' do it – as she had come here from Loughborough where church bells are made and indeed where ours used to go for repairs and T.L.C. etc.

At the time the captain at St Faith's was Morgan Marshall and when approached he was surprised, very pleased and willing to teach us the ropes (no pun intended – well sort of).

This opened up a whole new scenario as not only were we able to ring our bells but were welcomed in all churches in turn in our area – covered by the Winchester and Portsmouth Guild of Bellringers – on Saturday afternoons where after ringing the bells the host would provide refreshments. We were able to get there crammed in a couple of cars, Morgan's and Michael Johnson using his fathers' car. We would ring on Sundays for Evensong and it would always be 'touch and go' whether I would be able to get down from the belfry and over to the south transept to join my sister Joan before the choir started the procession through the church to the choir stalls.

That's enough for now I think!

Very happy days.

Leigh Park Citizen's Advice Bureau – 1980-1995
by Julia Hancock – 14 August 2020

Even as I listened to the question posed me as an Adviser at the CAB on my first sitting "we have broken our engagement, can I keep the ring he gave me?" (answer, 'yes - it's a gift') I was trying to think into which of the 13 CAB categories this would fall. Might it be Consumer, or legal rights perhaps? The National Association's information system was second to none and updated monthly, a laborious task involving cutting and pasting and hours of work. With the arrival of the digital age as I left 17 years later, all that changed and information was accessed at computer terminals.

The Bureaux are mostly funded by the Local Authority and Havant was fortunate in running 3 offices, Havant, Leigh Park and Waterlooville. To set up the Leigh Park Bureau we begged for additional funds from local industries, some of whom made generous donations. A local fishmonger gave us a used typewriter which announced its presence with an unmistakable and lingering smell!

CAB's offer free, impartial and confidential advice on any subject and we also offered home visits and personal support to those dealing with the then DHSS and Tribunals and County Courts.

Among the light hearted queries was one concerning false teeth, lost down the lavatory. Could the Water Company retrieve them? They could, and after sterilization returned them to the grateful owner! Most queries were of a more serious nature and none more so than debt counselling which became a large portion of our work as easy credit became available.

I can think of few other unpaid jobs that offer such a variety of challenges and chances to learn how life ticks than the work of the CAB.

Memories of Jamaica

by Nina Hartley – 14 August 2020

One night we watched a television programme about the forthcoming Commonwealth Games that were being held shortly in Jamaica. This was the first time an important event was going to take place since the country had become independent in 1962. Sam thought he would like to go take me to visit his family. We had married friends who were very reliable had offered to look after children for a week and that was all we needed.

After a long flight in a cool air-conditioned atmosphere, stepping out of the plane you felt the full force of the sudden heat as if an oven door had opened. We were met at the airport by Sam's sister who had offered us a place to stay. It took a couple of days to overcome jetlag and to adjust to the intense heat. Sam hired a car and we journeyed through the beautiful countryside. It was very green and lush with rivers and natural springs. Palm trees proliferated everywhere, fruit trees, delicious mangoes, bananas, coconuts, avocado pears and bread fruit all grew in abundance. After weaving our way over bumpy winding roads we reached uncle Jim's house. I was astonished to see a wooden single story house with grapefruit growing around the front porch. he welcomed us in, he had been busy looking after his grandchildren whilst his daughter was at work in Kingston.

Later we drove on further into the countryside to visit another cousin. I was shocked when I overheard a child say on passing, "Look, there is a white woman". I felt very odd indeed being described by the colour of my skin. Not a pleasant experience!

We spent time with Sam's cousins, aunts and uncles who gave us a warm reception. They made a great fuss of Hartley, which was my husband's real Christian name, not the nickname Sam he'd acquired in the air force. We were invited to a lovely house of relatives near the beach who had laid on a party with a delicious spread of exotic food. I was amused when a cousin described his house as "Ideal because it's very draughty and the breeze just flows through the open spaces." "Oh really? That's exactly the opposite to what we desire back at home in a cold climate you must try to come on holiday one day and experience a different climate as well as our rich historic culture." That was a bit ironic I thought after I'd said that.

Through general conversations I began to learn more about the Jamaican way of life. I admired the fact that despite the country's political struggles they eventually secured a peaceful independence.

Historically they had an embittered past with many battles fought and raged in order to control the island. The last battle was when Britain fought the Spanish and won that war in 1665. The Spanish left 400 slaves behind. England became involved and used the extra slaves for labour to increase the production of sugarcane. This generated enormous wealth in our country. Sugar was in great demand.

Now in modern times people were free from the legacy of slavery. They have become emancipated and spearheaded the way forward. Huge advancements have been made in education, industry and exports; for some time, they had mined bauxite, alumina and other chemicals. Many varieties of fruit, coffee, cane sugar, spice and rum are all exported and of course Jamaicans have excelled in many sports. Triumphantly they had won their liberation and the colony was finally released from British imperialism in 1962. I was determined next time when we visited we would bring the children, so they could discover more about their past ancestry. When it was time to say goodbye I knew I would miss Sam's affectionate family and the beautiful scenic island of Jamaica, a jewel in the Caribbean.

Take a letter Miss Acworth!

by Carol Acworth – 21 August 2020

I had just finished a year at a Secretarial college, my father could not wait for me to get a job and be off his hands. 'I shall be hopeless at it,' I complained. 'Don't worry Darling, you will only have to do it for a little while, until you meet a nice young man.' (Misplaced optimism)

So I looked for a nice stress free job with kind people I found just the thing with the Scripture Union, also known as the Children's Special Service Mission, with their shop on Wigmore Street in London.

So on the last day of December I presented myself before Miss Brown in her small office over the shop. 'This is really the Lord's doing,' she told me. ME. 'The Lord's doing?' Had I indeed come from the Lord? This was instant status.

'I have all these letters to write to children,' she continued, to arrive on New Year's Day. I could not have possibly done it alone, so let's start right away. Take a letter Miss Acworth.' My career as a shorthand typist has just begun. I do hope I can read my own shorthand).

Somehow I managed to read my squiggles and then get the letters typed. 'Bless the Lord,' said Miss Brown as she signed them. 'We can get them into the 5pm post.' I licked the envelopes then the stamps. Miss Brown put on her coat, very pleased with our day's work. 'I'll see you in the morning,' she called as she left the office. Well, I thought, perhaps I can manage this after all. I put on my coat and went home.

The following morning into the office I went, to behold, to my horror, all the unposted mail of the previous day. Thinking fast on my feet, perhaps I can get it to the post box before Miss Brown gets here! Scooping them up, I rushed downstairs, skedaddled past the bibles in the Scripture Union bookshop and hurtled down Wigmore Street and started shovelling it all in the box. Who should come round the corner from Cavendish Square, but Miss Brown. She went straight into the office and I finished my shovelling.

I meekly followed in, expecting the worst. To her credit, she never said a word. To this day I don't know if she saw me, but I suspect she did. Maybe she just thought perhaps the Lord wanted the children to get their letters on January 2 this year. His ways are past finding out.

Readers who are puzzled by Carol's maiden name being the same as her married name will be interested to know that Richard and Carol are actually fifth cousins! Ed.

Beryl Carter's story continues…

by Beryl Carter – 28 August 2020

In the article I wrote in Volume 11 of the Corona Chronicle I ended it "by the end of 1955 I had met a handsome sailor who became the love of my life - but that's another story!" So here is the "another story"!

Within two months Colin proposed and we arranged to meet at London Bridge to buy my engagement ring. I was all excited and arrived on time but no Colin. We had no telephone at home and his ship was delayed 24 hours by bad weather. You can image how I felt when the girls at work wanted to see my ring and I said I think the ship didn't come in! Little did I know that this would be the pattern of many times in my life as lots of naval wives will know.

We were very happy courting and then the navy decided to send him to a ship in the Far East for 18 months! However, we decided to wait for each other and get married when he came home! He bought me a carpet making kit to do while he was away - he certainly knew how to occupy my time! After 18 months and writing over 400 letters each and receiving many presents, when he came home it was as if we had never been parted.

We had a lovely wedding and honeymoon in Holywell Bay in Cornwall. We settled in our first home in Fawcett Road in Southsea while Colin was on a course but that was to last only 6 months before the navy decided to put him in a ship on Icelandic Fishery Patrol that was based in Scotland.

We decided that I should move to Edinburgh so that we would be together when the ship came in. We arranged to meet at Waverley Station in Edinburgh at 5pm when the London train arrived - but guess what? No Colin at the station - so I looked for the nearest policeman because that's what you did in those days when you needed help. When I found a policemen and tried to explain my stress he had a broad Scottish accent and I still had my South African accent and we couldn't understand each other but a very nice lady came and helped us.

The policeman telephoned the naval authorities and they told him the ship had been delayed by bad weather and was coming in later and that I should wait in the ladies' rest room at the station. Colin eventually arrived in uniform and we booked into a hotel off Princes Street.

The next morning Colin had to leave very early to be onboard and you can imagine the looks I got when I went down alone for breakfast with no uniform man! The ship was in for a few days and in that time I found somewhere for us to live and employment in Castle Street. We were very happy in Edinburgh for although Colin went away on 28 day patrols the ship always came back to Port Edgar when we had some time together. I made many good friends and got to love Scotland very much.

After 2 years in Edinburgh we moved to Lovedean and then Horndean while Colin qualified as a commissioned naval Communications Officer. His first ship as an officer was based in Devonport so we moved to Plymouth and again in a few days I found a place in Hooe to live and employment in the Town Clerk's office in the city.

Although there were many disappointments when the ship didn't come in I will always remember when the ship did come in on time. Colin told me to be on the cliff at Jennycliff Bay at 7 o'clock in the morning and I would see the Home Fleet sailing in with the ship he was in leading with the Commander-in-Chief (Colin was acting as his Flag Lieutenant). When I arrived on the cliff I couldn't see any ships and then in a little while slowly they appeared on the horizon like dinosaurs coming out of the water one after each other and as they passed Jennycliff, a light from Colin's ship flashed on the cliff and I knew it was for me as there was no one else around.

From Plymouth we moved to Drayton as Colin was appointed to the staff of the Commander-in-Chief, Portsmouth and then the navy sent him to Borneo for 6 months.

After 3 years in Drayton we settled in Havant in 1967 when our lovely Colleen came into our lives and our happiness was even more complete and the three of us spent two years in Singapore. This was the start of our association with St. Faith's Church.

The older naval wives told me at the beginning that life would be all heartaches and honeymoons - yes they were right. The goodbyes were the heartaches but the honeymoons were wonderful!

In the 62 years that we have been married, I wouldn't change a thing.

A Different Sort of Christmas … 1952

By Margaret Tait – 28 August 2020

My Uncle Frank had a wooden leg. He got it in the war. He was funny and always made me and my sister laugh. Uncle Frank and Aunty Mary would sometimes spend Christmas with us.

Life was hard although we didn't know any different; we lived in a rented terraced house in Milton, Portsmouth. It had no front garden but we had the whole road to play in; no-one had their own car in 1952, not in our street anyway.

Our house had a "front room" that was hardly ever used, a living room and a scullery, where dad had installed a proper bath with a removable worktop that he covered in oil cloth for mum to roll out her pastry. The toilet was outside the back door. We had a tiny garden with the remains of a corrugated-iron bomb shelter. Dad also had an allotment not far away and I loved going with him on the back of his push bike to help with weeding – he would take a screwed up brown paper bag with desiccated coconut for me as a snack. I think that must have been before I started school. Dad worked evenings and nights at the telephone exchange and mum was a machinist at Twilfit corset factory. They wanted to own their own home and I recall going by bus to Clanfield (right out in the countryside) where we looked at a brand new bungalow with two bedrooms. But mum said as they had only recently bought twin beds for us girls, the bedroom in the bungalow was so small they would have to buy bunk beds. Also dad was frightened of debt as many were in those days.

So – Christmas 1952: I was nearly six and my sister, Valerie, eight. In the days before Christmas we would take long paper streamers and go skipping along the local streets, singing carols. We were not allowed to ask for money; we did it for the joy of the festive season. Dad had hauled home a small Christmas tree from the local market and we girls had made paper chains. I still have several of the original decorations from that time; a couple of jingly bells and an angel.

Aunty Mary and Uncle Frank came to us on Christmas Eve when mum was busy preparing the vegetables for the Big Day. She had made a Christmas pudding months before and Christmas cake and mince pies too. They had my parents' bedroom and mum and dad slept on the floor in the front room.

We didn't have a television so I suppose we must have spent the evenings listening to the radio, and mum was always knitting. Or we'd have played games, we had ludo and snakes & ladders, and I loved my dolls. When I was about four, dad made me a dolls' house from a cardboard box. I played with it for hours.

On Christmas Eve, we hung up our stockings which were dad's home-made knitted long socks, and eagerly awaited the arrival of Father Christmas but it was hard to get to sleep.

We must have snoozed eventually but on Christmas morning …. Oh horrors! Our stockings were empty! I was in floods of tears, Valerie the same, as we went downstairs. It turned out that due to our staying awake until late, Father Christmas had given up waiting! All was not lost; our stocking gifts were in brown paper bags under the Christmas tree. We found a comic, a colouring book and crayons, a bar of Five Boys chocolate and an orange. Mum was busy in the scullery all morning, with the big pan steaming away with the pudding. Dad always had a small cigar on Christmas morning. We girls helped to lay the table, it looked very festive with paper napkins. Uncle Frank was called upon to carve "Herbert" – the Christmas capon was always called that. I remember there were silver sixpences wrapped in greaseproof paper hidden in the pudding, Valerie and I always found one in our bowl.

After it was all cleared away we performed our nativity play. This involved Valerie and I dressing up as Mary and Joseph. Valerie was always Mary with one of our dolls while I had to wear a striped towel on my head as Joseph. It always ended in tears for one reason or another! To calm things down we were allowed to open the remaining gifts from our parents and relatives. That year I opened a brand new doll from mum and dad. She came with a full set of hand-knitted clothes; a dress, bonnet and bootees in red and white. Mum had stayed up late at nights to finish it all in time. My Aunty Mary asked me if I preferred gloves or mittens and I said "oh mittens, they keep my fingers warmer", then she said did I like coloured things or white? I replied that white things would just get dirty. Then, believe it or not, she gave me their gift: a pair of white gloves. Even at that age I knew I should be tactful so I thanked her profusely and said how much I loved them.

Valerie and I had been given some money from mum's Co-op divi to buy Christmas presents. We never varied in our gift buying: pipe cleaners or a comb for dad and hankies or toilette water from Boots for mum.

On Boxing Day Aunty Mary and Uncle Frank went home to Paulsgrove, and we all went to the Kings Theatre for the pantomime. We sat in The Gods, which are the highest seats in the house and I hate steep steps and heights to this day!

Anyone can see how different Christmas is in the twenty first century to how it was nearly seventy years ago. We all moan about the commercialism then buy our little darlings everything on their wish list! Personally, I wouldn't want a return to "The Good Old Days" because I do not believe they existed. Life was hard and for our family it got harder when in 1957 my brother, Colin, was born.

Mum had to give up work for a while so there was less money to put food on the table. Dad, being the breadwinner, always had the best. That was how most mothers managed their housekeeping, nothing wrong with that. But she would sometimes sit down to dinner with an empty plate or a tiny portion saying she wasn't hungry. I was always hungry – not helped when Colin started eating proper meals and I had to share mine with him. A pack of 8 sausages between 5 hungry mouths didn't go far! My favourite was bacon suet roll on Saturdays; not much bacon but the suet pudding helped to fill us up. On Sundays there was a roast dinner but the apple pie and custard was saved for tea. On Fridays we had fish paste sandwiches, the rest of the week for tea it was bread and dripping.

I hope this will give a snapshot of how some of us spent Christmas back in the days of food rationing after the war. We should thank God for the plentiful food and choices that we now take for granted.

More from Bombay

by Alan Hakim – 28 August 2020

A recent news item about a proposal from the BJP Hindu Nationalist Government to downgrade the status of English brought back a memory of 1964. There are innumerable languages in India, but under the Constitution, there were two National languages (Hindi and English) and another 13 official languages which all appeared on the banknotes. But in 1965, English was due to be dropped. This led to protests, since the exams for Civil Service jobs would then be only in Hindi. For many North Indians, that is their native language, but not for those in the south. To do the exams in English meant that everyone would be using their second language. The proposal was quietly dropped, but now Mr Modi has raised it again. Does he know about 1964?

I did sometimes wonder why Cooks was still operating in Bombay. The 1960s were difficult times for travel for Indians. There was a permanent shortage of foreign currency, which meant that the only people encouraged to travel abroad were successful exporters.

The first hurdle was to get a passport issued. Then, in order to buy an air or sea ticket you had to get a 'P form' approved, which gave a good reason for travelling. That was quite straightforward for a Muslim going on the Hajj, but more difficult when a wealthy citizen wanted to go on a shopping trip in Europe. Only with that form in hand could your travel agent book a ticket. I later met my predecessor at Bombay, who had been promoted to Hong Kong. On his first day there, his customer was very surprised to be asked for his authority to buy a ticket.

You may have seen documentaries on television that mention Indian immigrants arriving in England with only £3. That was the ordinary travel allowance, defined as the amount you might have in your pocket after getting from home to the departure airport. Only the exporters got more.

The end result of all this was that few people booked to travel overseas. But inland travel was difficult too. We had a very efficient railway department, but the internal flights of Indian Airlines were full of red tape. Almost all flights had a waiting list, and if you were near the top, you had to buy a ticket, and then get a refund after missing the flight. That kept us busy.

Another curiosity of that time was Prohibition. This varied from state to state. In Delhi, drink was allowed on five days of the week, but the night before a ‘dry’ day, a notice appeared on the hotel menu advising you to order drinks for tomorrow, now.

Maharashtra (the state Bombay was in) had permits. Resident foreigners were thought to be beyond redemption, and could claim a permit as of right, as could tourists. (It was actually called a ‘Foreign Liquor Permit’.) But an Indian could only have a Health Permit, and then only if you were over 40. The travel trade had occasional parties at which drink was served, and the head of my Ocean Travel department got worried she might be raided at a party. So she applied for a Health Permit. Her doctor said she would have to go before a Board. “Any question they ask you,” he said, “say ‘Yes’” She got her permit.

Armed with your Foreign Liquor Permit, you could go to a ‘wine merchant’ and buy beer, gin, vodka and whisky. It was all Indian, and no actual wine was available. One of our periodic pleasures was watching the Australians come off the boat from Sydney, boasting of their strong heads, and being overcome by the much stronger Indian beer.

With a permit, you could also go to the tourist hotels, not to the bar, but to the ‘Permit Room’. You handed in your permit, which was given to a clerk in khaki drill uniform, sitting unobtrusively in the corner, entering everyone’s orders in a vast ledger, as well as deducting the orders from your monthly ration. I assume all my drinks in those years are recorded for ever in the state archives. We were allowed 6 units per month, a unit being a bottle of spirits or a dozen beers. So when I am advised now to restrict my drinking to no more than 14 units a week, I find it difficult to adjust to the smaller British unit.

After two years, my General Manager Frank Lofthouse reached retirement, and was to be replaced by Norman Woolley, the Branch Manager in Colombo. I was sent to Colombo to take over from him, and a new Travel Manager was sent out from London. He arrived with the best references, having achieved the highest marks ever in Cooks’ training course. Unfortunately, the training didn’t cover running an Indian office, and I heard later he had been sent home before his three-year tour was completed.

The Grey Lady of Cader Idris

by Clive Barnett

In the academic year 1970-71, I was studying for my postgraduate teaching certificate. At the end of each academic year, the geographers took their first year A Level students on a week-long field trip to mid-Wales, basing themselves at Aberystwyth University. They invited me to join them (as a responsible adult!). So it was, in mid-July 1971, I found myself driving off to mid-Wales with four geography lecturers and some 40-odd students.

One of the trip's key activities was a visit to Cader Idris, the highest mountain in Mid-Wales, and a notable example of the effects of glaciation on the landscape. In particular, some way up the mountain there is a corrie lake, formed by the action of the glacier. It looks like a chair with a steep 'back', semi-circular 'arms' and a flooded 'seat'. We arrived at the lake close to mid-day and, the weather being particularly hot, decided to rest there and eat our packed lunches. Many of the students took the opportunity to paddle – some to swim – in the icy water of the lake.

In the course of lunch, Robin, one of the lecturers who was something of a fell walker, persuaded a couple of us that it would be much more fun to attempt an ascent by the far more difficult route of scrambling up the steep scree slope at the 'back' of the chair. Looking back, it was a particularly foolhardy venture. We had no appropriate climbing equipment, clothing or boots; I seem to recall that I had on a pair of what today we would call trainers. However, in those far-off days the great god of health and safety did not hold all in its thrall as it does now, and at 22 you believe yourself to be immortal. Furthermore, I suffer badly from vertigo and, growing up this had held me back from joining in some of the exploits which my friends had got up to. 'Right', I thought, 'here's my chance to challenge my fear of heights … and overcome it'. So off we went, Robin, another lecturer called Andy, and me – sans hard hats, sans ropes, sans crampons etc.

All went well to begin with although I do admit to a few heart-stopping moments as the scree gave way under my feet. Nevertheless, with Andy in front and Robin behind me, we worked our way up and beyond it and then it was a matter of steady if painstaking progress using hands and feet for footholds in the bare rock. As I approached within nine to twelve feet of the top, I remember thinking that I was doing remarkably well and that I would be able to boast to my friends back home that I had at long last conquered my fear. That was when I made my BIG mistake. I looked down …. and I froze.

The stark realisation of our height above the lake and the fact that we had none of the equipment required for what we were doing induced a sense of panic the like of which I had never experienced before nor since. I simply could not move however much Andy and Robin encouraged and then cajoled me. I just remained motionless, my hands holding vice-like to a rocky outcrop and my feet welded to a ledge. It wasn't that I didn't want to move – I did, badly – I simply couldn't. Looking back, I could have been there for the rest of the day and even Robin, usually so calm in a crisis, subsequently admitted that he was running out of things to do or say.

We must have been stuck in our frozen tableau for maybe ten minutes – it seemed far longer – when I happened to look to my left where there was a slightly less steep, overhanging and grassy outcrop of rock. There, walking on the grass near to the cliff edge with her black and white collie dog, was an elderly lady – in those days, to me anyone over 40 counted as 'elderly' but on reflection I think she was probably in her sixties. She was dressed in a light grey two piece, of a design popular at the time although it seemed to be made out of the sort of heavy material which was singularly inappropriate on such a warm day, and she had on a pair of stiff walking shoes, which were altogether more suitable than the trainers I had on.

I remember thinking, 'Right, if that old dear can walk so near to the edge, I can certainly climb these last few feet' and thereupon I did. Helped by Andy who pulled, and Robin, who pushed, I finally made it to the top and collapsed on the ground utterly exhausted. Andy asked me what had finally galvanised me into moving when all of his and Robin's encouragement had failed so I told him about the elderly lady and how her example had first shamed and then spurred me into action. At the time, both said that they hadn't seen her but that was hardly surprising as all their efforts were focused on me. Anyway, I was left to recover my wits. Needless to say, there was no debate about which route we would take for the descent!

We arrived back at the foot of Cader Idris around 6 pm and, as our coach wasn't scheduled to collect us until 7 pm, we did the only thing possible in such circumstances: we retired to the pub.

The pub in question was much favoured by the hiking and climbing community. Its walls were covered with photos of well-known walkers and climbers who had passed through, as well as newspaper cuttings of incidents which had occurred on the mountain. A pint in hand, I started scanning the various photographs and stories. It was then that I came across one that told of an elderly lady who used to walk her dog on

Cader Idris until, one day in November 1938, a thick mist suddenly enveloped the mountain. No one knows exactly what happened but the next morning her body and that of the dog's were found close by the corrie lake. The supposition made by the mountain rescue team and accepted by the coroner was that she had become disorientated in the fog, lost the path and had thus fallen to her death.

The report of the coroner's findings was accompanied by a photograph of the lady. She was dressed in a light grey two piece and was standing beside her black and white collie dog…

Christmas in the Orient

by Alan Hakim

At the end of 1966 I was promoted to be Branch Manager in Colombo, Ceylon (now Sri Lanka). There was a convenient French liner, the M.V.Laos going direct from Bombay at the right time, so I was able to store my 15 pieces of luggage on the cabin balcony, and save the complications of going by air and waiting for the luggage to catch up.

Arriving in mid-December, I was just in time for a lot of holidays. Not only were there Christmas and New Year, but I now had to live with the Buddhist lunar calendar. This had been introduced a year earlier as an election pledge, and resulted in work following an 8-week pattern, with 8 days in weeks 2, 4 and 8. The newspapers carried an item every day, "Your next 3 weekends are ..", Tuesday/Wednesday, for example, followed by Wednesday/Thursday twice. My predecessor Norman Woolley and his wife were packing up to go to Bombay in the New Year, so I moved into the guest room of the company flat, full of packing cases, and we decided to go away for Christmas to Nuwara Eliya.

After two years in the tropics, I was a bit surprised to be told to bring my warmest clothes. We were going up to over 6000 feet (half as high again as Ben Nevis) and the town is very popular as a place to get away from the steamy heat of Colombo.

We went up on the night train, in a somewhat antique sleeping car, and arrived in the morning to find a small town like Bowness-on-Windermere set down in the highlands near the equator. We were to stay at the Grand Hotel, an enormous mock-Tudor building that had been built at the height of British rule. I don't think it had been greatly modernised since then. At least, unlike one of the other hotels, it didn't have a steel engraving of Landseer's "Stag at Bay" in Reception.

I don't remember much of our visit. Mostly, the thing to do is walk around the very attractive country. The more vigorous tourists climb up Mount Piduratalagala, another 2000 feet up, but surprisingly easy.

The most memorable item of the weekend was Christmas Dinner itself: a completely traditional British meal. The waiter brought round the turkey on a trolley, to carve in front of us. He had some trouble cutting its leg off, so he tucked it under his arm, and pulled.

A year later, things were very different. By then, I had met Elene (older parishioners may remember her) and we decided to go to South India. On Christmas Eve we arrived in Madras, which was as hot as Colombo, and we thought the Midnight service at the Cathedral would be the best.

Madras Cathedral, instead of windows in the walls, has large double doors all the way along. When we arrived, the congregation was already bursting out of every door, like the London Tube in the rush hour. But Indians are very hospitable. Seeing we were foreigners, they made enough space for us to get just inside, for a distant view of the celebrant.

Christmas Day itself is a holiday, but no more important than Hindu and Moslem holidays, with most shops and entertainments open. We went to the beach, and in the evening to a performance of Classical Dance, avoiding the invitations for "Foreign friends" to join them on stage. I don't remember dinner, so no trouble with the turkey this time, but Madras was "dry".

Elene had brought a bottle of wine with us, obtained through the diplomatic bag, but it wasn't to be had with our food. When we went on to Bangalore next day, we found drink was permitted, so our bottle joined us at dinner. After a time, I noticed a Frenchman at the next table had called for the wine list, and was looking baffled, after all, it had nothing on it except beer and spirits.

Poems

Social Isolation
By Margaret Tait
29 March 2020

In social isolation, what more can I do?
Cos my hair salon is closed now and my roots are coming through.
In another week or so my nails will need attention
I'm not sure that I can cope with social isolation.

Without some retail therapy how will we cope at all?
For myself and others like me, we may go up the wall.
The garden's looking good now, if only I had thought
To buy some nice Spring flowers at a time they could be bought.

We cannot see our grandkids except upon our screens.
I hope that I will see mine before they reach their teens.
Shopping is a nightmare, panic buying's not a hoot,
And if you need those loo rolls, be sure to hide them in the boot.

So this is where it starts folks, a whole new way of life,
We all play happy families, never mind the strife.
Will there be lots of babies born a year from now?
With social isolation – the question must be... HOW.?

Allan's Allotment

by Margaret Tate - 21 May 2020

(in semi-fictional tribute to her son-in-law)

Allan took on an allotment
where he hoped to grow some leeks,
The land resembled a jungle
and clearing it took several weeks.
There were compost bins, a potting shed
and a water butt down by the hedge,
After months of very hard digging,
Allan was growing fresh veg.

The children wanted to help
- and painted the shed blue and green,
Their design included some flower pot men,
with straw where the hair should have been.
They all chipped in at planting time,
sowing packets of vegetable seeds,
But when green shoots started to show,
it was hard work stopping the weeds.

Soon there were runners, carrots and peas,
potatoes and lettuce galore
Cabbages, parsnips, leeks and a swede,
till the children could carry no more.
Proudly they hauled their harvest home,
In an old and creaky wheel barrow,
Daunted by thoughts of the prepping to come,
You should see the size of the marrow.

The sun set over the bean poles
- "Now what shall we have for dinner?
With so much fresh food to consume,
our diet will be a winner."
But burgers, egg and chips were planned,
now we all know what that means;
"Forget about the veggies love.
This calls for a tin of baked beans!"

Havant First Aid Post.

by Judith Glenister. - May 1942

The present international Corona Crisis has elicited a sense of 'war-time' spirit in some of us. This poem, by a recently departed and very dear member of St Faith's was written when she was 12 years old, in the middle of 'wartime Havant'.

When the sky is summer blue,
And the grass is drenched with dew,
And the weary flowers sway
Through the sleepy noon of day,
I wander to a well—loved spot
Few trees for shade in summer hot,
And where should grow the Pink and Phlox
A vegetable garden grows.

And there the Church Hall used to be,
And there were feasts for charity
And children's treats at Christmas—tide
And Mothers' Meetings there beside
But when hostilities began
Some sensible and brainy man
Knowing we were so near the coast
Thought we should have a First Aid Post –

In case the German bombers came
And put our A.R.P. to shame,
And now our peaceful Parish Hall
Joined the war effort after all;
They wait indomitable brave
To dare all peril, and to save
Those who suffer, filled with pain
Bring them back to peace again.

Gay friends are these, they like a joke
A cup of tea, a little smoke
A game of Ping—pong after dark,
Or tennis in the village park.
From morning ‘till the sun goes down
They camouflage nets green and brown.
How glad this little group could be
If they could live in unity.

But still I know that I can find
Friends that are happy, quiet and kind,
That keep the place serene and bright,
Ana face the dangers of the night.
Then at the dawn of a new day,
They say farewell and creep away,
And in their country gardens fair
They take their rest in comfort there.

And those who through the day stand by
Await the peril from the sky,
Amuse themselves in rain or sun,
And watch ‘till each long day is run;
And as the sun rests on the hill
And all the sea is gold and still,
They wander back to home and fire,
A woman's pride, a man's desire

A walk to Langstone

by Margaret Tait – 28 May 2020

If you walk to Langstone, go the scenic way,
You will pass the bug hotel where beetles come to play.
The path is on the Billy Trail where steam trains used to run
Now it's used by cyclists and walkers just for fun.
Long ago the Terrier chugged along the shore,
But Hayling Bridge was deemed unsafe, now the railway is no more.

Walk beside a babbling brook, cross a wooden bridge or two
Once you've seen the ponies the sea comes into view.
There are no cafes here serving lunch and tea
With two pubs on the water's edge, it's good enough for me.
On the path there is a mill, restored and looking grand
Tall and black it proudly watches swans upon the sand.

Walk along the shore to the church that's very old,
With lichen covered gravestones, where history will be told.
Of Langstone's ancient tower where the story goes
King Henry's cousin was interned reflecting on her woes.
Now go towards the Royal Oak where you can meet some friends,
We hope you won't have long to wait – until the lockdown ends!

End of Lockdown barbecue
by Margaret Tait

I think I'll have a barbecue when this lockdown ends,
But only six will be allowed, so family or friends?
I'll go shopping for some burgers and sausages and steak
Then rustle up a crumble and set aside to bake.
I'll get some wine and salads and a case or two of beer,
But deciding who to ask is what I really fear.

I can't invite old grandad as he'd need the you-know-what,
And going in another house - permitted it is not!
My children fight like cat and dog, my daughters and my son.
They haven't been together since 1991.
My friends are all too busy, another pal's in Spain,
And judging by the sky above I don't think it will rain.

So instead I'll ask the neighbours, I'm sure they'd like a treat.
I pray there are no vegans and they'll happily eat meat.
But they are with their families enjoying summer sun.
So a quiet day for me – a barbecue for one!

The Big Clear-out

by Margaret Tait – 12 June 2020

We cleared out the attic, we cleared out the shed
We cleared out the drawers from under the bed
There were old shoes and toys, and dresses size ten,
I don't think that those will fit me again.

We found an old rug that we've not used for years
and photos of family that brought me to tears.
There was an old chair with a leg that was broke
Can't think why we kept it, must be for a joke.

There were comics and books whose pages were torn,
A Christening gown, precious but worn.
What will we do with this unwanted stuff
I'm dusty from cleaning and I've had enough.

Shall I queue at the tip or give it away?
Or just burn the lot on a dry sunny day.
So don't store old things in the attic or shed
No one will want them after we're dead!

My Journey

by Liz White – 12 June 2020

(in the voice of her grandson)

It has taken a long time
To be where I am today
It has not been easy
It's been hell along the way.

The friends I used to go with
The good times that we had
Have all gone and left me
Now that things are bad.

This illness is a nightmare
It cannot be seen
The ones that are affected
Will know only what I mean.

I have struggled with my torment
Not knowing what to do
Who can I turn to?
To get my mind in cue.

My family were anxious
Each coping with their pain
Supporting me with kindness
But mostly more in vain.

The staff in the places
That I've been made to go
Have said that they could help me
When I've been feeling low.

They encouraged me to tell them
How I am feeling now
I didn't want to tell them
Because I didn't quite know how.

My medication's vital
Or so they would say
I didn't want to take it
And refused along the way.

But they would not be beaten
Were determined I'd pull through
And conquer this condition
If they showed me what to do.

I feel I've nearly made it
My attitude has changed
The voices I was hearing
Seem somehow re-arranged.

They now do not torment me
And have almost gone away
It is much more peaceful
That's all that I can say.

I now can see the daylight
And feel I'm back on track
My family are now happy
'Cause they know they have me back.

Book Knowledge

by Chris Elmes – 25 June 2020

I'd feel at home in an American courtroom
Because I know how the jury is picked,
I know how to design a Cathedral from scratch
With a sand-tray, some rope and a stick.

I know how a wolf pack shares food
And organises, by status, its life,
And I know how to clear dirty water
Using leaves, some sticks and a knife.

I know that horses came to Egypt
Brought by the Hyksos invaders,
And I know of their gods and goddesses
That they later forced on their neighbours.

I've felt sorrow and joy in some measure
And known pleasure and pain in their time,
I've fallen in love with men of all types
Kings and Paupers, all have been mine.

I've waited with Scarlett for Rhett,
And learned the laws of robotics,
I've learned the tricks of an underground cop,
As he joins in the hunt for narcotics.

All of this wonderful knowledge
Is still waiting there in my brain
As week follows week I wonder
When shall I ever need it again.

I didn't set out to learn facts
That was never intended
It all just arrived in my head
As each of my books was ended!

The Uninvited Visitor
by Marion Porter – 25 June 2020

Midsummer Day – June twenty-four,
A bird flew in our kitchen door.
He sat upon a cupboard top
And seemed as though he'd like to stop.
Now, we're not good with feathered things,
Don't like the flapping of their wings;
We love to see them in the garden
But not indoors: we beg your pardon.
So, what to do we did not know.
We wished that little bird would go
Back through the door out in the sun,
Off to find his Dad and Mum.

Man of the house picked up the broom;
He'd gently shoo him from the room,
But every time he neared the pest
He'd find another place to rest.
From curtain pole to top of door,
The boiler next, then round once more
And as he flew around and round
Little feathers fluttered down....
Upon the work tops and the floor
And I'm afraid that was not all!

Yours truly took a turn to see
If she could set the captive free.
More windows now were opened wide
Enticing him to fly outside;
He was a youngster after all,
I think he heard his mother's call
For suddenly he saw the way
And out he went into the day.

Then out came Dettox, cloths and mop.
The cupboards, floor and each worktop
Were disinfected with great zest,
Removing traces of our guest.

Our small friend's visit had a meaning.
A little late, we've been spring cleaning.
So thanks for flying through our door;
The kitchen's cleaner than e'er before.

Storms

by an anonymous member of our Monday Club
(25 June 2020)

We all go through storms in our lives
and none of us escape them.
You're in a boat.
Rain is pouring down.
The sea is rough, thunder deafening
and lightening blinding.
Yet you're in the boat.
You're bailing out the sea.
You're soaked through.
You're cold and the wind is bitter.
You're longing for calm waters
and the warmth of the sun,
yet you're hanging-in there.
You're still bailing out water.
Yet faith, hope, love still remains
and you're longing for the joy of calm, still waters.

On finding myself strapped for cash during the lockdown
or
Twenty-first Century Timon to the Halifax Bank plc

by Felicity Kay – 2 July 2020

Note: At the beginning of the play, Timon of Athens by William Shakespeare, the titular hero, discovering he has lost all his wealth, and with it most of his friends, runs from his house to a place of sanctuary in the hills where he adores nature and abhors wealth.

There is a place I go call my own,
where everything is mine to hear and see
where thistle flowers take flight like gossamer stars
and brambles hang with rich obsidian.
Where coin of autumn wheat and robin's song
fills my winter purse and I run free,
for running's sake, not fear or ambition,
nor to quiet the clamour of your abacus.
Where sky-pinned in bright cerulean blue,
my joys are held on expert kestrel's wing
and strong and still they fly against the wind,
while beneath my feet, the quarter chiming
sombre voice of care diminishes,
made dull and mute in earthy labyrinth.

The Monday Club Song

from Bill Jones and Wyn Clinnick - 2 July 2020

Bill has kindly sent in the song lyrics below, which were passed to him by Wyn Clinnick. He says: "Apparently, this was written by the sister of Edna Martin. Edna and her family (whom I remember very well) were a staunch supporters of St Albans Church, West Leigh, in the days when this church was in St Albans Road. This song/poem was used each week when a group met in Emsworth called "The Golden Age Club" possibly a forerunner of "The Monday Club". Wyn wanted us to use this as our weekly prayer in St Faith's on a Monday morning."

Golden Age Song.

To do the kind and genuine deed,
To see the want and meet the need,
To seize the chance that comes a long,
To ease the stress and right a wrong.

To bring a smile to a frowning face,
To flash a light in a gloomy place,
To spread the sound of happiness,
Where hearts are heavy, and in distress.

To help each other along the road,
To lend a hand to share the load,
To take the best and brightest view,
That is what we are on earth to do.

My friend Sue…

by Liz White – 30 July 2020

I want to relay a tale to you
To give you all a laugh
I think you'll end up thinking
That I'm rather daft.

About seven or eight weeks ago
A nice lady phoned to say
She's checking on some people
To see if they're ok.

She said that she went to church
And that her name was Sue
But as to who she was
I didn't have a clue.

I asked her where in church she sat
To give me some idea
Of just what she looks like
And make things a bit more clear.

After she explained to me
And told me where she sat
I now can put a face to her
And we have a good old chat.

The other day I walked into town
To buy a thing or two
And who should I bump into
None other than my friend Sue.

I greeted her most warmly
And we chatted as you do
But just as I was leaving
She said her name's not Sue.

Oh Dear what have I done
I'm feeling very sad
I wish the ground would open up
'Cause I think I'm going mad!

Now I don't want to bore you
But I know what to do for sure
I think I'll go round to Sue's house
And knock on her front door.

I phoned to say I'm coming
And asked if she would mind
She said she'd like to see me
I think she's very kind.

We sat in her front garden
And I told her what I'd done
She said not to worry
It could happen to anyone.

I want to get back to normal
When the (Corona) sad time has past
When the church and (charity) shop is open
And we can meet up with friends at last.

Coronavirus

by Bridget Wade – 14 August 2020

Coronavirus, who'd have thought it,
in 2020 we would be ordered to stay home.
Isolate, social distance, only go out for essentials,
Didn't we all moan!

As the weeks went by and the death toll rose,
we realised that life really wasn't that bad.
If we obeyed the instructions, if we did as we were told
we could be sure of escaping what a lot of others had.

Lots started knitting, some tried sewing,
many baked to their hearts content.
As long as we stayed home and listened to Boris,
the guidance we (sort of) understood what it meant.

And so it began, the birth of live-streaming,
From Mothering Sunday to Trinity.
A few minor hiccups, some angle sorting.
but we soon got the hang of it, hoorah for IT?

It became apparent that the streets were cleaner.
the air was fresher and the sea was even bluer.
The birds sang their merry song ever louder,
Covid I9 cases were becoming fewer.

So, as we turn a corner, as we reach a newer phase.
let's reflect on our time in lockdown and learn from it.
The calls, the letters, the coffee morning zooms,
the flowers, the cakes, the videos, all lifting our spirit.

We thank all those key workers, many there are,
let's raise a glass for all.
But once we're back to 'normal', let's not forget,
the fellowship, the faith and the cake most of all!

Green fingers

by Margaret Tait – 21 August 2020

I'd like to be green fingered and not always have to strive
To struggle all the time just to keep my plants alive.

My marigolds are not so gold, they're eaten by the slugs
Bizzie lizzies make a snack for numerous hungry bugs.
The roses have some black fly, I spray them every night,
It's made no difference to the blooms, I still can't get it right.

I thought I'd grow tomatoes or maybe runner beans,
But they're just good for snails and they grow into their teens.
I'll put them on the compost heap if they don't grow any stronger,
They're looking rather sad today and I can wait no longer.

Shall I give my garden up, and lay plastic grass instead?
With plastic flowers in plastic pots, to fill the flower bed?
But I really like a challenge, why should the slugs win this?
I would banish all the bugs if I could have one wish!

Church bells

by Ann Plater – 8 October 2020

We ring the bells on Sunday
And call all folk to pray
A few will heed the message
But more will stay away.

The bells they sound so lovely
We hear them all quite near
They're part of our tradition
And maybe more that's clear.

God's bells give Him much pleasure
And we enjoy them too
So when we sound our message
What does that mean to you?

The bells can speak of Jesus
And what he came to do
There's blessing there for all of us
And for our children too.

So when you hear our ringing
Just offer up this prayer
"Lord Jesus, please bless me and mine
And keep us in Your care."

Arachnophobia

By Margaret Tate – 22 October 2020

I am arachnophobic, scared of spiders big and small,
Whether hiding in a corner or climbing up the wall.
If the weather's stormy, they shelter from the rain,
I see them in the bathtub where they've climbed right up the drain!

Some have lots of dangly legs, with bodies plump and round,
All summer long they multiply, in garden sheds they're found.
At night I lift the pillows and check beneath the bed,
To avoid nocturnal visits which fill my heart with dread.

Cobwebs have been swept away, so spiders cannot rest,
My broom is at the ready to send them flying west!
I need to make my home a place that's spider free,
So here is what I found if you feel the same as me!

One remedy is conkers: I hear they hate the smell,
And electronic plug ins will do the job as well.
So now my mind's at rest with these remedies as said,
Oh no!! What's this I see .... a giant octoped!!!!!!!

A church fayre
by Margaret Tait – 22 October 2020

To raise funds for the needy
Our church will hold a Fayre,
They need plenty of donations
Do you have things to spare?

I hope to make a lemon cake
And pray it doesn't sink,
Perhaps a marble one as well
In shades of blue and pink.

I have unwanted gifts to bring -
A manicure set or two,
Christmas socks which aren't my style
And a candle for the loo.

I'll bring along some books I've read
And winter shrubs and flowers,
They aim to hold the fayre outside ....
If we avoid the showers.

So gather all and please attend,
Buy jars of local honey,
A lovely way to spend and spend,
Bring a wallet bulging money!

The second Lockdown
by Margaret Tait

The second lockdown has started this week,
With lots of restrictions that we didn't seek.
They've cancelled our Christmas Fayre that was planned,
Boris says indoor meetings are banned.

We can't see our friends except in the park,
But it's cold out and windy and by four nearly dark.
In the previous Lockdown we had warm sunny days
As we pottered in gardens finding various ways

To keep up our spirits and stay looking ahead.
But hard times are returning that fill us with dread.
Count all your blessings, we all have so much
See loved ones on zoom but long for their touch.

So chin up and smile as day follows night,
We'll soon be together to continue the fight.
We will beat this Covid, the virus we hate,
And meet back in church on an uncertain date.

Thank you for purchasing this volume of our writings.

All funds raised will do towards making St Faith's an even more welcoming place for the whole community.